W9-AJT-473

# It's Not TV

## Watching HBO in the Post-television Era

Edited by
Marc Leverette, Brian L. Ott,
and Cara Louise Buckley

Routledge
Taylor & Francis Group

NEW YORK AND LONDON

First published 2008
by Routledge
270 Madison Ave, New York, NY 10016

Simultaneously published in the UK
by Routledge
2 Park Square, Milton Park, Abingdon, Oxon OX14 4RN

*Routledge is an imprint of the Taylor & Francis Group,
an informa business*

© 2008 Taylor and Francis Group

Typeset in Perpetua by RefineCatch Limited, Bungay, Suffolk
Printed and bound in the United States of America on acid-free
paper by Edwards Brothers, Inc.

All rights reserved. No part of this book may be reprinted or
reproduced or utilized in any form or by any electronic,
mechanical, or other means, now known or hereafter
invented, including photocopying and recording, or in any
information storage or retrieval system, without permission in
writing from the publishers.

**Trademark Notice**: Product or corporate names may be
trademarks or registered trademarks, and are used only for
identification and explanation without intent to infringe.

*Library of Congress Cataloging in Publication Data*
A catalog record has been requested for this book

ISBN10: 0–415–96037–1 (hbk)
ISBN10: 0–415–96038–X (pbk)
ISBN10: 0–203–92886–5 (ebk)

ISBN13: 978–0–415–96037–3 (hbk)
ISBN13: 978–0–415–96038–0 (pbk)
ISBN10: 978–0–203–92886–8 (ebk)

AMKinahan

# It's Not TV

Since first going on the air in 1972, HBO has continually attempted to redefine television as we know it. Today, pay television (and HBO in particular) is positioned as an alternative to network offerings, consistently regarded as the premier site for what has come to be called "quality television."

This collection of new essays by an international group of media scholars argues that HBO, as part of the leading edge of television, is at the center of television studies' interests in market positioning, style, content, technology, and political economy. The contributors focus on pioneering areas of analysis and new critical approaches in television studies today, highlighting unique aspects of the "HBO effect" to explore new perspectives on contemporary television from radical changes in technology to dramatic shifts in viewing habits.

*It's Not TV* provides fresh insights into the "post-television network" by examining HBO's phenomenally popular and pioneering shows, including *The Sopranos*, *The Wire*, *Six Feet Under*, *Sex and the City* as well as its failed series, such as *K Street* and *The Comeback*. The contributors also explore the production process itself and the creation of a brand commodity, along with HBO's place as a market leader and technological innovator.

**Marc Leverette** (Ph.D., Rutgers University) is Assistant Professor of Media Studies at Colorado State University.

**Brian L. Ott** (Ph.D., The Pennsylvania State University) is Associate Professor of Media Studies at Colorado State University.

**Cara Louise Buckley** (Ph.D. candidate Indiana University) is Lecturer in Communication at Emerson College.

For Pooty, Penley, and Lola
—and why not?

"It's not TV?" It's TV. Why do they think people watch it?
You watch it on TV, don't you?
You don't go to the movies to see it.

Larry David to HBO Executive Alan Wasserman,
in the *Curb Your Enthusiasm* episode "The Shrimp Incident".

# Contents

# Foreword: It's television. It's HBO

*Toby Miller*

As the fall season of 2007 drew close, discussion of HBO tended to focus on life after *The Sopranos*, the network's biggest hit alongside the dearly departed *Sex and the City*. Other popular or acclaimed dramas, such as *Six Feet Under* and *Deadwood* had ended, and hopes for *John from Cincinnati* had been dashed on the shores of Imperial Beach and a few addled *avant-garde* minds. Meanwhile, *Weeds* and *Dexter* were being heralded as the best drama on television—and they were on the network's great rival Showtime. Meanwhile, nonpremium cable franchises were doing drama as per the HBO model. Many male producers and female stars from Hollywood cinema had migrated to TV, or at least kept weekend homes there. The men shifted because of the routine pay-packet— think of Jerry Bruckheimer with *CSI* or Brian Grazer with *24* (Caldwell 2005: 90–91). The women shifted due to the limited opportunities they were afforded by the action and fantasy predilections of the major studios. Glenn Close in *Damages* on F/X and Holly Hunter in *Saving Grace* on TNT were two examples, along with many leading lights of what used to be independent film, who were also floating around decoders on one-hour shifts (McNamara, 2007). Far from HBO being a lonely quality holdout against reality genres, far from the network being able to say "It's not TV. It's HBO," Time Warner's subsidiary had been overtaken, or at least rivaled, by cable stations who had targeted its own specialty.[1]

This transformation occurred because the network's *modus operandi* became common across the medium. With video compression and fiber optics emerging by the mid-1980s, spectrum scarcity was clearly soon to be a thing of the past. In 1986, HBO became the first TV station that scrambled its entire output, so it couldn't be pirated. This set the network apart as a premium service that had to be purchased. HBO's decision to encrypt made the ownership of original content, and its protection, a byword of US cultural capitalism (Gomery, 2006). Others followed suit. But whereas that decision was to do with carefully administering boundaries, another side to the company was about achieving as loose a set of arrangements as possible. For just as HBO wished to avoid the way rabbit ears could pick up network TV *gratis*, it also wished to avoid the tight nexus that broadcast television had with a unionized workforce and job security. In this sense, HBO represents the organized, centralized, inflexible post-Fordism of contemporary cultural capitalism, because it is part of a huge conglomerate's vertical integration through basic cable, premium cable, and pay per view; for all the world cloned from a movie studio of the classical Hollywood era. At the same time, it represents the disorganized, decentralized, flexible post-Fordism of contemporary cultural capitalism. It relies on a wide variety of workers, many of whom do not have tenure and benefits, who are employed by small companies even when they sell their labor to the giant corporation of Time Warner that is the network's parent organization (you can register your desire to join the production pre-cariat at HBO via its website).

The network operates like the model for cable stations: very old-fashioned Top-40 radio with high rotation of a tiny amount of programming. It thereby avoids the classic capitalist problem of overproduction by recycling rather than exhausting its resources. Like the makers of *Fawlty Towers* or *Monty Python's Flying Circus* in the old days of the BBC, HBO's hegemons know that scarcity improves the productivity of talent (as described in Tony Kelso's chapter here). So whereas today's broadcast network drama requires 22 episodes a season, *The Sopranos* generated about half that number. HBO's production values were commensurately high—shooting on film, using long takes, filming at night, cameras on the move, single-camera production to permit multiple set-ups, and loads of reaction shots as per the movies (O'Donnell, 2007: 34, 58–59).

The rhetoric around such artistic decisions inevitably raises the specter that haunts this book (and all discussions of HBO that largely avoid boxing). I am referring here to the Q-Word—quality, or what Rupert Murdoch termed "drama run by the costume department" in deriding class-laden notions of history on television (1989: 5). And indeed, if we look at the history of the discourse of quality surrounding cable television in the United States, it is clearly articulated to a snobby ruling-class doctrine of cross-subsidized eleva-tion. In the 1950s and '60s, pay-TV advocates such as the anti-Marxist liberal left, represented by Americans for Democratic Action, called for innovation *contra* network fare of game shows, soaps, westerns, and situation comedies, twinning a rhetoric of cultural uplift with consumer sovereignty through choice. The working class stood against the idea, with Catholic War Veterans, Jewish War Veterans, and Veterans of Foreign Wars opposing such exploitation of the investment that ordinary people had made in TV sets based on the understanding that this would enable them to receive each signal that was technically available in their region (McMurria, 2007: 45, 49, 54).

Chapters in this volume by Avi Santo and Janet McCabe and Kim Akass rightly focus on HBO's reassurance to subscribers that they have sufficient cultural capital to appreciate the Q-Word (although this is not the address used in boxing bouts, for example). That interpellation might even suggest a new slogan: "You're Not a Viewer. You're a Connoisseur." And this is itself achieved with a knowing postmodern quality that makes fun of itself, as per Larry David's on–screen encounters with HBO that Lisa Williamson details.

How can all this be understood by academia? Like most domains of the human sciences, the study of television is characterized by contests over meanings and approaches, not least because its analysts "speak different languages, use different methods," and pursue "different questions" (Hartley, 1999: 18). Broadly speaking, TV has given rise to three key concerns of academic research:

- ownership and control—television's political economy;
- texts—its content; and
- audiences—its public.

Within these categories lie several other divisions:

- approaches to ownership and control vary between neoliberal endorsements of limited regulation by the state, in the interests of guaranteeing market entry for new competitors, and Marxist critiques of the *bourgeois* media's agenda for discussing society;
- approaches to textuality vary between *hermeneutic* projects, which unearth the meaning of individual programs and link them to broader social formations and problems, and *content-analytic* instruments, which seek patterns across significant numbers of similar texts; and
- approaches to audiences vary between psychological attempts to validate correlations between watching TV and social conduct, and culturalist engagements with viewer's sense-making practices.

Effects work is not on display in this volume—it doesn't ask questions like "Does Tony Soprano induce feelings of violent intent in members of the freshman psychology class at a large mid-Western university?" or "One time I became titillated during *Sex and the City* was when. . . ." But we do see chapters fulfilling other functions, and in an interdisciplinary way that frequently blurs the very boundaries I have erected. If this is tomorrow's top-tier TV studies, sign me up for premium service—but anticipate some churn.

## Note

1 Meanwhile, HBO continued to attract viewers to its longstanding coverage of sports, especially boxing. (Sport rates ahead of films on the network, provides 6–7 percent of video–on–demand, and is prominent through websites and archival sales on line.)

## Works cited

Caldwell, J.T. (2005) "Welcome to the Viral Future of Cinema (Television)", *Cinema Journal* 45 (1): 90–97.

Gomery, D. (2006) "Cable Television—US", in D. Gomery and L. Hockley (eds), *Television Industries*, pp 23–25. London: British Film Institute.

Hartley, J. (1999) *Uses of Television*. London: Routledge.

McMurria, J. (2007) "A Taste of Class: Pay–TV and the Commodification of Television in Postwar America", in S. Banet-Weiser, C. Chris, and A. Freitas (eds), *Cablevisions: Television Beyond Broadcasting*, pp 44–65. New York: New York University Press.

McNamara, M. (2007, August 28), "Film Loses its Feminine Touch", *Los Angeles Times*.

Murdoch, R. (1989, August 25), *Freedom in Broadcasting*. MacTaggart Lecture. Edinburgh Television Festival.

O'Donnell, V. (2007) *Television Criticism*. Thousand Oaks: Sage Publications.

# Introduction

## If it's not TV, then what?

The premiere episode of NBC's new Emmy-winning series, *30 Rock*, featured the following conversation about "quality TV":

LIZ:  So Tracy, we should talk about the show.
TRACY:  Man, I ain't doin' it unless I get to do it my way, you know? I want it
to be raw, HBO-style content.
LIZ:  Well, it's not HBO. It's TV.

It may seem ironic that we chose to begin a book about a cable channel that markets itself as "*not* TV" with a quotation from a show that airs on NBC—a commercial network that "*is* TV," perhaps more so than any other (it is "America's network," after all [see Hilmes, 2007]). But the juxtaposition is a fitting one, as this book is interested in precisely how the industry, production practices, branding, aesthetics, images, genres, audiences and reception of HBO differ, if at all, from commercial network television.

Since going on the air in 1972 as one of the first nonterrestrial cable networks (and becoming one of the first to broadcast via satellite in 1975), Home Box Office has continually attempted to redefine television as we know it, gaining a reputation for offering high quality original programming, in addition to the showing of feature films, adult content, and televised sport, such as boxing. Today, pay television (and HBO in particular) is positioned as an alternative to network offerings, consistently regarded as the premier site for what has come to be called "quality television," and hailed critically as well as by audiences. In recent times, HBO's influence has reached across the television landscape. Other networks have begun to imitate the HBO formula in terms of style and content, the "HBO effect," if you will. Cable channels such as FX, with shows like *The Shield* and *Nip / Tuck*, AMC with a series like

*Mad Men*, and Showtime, with *The L Word*, *Californication*, *Dexter*, *Weeds*, and *Queer As Folk*, have seemingly stolen a page from the HBO playbook, as well as networks like ABC with *Desperate Housewives* and *Lost*, Fox with *24* and *Arrested Development*, and NBC with *The Office* and *My Name is Earl*, have all brought the HBO "quality" formula to mainstream audiences. The current collaborations between HBO and the BBC, with its international reputation for producing quality programs, are HBO's latest ventures to reaffirm its position as a leader in quality programming (though the actual success or lack thereof of *Rome* and *Extras* may speak otherwise). This book suggests that HBO, as part of the leading edge of television, is at the center of television studies' interests in market positioning, style, content, technology, and political economy. As such, we focus here on pioneering areas of analysis and new critical approaches in television studies today.

### An extremely brief (but necessary) history of HBO

The story of the network that insists it's "not TV" began when early cable pioneer Charles Dolan won the franchise to bring cable to lower Manhattan in 1965.[1] Dolan's new system, Sterling Manhattan Cable, was the first underground system in the country. After Sterling Manhattan laid those wires, in an attempt to deal with the problem of blocked signals due to New York's tall buildings, Time Life Inc. purchased 20 percent of the company.

This afforded Dolan the opportunity to pitch his idea for a new cable channel to the Time Life Channel, something he was then calling "the Green Channel." However, with satellite technology still on the horizon and not yet at its full potential, Time Life agreed to back his experiment and HBO was created on November 8, 1972, then using microwave instead of satellite. And while HBO is primarily thought of today in terms of Tony Soprano's postmodern mélange of masculinity and meltdowns or Al Swearengen's particular linguistic patois, the first program ever aired on the pay channel was, in fact, a hockey game between the New York Rangers and the Vancouver Canucks via a Community Antenna Television system in Wilkes-Barre, Pennsylvania (where a plaque now can be found in the downtown public square commemorating this event). According to legend, the game was followed by the airing of the first film to be screened on HBO.

During this time, however, Sterling Manhattan was hemorrhaging money—largely due to the fact that it only had 20,000 customers in Manhattan. At this point, Time Life gained an 80 percent control and decided to kill this Manhattan project. It dropped the Sterling name, becoming Manhattan Cable Television, and effectively gained control over HBO in March 1973, when Gerald Levin took over Dolan's position as President and CEO. In September of that year Time Life completed the acquisition and soon thereafter HBO was available on 14 systems in New York and Pennsylvania. But it is worth noting, particularly with regard to the apparent crisis in "not" television's success that Kelso writes about in his chapter, that the churn rate was exceptionally high even then. Much like the problem HBO faces today when people cancel their subscription after their favorite series concludes its current season, viewers 35 years ago would often subscribe for a few weeks, get weary of watching the same loop of second-run movies, and cancel. At this point, HBO begins its long history with experimentation and its struggle for an identity. In Lawrence, Massachusetts, around this time, for example, viewers could subscribe to a free preview on channel 3. After they watched for a month, the service then moved to channel 6 and got scrambled. This pattern proved highly successful for HBO and the concept was used elsewhere and by other pay channels.

Then called simply "Home Box," HBO broke technological ground again on December 13, 1975 when it became the first network to broadcast via satellite, airing the "Thrilla in Manila" fight between Muhammad Ali and Joe Frazier. Then, on December 28, 1981 the network expanded its programming to 24 hours a day, seven days a week. Interestingly, even though HBO is often considered to be on the industry leading edge, Showtime and The Movie Channel were on 24/7 earlier (March 7, 1978 and December 1, 1979, respectively—though TMC had been around since 1973 as Star Channel, a pay movie service of Gridtronics), and Cinemax, HBO's own answer to Showtime, was 24/7 from its first day in August 1980. However, the key from an industry perspective here is that in January 1986, as Toby Miller alludes to in his preface, HBO became the first satellite network to digitally encrypt its signal, essentially putting an end to unauthorized—unpaid—viewing through its use of the Videocipher II System.

In 1983, HBO premiered *The Terry Fox Story*, a biopic of the Canadian athlete, amputee, and humanitarian. Even though the film had a Canadian theatrical release (and went on to win six Genie awards, including Best Picture), it is the first television film ever made for distribution on a cable network.

In addition to the more successful Cinemax (or Sin-a-Max and Skinemax as it became known for its large quantity of "adult" programming), HBO launched Festival, a short-lived effort in the late 1980s, which featured classic and contemporary films, as well as HBO's original comedy specials and documentaries. Unlike HBO and Cinemax, however, where the network could show what it wanted outside of FCC parameters, Festival's R-rated screenings were edited down and HBO claimed that they would show no "low quality" movies or programs. In line with this early branding of "quality"—a word that gets much play in this collection—Festival subscribers, who paid significantly less than those of HBO and Cinemax, received a 20-page monthly color programming guide. The channel's slogan is "Quality Entertainment You Can Welcome Home." The programming consisted of classic Hollywood films from the golden age of the studio systems, "Star Salutes" that focused on the body of work of a particular star (not unlike what Starz! and Encore do today), documentaries without controversy, such as nature shows or straight A&E-esque biographies, and, finally, "Centerstage" ("Here's your front row seat to great entertainment."), which included concerts from popular artists at the time, ice skating (as opposed to the more brutal boxing on HBO), as well as highly inoffensive comedy specials from performers such as Bill Cosby and Jerry Seinfeld. It is also worth noting that HBO edited its R-rated movies down to a PG-rating (though still being commercial free), since, as Leverette argues in his chapter, HBO now offers its customers something they can't get elsewhere, namely profane, violent, and sexual content. As such, and with only a few cable systems throughout the country carrying Festival, the channel failed after only one year.

With that having been noted, HBO was involved in several related lawsuits during the 1980s with cable systems and local statutes, including city and state, which attempted to censor HBO and other pay networks for broadcasting indecent material.

One of the strangest incidents in HBO's history occurred when "Captain Midnight," the alias of electronic engineer John R. MacDougall, intruded into HBO's broadcast signal, as a protest of the then-high $12.95 monthly fee and of HBO's use of scrambling equipment. After overseeing the uplink of *Pee-wee's Big Adventure* to HBO's satellite while working at Central Florida Teleport in Ocala, Florida, MacDougall repositioned the dish in its storage position, which happened to be the location of Galaxy 1, HBO's carrying satellite. And at 12:32am on April 27, 1986, he transmitted a signal that overrode HBO's broadcast of *The Falcon and the Snowman*. For four-and-a-half minutes, HBO subscribers up and down the Eastern time zone received a test pattern image with the words:

GOODEVENING HBO
FROM CAPTAIN MIDNIGHT
$12.95/MONTH?
NO WAY!
[SHOWTIME/MOVIE CHANNEL BEWARE!]

After industry and media pressure, the Federal Communications Commission (FCC) fined MacDougall $5,000 and placed him on one year's probation.

In the 1990s, HBO's expansion of their swathe of the commercial television landscape became more apparent with each passing year, with it and Cinemax becoming the first premium networks to offer a multiplexed service to their subscribers with HBO2 (which was called HBO Plus from 1998 to 2002) and Cinemax 2 (which is now called MoreMax). They premiered this service to three cable systems in Kansas, Texas, and Wisconsin and, upon proving successful, launched additional channels across numerous cable systems. HBO3 was launched in 1995 and was renamed HBO Signature three years later. HBO Family was launched in 1996. HBO Comedy and HBO Zone were both launched in 1999. HBO En Español began in 1998 and was followed-up with HBO Latino in 2000. During this time period Cinemax followed suit and began Cinemax 3 in 1996, relaunched as ActionMax in 1998, ThrillerMax in 1998, and WMax, @Max, 5StarMax, and OuterMax all being launched in 2001. HBO viewers who subscribe to the complete package receive what became known in 1998 as "HBO The Works," similar to Cinemax subscribers who can get the "MultiMax" package of channels. Currently these two packages are available as a merged combo from most cable providers under the label, "HBOMAX Pak."

In addition to its growing number of services and channels, HBO was also one of the first cable networks to broadcast a high-definition version. And in 1990 it launched HBO Independent Productions, discussed by Santo here, as a production house for a number of broadcast and basic cable channels (producing mainly sitcoms throughout the 1990s). HBO Downtown Productions was launched the following year to produce comedy specials for the network and its sister channel Comedy Central (which formerly had been an HBO company). As HBO was originally part of Time Inc., when Time Inc. merged with Warner Communications in 1989, HBO became a flagship part of the emergent parent corporation's (Time Warner) vast media empire.

While subscription numbers vary from month to month, 30 percent of the households in the United States currently (2007) receive HBO, despite the fact that subscription rates have become increasingly expensive over the years (adding a standard HBO package in some areas can increase a cable bill by as much as 40 percent). HBO is also quite popular globally, as McIntosh discusses in Chapter 3 on the potential of HBO Asia, with international operations in Bulgaria, Croatia, Czech Republic, Hungary, Latin America, Poland, Romania and Moldova, Serbia, Slovenia, Slovakia, and South Asia (including the People's Republic of Bangladesh, India, and Pakistan). As of this writing, HBO is currently moving into other "key" markets such as Japan and Western Europe, specifically France, Germany, Italy, and Spain. HBO had an early deal with New Zealand's Sky Network to bring the channel there and customers in the United Kingdom can already receive HBO content via Tiscali TV's video-on-demand service, through Internet Protocol Television, and through normal HBO On Demand services within Virgin Media's cable platform.

So, despite being just one of Time Warner's many holdings, HBO is a media empire in-and-of itself. In addition to operating all of the HBO and Cinemax networks, HBO also controls HBO films, HBO Pictures, and HBO NYC Productions (which was, prior to 1996, called HBO Showcase). It has held joint ventures with Tri-Star Pictures during its initial creation under Columbia Pictures and CBS. Comedy Central was created when Viacom's HA! merged with HBO's The Comedy Channel. In 2003, HBO sold its half of Comedy Central to Viacom, who folded the network into its MTV family. HBO is the primary sponsor of the annual U.S. Comedy Arts Fesitval. It has pioneered the use of On Demand services with Comcast in the U.S. and Virgin Media in the U.K. It had a joint venture with Liberty Media and operated the Movie Time Channel (now E!), which it sold in 1997 to Comcast and The Walt Disney Company. In 2005, HBO launched Picturehouse with New Line Cinema, taking over what had been Fine Line Features (formerly a New Line Company). In its first two years, Picturehouse has released a number of critically acclaimed films including *El Cantante*, *Fur: An Imaginary Portrait of Diane Arbus*, *Gracie*, *The King of Kong: A Fistful of Quarters*, *Last Days*, *The Notorious Bettie Page*, *Pan's Labyrinth*, *A Prairie Home Companion*, *Rocket Science*, *Run Fatboy*, *Run*, *Silk*, *Starter for Ten*, and *Tristram Shandy: A Cock and Bull Story*.

But despite its impressive resume of assets and ventures, HBO's success is always in question. Being squarely centered since its inception in debates surrounding broadcast vs. pay television, as well as decency and censorship issues, HBO's stability is under constant threat. As this book was being produced, HBO had lost nearly all of the recognizably "HBO" shows, perhaps the key works that made it "not TV." Since we've now seen the last of *Sex and the City*, *The Sopranos*, *Six Feet Under*, *Deadwood*, *Da Ali G Show*, *Carnivàle*, and *Rome* among others, HBO's "original programming"—which is, as a number of these essays argue, central to its brand identity—perhaps no longer holds the weight it once did, particularly in an age where Fox, FX, Showtime, AMC, and the traditional "Big Three" all now know the rules and are seemingly winning the game. HBO's *John from Cincinnati*, arguably one of the only post-*Sopranos* shows that anyone seemed to care about, came and went as quietly as John Monad repeated others on Imperial Beach.

Moreover, at 3:00am on May 6, 2007, HBO chairman Chris Albrecht, who many deemed the figure most responsible for HBO's late-1990s–early-2000s innovations and successes (Kubey, 2004: 475–480), was arrested for assault in Las Vegas. Albrecht blamed his attack on a woman outside of the MGM Grand on alcoholism. But this was not the first such incident. As the *Los Angeles Times* quickly reported after the arrest, in 1991 Albrecht settled a pending lawsuit for $400,000 with a female subordinate at HBO with whom he was romantically involved, but frequently physically abused. When HBO's execs start looking like its characters, when quality programming starts to seem formulaic, and when the distinctions between "TV" and "not TV" start to sound like a bizarre joke, the question must be raised, adjusting David Lavery's (2006) concern about Tony's future: "Will this be the end for HBO?" Or perhaps, in a more serious vein, this book is about one HBO, one at a particular time and place, one marked by a specific group of series, one existing in a specific cultural zeitgeist. Perhaps it isn't TV. Perhaps it is. Perhaps the answer that comes from these pages is more complicated considering HBO's pioneering work, its relationship with what Toby Miller refers to here as "the Q-word," and how the televisual landscape looks awfully good in the post-network, post-television, post-HBO era. Perhaps it *wasn't* TV. It *was* HBO.

### A brief (but necessary) explanation of It's Not TV

Several books that we feel are important contributions to the field of media studies and are along the same lines as this one in terms of presenting a sustained commentary on a specific channel are Heather Hendershot's *Nickelodeon Nation: The History, Politics, and Economics of America's Only Channel for Kids*, Piers Robinson's *The CNN Effect: The Myth of News, Foreign Policy and Intervention*, and the now numerous books on Al-Jazeera to emerge post-9/11. While the latter examples are specifically about news organizations, their sustained commentary on the place of a "network" opens a space where critical discourse surrounding pay television can, and should, occur.

In addition to the issues raised above, HBO has also been a major player in providing sports content, often serving as an alternative to network coverage or ESPN, specifically with programming such as *Costas NOW, Real Sports*, and *Inside the NFL* among others. Furthermore, HBO's documentary brand, "America Undercover," has pushed the envelope of nonfiction programming with its provocative series such as *Real Sex, Cathouse, Pornucopia, Autopsy, Last Letters Home, Ghosts of Abu Ghraib*, and *When the Levees Broke: A Requiem in Four Acts*. While HBO miniseries are standard fare at end-of-the-season award shows, with recent standout examples such as *Elizabeth, Band of Brothers, From the Earth to the Moon*, and *Angels in America*, the company has not stopped at the small screen with HBO films offering up such critical darlings in recent years as *Lackawanna Blues, American Splendor, Iron Jawed Angels, Hysterical Blindness*, and *Capturing the Friedmans*. Similarly, its stand-up comedy has, over the last three decades, been consistently thought-provoking and challenging—from George Carlin's controversial specials in the late 1970s through today's regularly scheduled specials and series such as *Def Comedy Jam, Bad Boys of Comedy, One Night Stand*, and the more avant-garde programming efforts behind shows like *Def Poetry Jam*. HBO's bread and butter, however, at least during its high watermark in the late 1990s and early 2000s, is without question its original programming, with many of the following shows leaving an indelible mark on the American (and global) cultural psyche: *Big Love*, *Carnivàle*, *Cathouse*, *The Comeback*, *Curb Your Enthusiasm*, *Deadwood*, *Def Poetry Jam*, *Entourage*, *Extras*, *Oz*, *Real Time with Bill Maher*, *Rome*, *Sex and the City*, *Six Feet Under*, *The Sopranos*, *Unscripted*, and *The Wire*. But this is not to dismiss the impact and importance of previous HBO efforts such as: *Aril$$*, *The Chris Rock Show*, *Fraggle Rock*, *Dream On*, *The Larry Sanders Show*, *The Mind of the Married Man*, *Mr. Show with Bob and Dave*, *Not Necessarily the News*, or *Tenacious D*.

Clearly this is a diverse set of shows and programs and we cannot touch on all of them here. What we do is touch on a variety of these shows in a variety of ways. Some contributions to *It's Not TV* situate an HBO within the current historical and cultural zeitgeist to analyze how HBO is figured into the tele-visual flow, while others offer polemic and personal responses to HBO's most celebrated, controversial, and, at times, ignored or misunderstood, original programming. As such, *It's Not TV* focuses on numerous aspects of the "post-television network," from HBO's political economy within the media industry and recent phenomenally popular and pioneering shows (such as *Sex and the City* or *Six Feet Under*) as well as its failed series (such as *K Street* or *The Comeback*) to the production process itself and the creation of a brand commodity, along with an understanding of HBO's place as a market leader and technological innovator.

Television's nature and constant presence demand we focus our attention to its most crucial moments. HBO's brand identity, technological innovations, and original programming have taken hold of the public imagination and emerged as unique in television's cultural production. Eschewing formulae and generic convention in its original programming, yet turning that into a formula itself, while remaining a leader in the distribution of movies on television, in addition to its status of producer and disseminator of sport, HBO's unique integration of production and distribution demands it be the focus of intense discussion among scholars of media and culture, as much as it is the focus of cultural pleasure for its millions of viewers.

What we intend to do with *It's Not TV* is reflect on the television zeitgeist, as well as its history and future, in order to be at once productive, predictive, and prophylactic in our criticism. By identifying HBO not simply as a channel, rather examining it as a phenomenon within the larger televisual context—at the height of its popularity and success and during its subsequent waning—this collection is an attempt to take the pulse of contemporary culture in order to consider how television is created and consumed in the information age, hope-fully offering a space wherein readers will find sustained investigations and varied responses to one of the most important sites of cultural production today.

The book's organization into three overarching sections encompasses much of what media studies looks like today: industries and economics, texts and contexts, and audiences and identities. We have organized this collection in a way that we hope creates a kind of meta-narrative regarding what television studies as a field looks like in the hopes of speaking to the following questions. If HBO is or is not TV—a debate you will find actively playing out in this collection—then what does it look like? What does the "not" TV industry look like? What does the "not" TV text look like? What does the "not" TV audience look like? How is HBO producing a unique answer to these questions? Is it producing a unique answer at all?

Finally, we must take this opportunity to heap thanks and praise on Matt Byrnie at Routledge for his initial interest, his thorough efforts, and his infinite patience. We also wish to thank our contributors for their individual contributions. As such, we extend our sincerest appreciation to those who lent us their insights here: Kim Akass, Rhiannon Bury, Joanna Di Mattia, Blake Ethridge, Tony Kelso, David Marc, Janet McCabe, Conor McGrath, Shawn McIntosh, Toby Miller, Avi Santo, and Lisa Williamson.

Finally, Marc wishes not only to thank his family, but also rub it in their faces that yes, though it is completely beyond belief, he gets "paid to do this shit." He also wants to thank Shawn McIntosh, Shawn Kildea, Guy McHendry, and Josh Riggs for so many great conversations about television and other important life issues, as well as all the assistants and students who he is always learning more from than they are from him. He also wants to thank Brian and Cara for lots of stuff. Thanks be to Pooty as well, for she is the best television viewing buddy anyone could ask for—except when her incessant barking interrupts whatever happens to be on. And the final thanks must go to Lehne for talking him into getting HBO and smartly talking him into getting rid of it at just the right moment. And Lehne, I love you, though Neruda can express it better: "I crave your mouth, your voice, your hair. / Silent and starving, I prowl through the streets. / Bread does not nourish me, dawn disrupts me, all day/ I hunt for the liquid measure of your steps. / I hunger for your sleek laugh,/ your hands the color of a savage harvest,/ hunger for the pale stones of your fingernails,/ I want to eat your skin like a whole almond." This book, or at least my portion of it, as with everything, is for you.

## Note

1   Much of this history comes from one of the only books devoted to the developing of HBO as a viable Time Warner commodity. For a much more thorough history of HBO, specifically its role in the home video revolution, see Mair (1988).

## Works cited

Hendershot, H. (ed.) (2004) *Nickelodeon Nation: The History, Politics, and Economics of America's Only Channel for Kids*. New York: New York University Press.

Hilmes, M. (ed.) (2007) *NBC: America's Network*. Berkeley: University of California Press.

Kubey, R. (2004) *Creating Television: Conversations with the People Behind Fifty Years of American TV*. Mahwah, NJ: Lawrence Erlbaum.

Lavery, D. (2006) "Can This Be The End of Tony Soprano?", pp 3–14 in D. Lavery (ed.) *Reading The Sopranos: Hit TV from HBO*. London: I.B. Tauris.

Mair, G. (1988) *Inside HBO: The Billion Dollar War between HBO, Hollywood, and the Home Video Revolution*. New York: Dodd, Mead & Company.

Robinson, P. (2002) *The CNN Effect: The Myth of News, Foreign Policy and Intervention*. New York and London: Routledge.

# Part I

# Industry and economics

# Introduction: The not TV industry

*Marc Leverette*

A specter haunts television studies—the specter of the media industries.

Within this specter loom other spirits as well. They go by many names: branding, political economy, globalization, production, and so on. And these ghosts have been called out by name for very explicit reasons in this section in its examination of HBO from a largely institutional and economic perspective. And so these spirits will be our guide in this section as the following four chapters each ostensibly ask: "If HBO is not TV, then how does HBO relate to the television industry?"

Part of HBO's success in the television industry is due in large part to how it defines and, perhaps more importantly, brands itself. And while many of the chapters in this book—not merely this section—challenge HBO's claim as to whether or not it's actually "TV," it is hard to deny that a key to good branding is, of course, a slogan. And while HBO's "It's Not TV. It's HBO." is a statement that gets thoroughly deconstructed throughout here, it wasn't always how HBO saw itself. For example, HBO, since its inception has had no less than 11 different catchphrases to help people remember the place of Home Box Office in their lives. From 1972 to 1978 it was "Different and First." Then came "The Home Box," which was used until 1982. The 1982–1983 season briefly heard the slogan "Start with Us on HBO." "There's No Place Like HBO" stuck around for two years, getting replaced in 1986 with "Let's All Get Together," which—somehow—managed to last until 1988. "Watch Us Here on HBO" wasn't very popular either, getting replaced in 1989–1990 with "Simply the Best," one of their more elaborate image campaigns constructed around the Tina Turner hit of the same name. Both 1992 and 1993 were privy to "We're HBO," elegant in its brevity. Beyond the understanding of this author (who was not a media critic at the time nor an HBO consumer) is how "We're Out of Town Today" managed to be the central branding slogan for four years. However, the HBO that has come to be central in today's cultural zeitgeist, the post-*Sopranos* HBO that opens all its shows with that familiar click of static with the logo coming quickly into focus, has been all about the two sentences from which the title of this book is hijacked. In addition to "It's Not TV. It's HBO," in 2006, the website began confronting viewers with the phrase "Get More," in addition to the former, more familiar slogan.

Avi Santo's chapter "Para-Television and Discourses of Distinction: The Culture of Production at HBO," seemingly takes up that last motto by way of considering whether or not HBO is offering us a chance or an ultimatum, though an investigation of how HBO's culture of production has "contributed to a series of programming and marketing strategies that position the channel (and its subscribers) in a complex and often contradictory relationship with the rest of the television universe." As Santo observes, HBO's efforts to brand itself in opposition to the rest of television contradict some of the basic operating principles upon which the pay network relies in order to remain profitable. Santo sees HBO executives as having seemingly bought into the pay station's own rhetoric, thus creating a work culture that, at times, appears at odds with HBO's own long-range profitability and sustainability.

Modern theories of political economy illuminate a capitalist society where profit is the absolute truth and those in control preach auspiciously from within the system. The problem is "classically" identified by Horkheimer and Adorno (1972) as an illusion of choice, where culture is being "engulfed by an insatiable uniformity," charging that "culture today is infecting everything with sameness." This illusion manifests itself across the spectrum of our cultural commodities. Our media is always and already infected, with everything going to the bottom line. For many interested in the media industries and their ideological and economic ramifications, effort to stress a connection among economics, society, and culture illustrates the necessity to critically evaluate the industry. Commenting on the importance of political economy, Ben Bagdikian (2004) argues that the quest for profit maximization has created a situation of deregulation, conglomeration, and integration, which the corporate giants—giants such as Time Warner, HBO's parent company—have taken advantage of in order to dominate the market. For media scholars, the theories of political economy are important because they deal directly with the production and consumption of *our* culture, which at the moment is dominated by the undeniable structures of capitalism.

This problematic relationship with risk/creativity and success/profit in the media industries is at the heart of Tony Kelso's chapter. As Kelso and his political economy perspective are quick to show, when it comes to creating commercial network programming, one implicit rule is clear: avoid risk (resulting in the "sameness" Horkheimer and Adorno so disdained). Television executives often feel pressure to provide an "advertising-friendly" environment that, while building ratings, does not threaten revenue by alienating sponsors.

Yet because HBO relies on viewer subscriptions, it must separate itself from commercial stations and, consequently, take chances. As such, Kelso examines some of HBO's recent, innovative content to establish this theme and argues that the network demonstrates greater respect for its audience than advertising-supported channels by more often giving viewers not what they are *willing* to watch, but what they *want* to watch.

Shawn McIntosh takes this question a clear step further—at least in geographic terms—as he asks, "Will *Yingshuiji* Buzz Help HBO Asia?" Concerned with what the network's expansion and various partnerships overseas provide, McIntosh finds that a look at HBO Asia offers an interesting window into how HBO may change its business practices in the future. McIntosh attempts to frame HBO within the global marketplace, a complex system that is not at first easily definable. Globalization is a large concept with many different inroads. A hotly debated notion, it has become *the* buzzword in contemporary discourse. McIntosh uses a definition provided by David Held and Anthony McGrew (2003: 4) that's as good as any:

> Simply put, globalization denotes the expanding scale, growing magnitude, speeding up and deepening impact of interregional flows and patterns of social interaction. It refers to a shift or transformation in the scale of human social organization that links distant communities and expands the reach of power relations across the world's major regions and continents.

In examining how HBO Asia positions itself within the Asian market, McIntosh discusses both implications for HBO as a whole and what the HBO brand means within the Asian media market—a market radically different from its European and North and South American counterparts. Whereas Kelso uses political economy as a starting point for tracking HBO programming decisions, McIntosh here eschews generalized political economy assumptions and offers a nuanced look at how a modern transnational media entertainment company such as HBO negotiates new (global) markets and how that very interaction may not only change the markets it enters, but the practices and assumptions of the company itself.

The final chapter in this section, Janet McCabe and Kim Akass's "It's Not TV, It's HBO's Original Programming: Producing Quality TV," links these broad-ranging industry-based questions with the recent aesthetic and content-based turn in television studies. Thus their chapter aims to situate HBO's original programming within the current "Quality TV" debate, a debate McCabe and Akass are at the center of (forthcoming). With this contribution, McCabe and Akass suggest how HBO emerged as an aggressive market leader at the moment when the landscape of contemporary US television was itself changing through

an assessment of how HBO instituted a policy of original programming, building as it did its groundbreaking reputation on notions of "quality" based on
branding, cost, and innovation as it sought to find a place for itself in an
overcrowded television landscape/marketplace. Additionally, McCabe and
Akass look at what impact this business strategy had on the formal style and
content of original programming, what we could call the HBO effect. By
focusing on the promotion of the author, aesthetic and formal innovations, and
controversy, they explore how notions of quality were used and asserted
to do different work, to boldly go where the networks and other cable channels (until recently) feared to tread, offering the suggestion that it is no
accident that a renewed academic interest in TV coincides with the rise to
prominence of HBO. For McCabe and Akass, the polemic debate is now
between the "quality" of HBO (that it's not regular TV) and the popularity of
network television, in addition to the struggle between good (expensive) TV
(eg *The Sopranos*) and bad (cheap) TV (eg reality TV, makeover shows, etc); the
existence of this polemic (good/bad; quality/popular) is at the heart of discussions—be they academic, critical or popular—defining contemporary U.S.
television.

What these four chapters offer then are snapshots of a particular company
that exists in a particular time and place. As these chapters show, when we
start to look at HBO outside of this particular time, and place things outside
of the snapshots' frame, and unravel, things change, and things get further
complicated. But these chapters are written knowing full well that these
complications are the object of critical media studies. In a globalized world
where corporate branding, programming, and production all exist within a
complex network of synergistic ebbs and flows, television studies must fully
recognize the ghost that is always at our backs. What these chapters argue for
is a better understanding of the ways in which HBO operates and the system
in which it both is and is not TV. HBO is interested in these contours for
economic reasons; the authors in this section illustrate that the media industries and the systemic interests that reify global, neoliberal capital have, as
Marx and Engels would say, "a world to win." For scholars, that world is ours
to understand.

Media critics of all countries, unite!

## Works cited

Bagdikian, B. (2004) *The New Media Monopoly*. Boston: Beacon.
Held, D. & McGrew, A. (2003) "The Great Globalization Debate: An Introduction",
    pp 1–49 in D. Held & A. McGrew (eds), *The Global Transformations Reader: An
    Introduction to the Globalization Debate*. Cambridge: Polity.

Horkheimer, M. & Adorno, T. (1972) "The Culture Industry: Enlightenment as Mass Deception", pp 120–167 in *The Dialectic of Enlightenment*, trans. J. Cumming. New York: Continuum.

McCabe, J. & Akass, K. (eds) (forthcoming) *Quality TV: Contemporary American Television and Beyond*. London: IB Tauris.

Chapter 1

# Para-television and discourses of distinction

## The culture of production at HBO

*Avi Santo*

HBO's recent success is often credited to the innovativeness of its programming and the effectiveness of its advertising. This claim has generated a slew of
articles, both academic and journalistic, debating whether or not HBO is TV in
the traditional sense. Despite the difficulty many scholars and commentators
have in identifying what television in the post-network era is, they nevertheless have highlighted "qualitative" differences between pay cable and standard
broadcast fare. Yet, very little commentary has directly addressed either the
historical development of original programming on HBO *in relation* to broadcast television or explored how HBO's unique culture of production has contributed to a series of programming and marketing strategies that position the
channel (and its subscribers) in a complex and often contradictory relationship
with the rest of the television universe.

It largely has been assumed that the deregulated and advertiser-free space
pay cable occupies is sufficient to explain differences in content, form, and
practice between HBO and network television. In contrast, I contend that
HBO's historical position within the televisual landscape has produced a set of
institutional imperatives and tensions that have greatly contributed to the types
of programming it produces and the marketing campaigns it runs. Among
these are HBO's requirements continuously to attract new subscribers while
keeping churn to a minimum and its need to distinguish its product from
standard network fare while simultaneously looking to broadcast and cable
networks as sites for future syndication and production deals. The end result
for HBO is neither television in the traditional network era sense of the word
(not that anything produced in the post-network landscape truly is) nor "not
television," but, as I will demonstrate, the production of para-television, which
purposely relies on mimicking and tweaking existing and recognizable TV
forms.

Furthermore, I argue that HBO's efforts to distinguish itself from standard
broadcast television are indicative of what the pay network believes it is selling

to subscribers. On a fairly simple level, pay cable must appear to offer something that subscribers cannot get either on free TV (the networks) or for the price of basic cable, and which viewers believe is superior to those cheaper alternatives. Thus, HBO must continuously promote discourses of "quality" and "exclusivity" as central to the subscription experience. These discourses aim to brand not only HBO, but its audience as well. In this manner, pay cable sells cultural capital to its subscribers, who are elevated above the riffraff that merely consume television, a medium long derided as base and feminizing in its unabashed embrace of consumerism. Thus, HBO has formulated a notion of what subscribers are paying for that often conflicts with its own institutional imperatives. "Quality" implies a distinction from network programming that is neither fully attainable nor desirable given HBO's historical reliance upon network television as an ancillary market and programming inspiration. "Exclusivity" implies a limiting of access that conflicts with HBO's stated desire to attract as many subscribers as possible. This contributes further to the institutional tensions that impact HBO programming and marketing, since assumptions about what subscribers are seeking conflicts with the pay network's continuous need to seek out new markets and develop closer ties with the broadcast networks.

Finally, I argue that HBO's efforts to brand itself in opposition to the rest of television not only contradict some of the basic operating principles upon which the pay network relies in order to remain profitable, but that HBO has seemingly bought into its own rhetorical position to such an extent that it has created a work culture that, at times, appears at odds with its own long-range profitability and sustainability. In other words, it is not simply that HBO's marketing strategy emphasizing its non-televisuality is misleading when examined with close regard to the pay channel's historical relationship to the rest of television, but that HBO has absorbed the cultural values it believes subscribers are seeking into its own culture of production, even to the detriment of its supposed economic bottom line. In this sense, cultural values inform economic decisions as much as they are shaped by them, complicating traditional political economy arguments that reduce culture down to its means of production and see economics determining such processes in every instance. Certainly, HBO's programming and marketing strategies are intended to serve a profit-generating purpose, but they are also informed by the particular cultural values HBO seeks to brand itself by, which, in turn, intersect and interfere with the pay channel's financial goals.

I will begin this essay by tracing briefly the historical emergence of original programming on HBO. I will discuss the key regulatory, industrial, and technological shifts that have influenced HBO's foray into the production of para-television. I then will analyze the particular institutional imperatives and tensions HBO faces and how these are negotiated through its programming and marketing choices. I will end by discussing how the cultural values HBO seeks to brand itself by have been incorporated into the cultural philosophy of the pay channel, and have, in turn, led to programming and marketing strategies that run counter to HBO's economic goals.

## Leading up to originality

HBO was launched in November 1972 as a small pay movie channel available as part of the Time Inc. cable package. The pay channel's initial audience comprised 365 subscribers in Wilkes-Barre, Pennsylvania (Miller, 1994: 1). In 1975, following the FCC's decision to allow cable operators to import long-distance signals and expand into the top 100 markets in the U.S., HBO leased a transponder on RCA's SATCOM 1 satellite and became the first pay network in operation (Gatesward, 1997: 783–784). HBO's initial satellite telecast was the Ali–Frazier boxing match from Manila. HBO's early lineups included feature films and sporting events, which would become the bread and butter of pay cable throughout the next decade.

HBO's first venture into original programming was a 1972 Pennsylvania polka special that clearly was targeted at the Wilkes-Barre community, which it initially serviced. While original programming existed on HBO from the very beginning, it primarily was intended to fill up space on the pay network's schedule while HBO took the FCC to court over restrictions on film broadcasts. As of 1969, FCC regulations prevented cable channels from showing films that were less than 10 years old or more than two years old. This was intended to ensure that broadcast network affiliates would have first claim to the most lucrative films produced by Hollywood, while cable was reduced to showing films that had already run on network television or had bombed in the theatre (Strover, 1997: 1722–1723). In 1977, the U.S. Court of Appeals for the District of Columbia declared that the FCC had exceeded its authority over the cable industry by imposing programming restrictions (Strover, 1997: 1723). HBO was now free to acquire and show any film it desired.

HBO's programming strategy throughout the late 1970s and early 1980s relied heavily upon showcasing previously exhibited theatrical features. The approach proved to be incredibly successful as the pay channel's subscription rate grew from 2 million to 11.5 million households from 1977 to 1984 (Shales, 1983: L1). By the mid-1980s, however, the market for pay cable had begun to stagnate. HBO's subscriber growth rate declined in the first quarter of 1984 to 300,000, 70 percent less than the pay channel had anticipated and approximately half of what it had gained in the first quarter of 1983 (Brown, 1984: G1). This decline was due primarily to the rising cost of basic cable (brought about by further deregulation of the cable industry under Reagan) and the advent of the VCR, which altered both the distribution pattern for feature films to ancillary markets and the viewing habits of pay cable sub-scribers (Lippman, 1990: 1). By the late 1980s, cable deregulation had led to an explosion of new channels, some targeting specific niche audiences (Lifetime, BET), others backed by Hollywood studios (USA by MCA and Paramount, TNT by Warner Communications and Turner Broadcasting) and showing feature films without the added pay-TV cost (Hilmes, 1990: 309). Moreover, pay-per-view and digital technologies were looming on the horizon, threatening to expand the field of competition even wider (Greenstein, 1991: 1). HBO needed to diversify in order to stay competitive. Original productions quickly became a means of justifying subscription rates and filling out HBO's schedule.

As early as 1982, HBO began producing its own made-for-pay-TV-movies, following in network television's footsteps. The networks had made a similar investment in made-for-TV fare a decade earlier in preparation for cable's cornering of the feature film market (Morgan, 1986: 50). HBO also experi-mented with series television as far back as 1983, when it premiered *The Hitchhiker* (1983–1989), a horror/suspense anthology series reminiscent of *Alfred Hitchcock Presents* in both mode of production and thematic content, featuring a different cast and crew for each episode and utilizing the fantasy/horror genre to tell (decidedly lurid) morality tales (Margulies, 1985: 6). In 1984, HBO premiered its first comedy series, *1ˢᵗ and Ten*, which ran sporadic-ally from 1984 to 1991. *1ˢᵗ And Ten* told the story of a fictitious football team and was a clear attempt to build off of HBO's prior success with sporting events. While *The Hitchhiker* and *1ˢᵗ and Ten* were generally successful for HBO, a lack of ancillary markets to defray the cost of producing each series hampered the shows' consistency and kept their budgets to a minimum. Over the next decade, however, HBO would develop the requisite syndication markets needed to produce high-quality television series.

Over the years, HBO successfully had launched the careers of many big name comics and had become renowned for its comedy specials throughout the television industry. Many comics had honed their routines on HBO specials and then successfully had procured prime-time sitcoms on network television. Roseanne Barr had asked HBO to develop a series for her before joining ABC's prime-time lineup (Stilson, 1991: 14). Other success stories included the Wayans Brothers, who created *In Living Color* for FOX, and Jerry Seinfeld. The successful crossover of these comedians made HBO aware that a market was opening up for the type of comedy it specialized in (Mitchell, 1990: 40). With all this in mind, HBO launched its independent production wing (HBOIP) in October of 1990 with the express purpose of creating series television for broadcasters and cable channels alike. The strategy of HBOIP was to market itself as a comedy boutique, specializing in sitcom development based on HBO's successful comedy exclusives (Mitchell, 1990: 40).

HBOIP's first (and best) client would be the FOX network, launched by Rupert Murdoch in 1986. By 1991, FOX was ready to offer a full prime-time schedule of shows and was in need of programming to fill its lineup. Since FOX wanted to target a younger demographic than the other three networks and sought to differentiate its product from standard broadcast fare, HBOIP seemed the perfect partner (Cerone, 1992: 8). HBOIP produced two series for FOX in 1991: *ROC*, described by Chris Albrecht, HBO's head of original productions as a "black honeymooner," and *Down the Shore* (Stilson, 1991: 14). Other network shows developed by HBOIP include *The Ben Stiller Show* and *Martin,* also for FOX. To this day, HBO produces series for network TV, including the highly successful *Everybody Loves Raymond* for CBS.

FOX's need for programming also resulted in the network purchasing the syndication rights to Showtime's *It's the Garry Shandling Show* in 1988 (Lowry, 1994: 3). This led pay cable operators to the conclusion that ancillary markets were becoming available for their products. This was further confirmed when, in 1992, Congress instituted a safe harbor block of time on network schedules from midnight to 6:00am, in which broadcasters could air edgier material. The block was eventually moved back to 10:00pm from midnight (Blumenthal and Goodenough, 1988: 193). Material that had previously been deemed too racy for other networks was now in high demand.

The opening up of ancillary markets was key to HBO developing its own original series programming. HBO felt confident that it could develop comedic series through HBOIP that could either be shown on pay cable or sold to the networks. Moreover, HBO knew that it now had syndication options for its original series, which guaranteed both supplementary income and free publicity for the pay cable channel (when FOX bought the syndication rights to *Tales from the Crypt*, it renamed the series *HBO's Tales from the Crypt*) (Cerone, 1994: 2). In addition, the explosive growth of commercial broadcast stations in Europe and Asia throughout the 1990s provided HBO with international syndication possibilities as well (Bigelow, 1988: 64). With this safety net in place, HBO developed its first hit series, *Dream On*, in 1990. Though the series, much like other HBO original productions, contained nudity and profanity, HBO also shot a cleaned up version of each episode with syndication in mind (Coe, 1990: 75–77). FOX eventually syndicated *Dream On.*

Thus, from the very beginning, HBO's foray into original programming has had an explicit connection with standard broadcast television. Whether in response to regulations limiting the types of movies HBO could show or in recognition of the possibilities networks like FOX offered in terms of production and syndication outlets, HBO's efforts at creating series cannot be separated from events happening on other networks. As the next section will elaborate, for these and other reasons, HBO's original productions have historically maintained a particular relationship with network television that is rooted in equal parts innovation and repetition. Rather than argue whether HBO is or is not television, I assert that its programming, at least, is best defined as a para-television, purposely dialoguing with existing television forms and practices in order to call attention to the variations HBO introduces into otherwise familiar television experiences.

## Institutional context

According to Amanda Lotz, HBO operates on a radically different economic model from network television. As a subscription-based service that bypasses advertisers and markets itself directly to its viewers, HBO is able largely to sell itself to subscribers based on the strength of only a few isolated programs (Lotz, 2003: 49–52). "The network is not exceptionally concerned with how often or what the individual subscriber views, so much as that each subscriber finds enough value in some aspect of the programming to continue the subscription" (Lotz, 2003: 59). Thus, HBO appears to be in a good position to experiment with its programming, since the network will effectively earn the same amount of revenue regardless of the success or failure of any given program.

Yet, it is my contention that despite this freedom to experiment, the types of original programming HBO historically has produced are more accurately defined as para-television than non-television. By para-television I am referring to production practices and programming choices that are purposely situated alongside recognizable television forms in order to confer particular meanings upon them. HBO might define itself as "Not Television," but most of the content appearing on HBO draws upon existing television forms, narratives, aesthetics, themes, and economic and institutional practices in order to articulate HBO's difference. HBO has relied upon various regulatory and economic differences between pay and regular television to add variation to its programming strategies, but very rarely produces anything non-televisual (and when it has, as shall be elaborated upon further along in this essay, such programming has largely been met with disinterest on the parts of subscribers).

Of course, while HBO's programming strategies have never veered too far away from recognizable television forms, they have also been informed by the particular cultural climates in which they emerged. For example, Thomas Streeter has identified a shift in public discourse surrounding cable throughout the 1960s and early 1970s, in which community groups, educators, industry representatives, and policymakers began to herald the untapped potential for cable to be used in socially beneficial ways that would allow for greater participation on the parts of local communities and disempowered minority groups (Streeter, 1987: 178).

As a cable station born into an era that stressed cable's utopian potential for diversity and public service, HBO's programming choices have, in part, been influenced by a public service model of television. Early HBO programming included Jim Henson's kids' show *Fraggle Rock* (1983), John Moffitt's political humor series *Not Necessarily the News* (1983–1990), and *HBO Showcase '86* (1986), which Bridget Potter, former senior vice president of original programming at HBO, compared with PBS' *American Playhouse* (Modderno, 1987: 1). Later efforts have included Robert Altman's experimental blending of reality television and fictional political satire in *Tanner 88* (1988), and Mike Nichols' adaptation of Tony Kushner's postmodern account of the impact of AIDS in the 1980s, *Angels in America* (2004).

To this day, HBO continues to produce documentaries (*America Undercover* [1993–]), comedy and variety specials (*John Leguizamo's Sexaholix: A Love Story* [2002], *Russell Simmons Presents Def Poetry Jam* [2002–]), mini-series (*From the Earth to the Moon* [1998], *Band of Brothers* [2001]) and musical concerts (*Janet Jackson Live in Hawaii* [2002], *Britney Spears Live from Las Vegas* [2001]) in much greater number than any of the four network stations. In particular, HBO has staked out a claim for itself in the field of documentaries, earning numerous Emmys, Peabodys, and Oscars. These awards have brought the pay station a great deal of prestige and publicity. Still, most HBO documentaries traffic in controversy.

One of the most significant outcomes of HBO's court battle with the FCC was that the Court of Appeals declared cable, which is purchased as opposed to "freely distributed" like radio and broadcast television, to be more akin to newspaper publishing, which is offered protection under the First Amendment (Strover, 1997: 1723–1724). This ruling would have a profound impact on the content of HBO's programming, which could incorporate nudity, violence, and vulgarity in ways that the networks could not. As a result, almost all of HBO's original series, from the dramas to the documentaries to the sitcoms, contain material that could not be included on network TV. The HBO documentary unit also produces programs like *Real Sex* (2000–) and *Taxi Cab Confessions* (1995–), which feature soft-core sex acts and illicit monologues from unsuspecting travelers, further blurring the line between discourses of public service and exploitation.

As HBO has responded over the years to various industrial, legislative, and technological challenges by diversifying its interests and reinventing its appeal to audiences as a site for groundbreaking television series in addition to feature films and sporting events, the pay station has also become increasingly invested in distinguishing itself from network television. This seems almost paradoxical, as HBO has, over the past two decades, gradually begun to resemble network TV more and more with each new foray into original programming. Knowing that a secondary market for HBO-originals existed bolstered the pay station's interest in producing original programming, but it also limited the degree of innovativeness HBO would be willing to pursue, as it attempted to cater to network interests in "edgier" but not radically different fare.

The networks' influence on HBO programming, however, goes beyond merely accommodating syndication needs. The networks have also provided HBO with a long history of production and programming choices, both successful and unsuccessful, to draw upon when creating their own series. As HBO's investment in original series production continues to grow, the pay station has also begun to compete directly with network offerings and must therefore walk a thin line between borrowing from established network genres and programming strategies and tinkering with them in order to distinguish itself from its broadcast counterparts.

Despite its claims of difference, HBO has historically relied upon proven commodities when producing original series, or as television consultant Paul Bortz suggests, "The cable industry historically has been able to sell successfully what has been pre-sold to the public" (quoted in Brown, 1984: G1). From the onset, HBO employed producers with television experience. Jim Henson had created and successfully syndicated *The Muppet Show* (1976–1981) to network affiliates before moving on to *Fraggle Rock* in 1983. Likewise, John Moffitt, the creator of *Not Necessarily the News* (1983–1990), had previously produced *Fridays* (1980–1982), a similar late-night comedy series for ABC. Later series would either continue this trend of relying upon experienced television producers (*Oz* by Tom Fontana and Barry Levinson, the creators of *Homicide: Life on the Streets* [1993–1999]; *Sex and the City* by Darren Starr, creator of *Beverly Hills 90210* [1990–2000] and *Melrose Place* [1992–1999]; *The Sopranos* by David Chase, producer of *I'll Fly Away* [1991–1993] and *Northern Exposure* [1990–1995]), or would be produced by individuals who would later have great success on network TV (Stephen Engel and Kevin Bright, the creators of *Dream On*, went on to produce *Mad About You* [1992–1999], *Just Shoot Me* [1997–2002], and *Friends* [1994–2004], while Brad Grey, the executive producer on *The Larry Sanders Show*, fulfilled a similar capacity on *News Radio* [1995–1999] and *Politically Incorrect* [1997–2001] before returning to HBO to produce *The Sopranos*). The steady crossover of producers from network television to HBO and back again is but one area of intersection.[1]

Over the years, HBO has also reworked its prime-time schedule so that it more closely resembles that of the networks, most especially early FOX and current-day NBC lineups. Until the late 1990s, even successful series like *Dream On* were simply used as lead-ins for HBO's principle product, feature films. Other formats, from documentaries to soft-core erotica were used to fill early evening and late night timeslots in between features. In 1997, HBO experimented with placing its original series *Oz*, *The Larry Sanders Show* and *Arli$$* in 11:00pm timeslots spread across the weekday schedule. The justification for this scheduling strategy was that HBO intended to complement network prime-time programming. HBO hoped that viewers would transfer over to the pay channel after they had finished watching their network shows (Richmond, 1997: 5). Today, HBO makes no secret of the fact that it seeks to challenge the networks head on for prime-time dominance (Carter, 2002: C1). The pay channel has carefully selected Sunday night (traditionally a weak network night for adult-oriented fare) as its starting point. When FOX emerged in 1987, it also chose Sunday night for its initial foray. HBO's series are shown back-to-back, from 7:00pm to 9:00pm estimated, usually beginning with the sitcoms (*Sex and the City*, *Arli$$*, *Curb Your Enthusiasm*, *The Mind of the Married Man*), progressing towards the family dramas (*The Sopranos*, *Six Feet Under*) and ending with the more hard-hitting (ie more explicit and controversial) dramatic or documentary series (*Oz*, *America Undercover*). In this regard, HBO has attempted to mimic the flow of NBC's successful 1990s "Must See TV" Thursday lineup, which featured a similar progression.

Further, following NBC's lead, HBO has also opted to program all of its hit series on the same night rather than dispersing them throughout the weekly schedule. As evidenced by HBO's "Sunday is. . . HBO" ad campaign, this strategy is intended to create audience identification with Sunday night as belonging to HBO, much as Thursday was long associated with NBC. By getting audiences to tune in for an entire evening rather than a particular program, HBO can ensure that new series both receive instant viewers and cultural cache when slotted into the Sunday night schedule. This, again, is a strategy borrowed directly from NBC, which, since the late 1980s, has used the strength of its Thursday night lineup to launch new series that have instantly scored well in the ratings simply because of their lucrative timeslot.

Still, as a pay network, HBO earns its revenue from subscriptions rather than selling spots to advertisers, which means that it does not have to tailor the content of its programming (as the networks do) in order to appease merchandisers seeking inoffensive material appealing to the greatest common denominator of viewers. Contrarily, the pay station can actually afford to be critical of consumer habits and poke fun at specific product brands without worrying that advertisers will pull their spots. It is important to note, however, that while HBO has long touted itself as an advertiser-free environment, many of HBO's series contain product placement (*The Sopranos* and Tropicana Orange Juice, *Sex and the City* and numerous clothing and shoe manufacturers, not to mention an entire episode devoted to Carrie upgrading to an iMac) and advocate the rewards of consumerism (entire romances are structured around shopping sprees on *Sex and the City*, while business is usually conducted around a restaurant table on *The Sopranos*). Although series like *Oz* and *The Sopranos* provide complex critiques of capitalism, their serial narratives epitomize the very act of repetitive consumption that television series demand of their viewers.

While in the end, a lack of commercials does not equal a lack of commercialism, the absence of advertising on HBO has still had an impact on original programming found on the pay cable station. HBO's series do not have commercial interruptions, which means that their pacing differs from network series that must rely on hooks to keep viewers watching through the advertisements (Lowry, 1999: 1). Rather than a series of crises and resolutions, HBO programs generally build steadily towards a climax through multiple examinations of a particular theme from myriad perspectives. Alternatively, climactic events can occur at almost any place in the narrative as, for example, when an assassination attempt on Tony Soprano, a plot that had been developing for several episodes, unceremoniously occurs two-thirds of the way through a first season episode of *The Sopranos*.

However, since the majority of HBO's potential subscriber pool already watches basic television (very few people purchase a television set for the first time with the sole intent of subscribing to HBO), the pay network must walk a fine line between offering up different, yet familiar, programming. As Horace Newcomb has argued with regards to HBO's signature series, *The Sopranos*, and the position it holds within the post-network era, "changes implied in the term 'post-network' are deeply reliant on the comfortable, generalized familiarity with 'TV' as experienced in the past. Rather than exploring a program such as *The Sopranos* as a distinct 'break' with that past, then, or considering HBO as somehow totally distinctive and new in its programming strategies other questions should be addressed. What, for example, could it mean that millions of viewers attending to [*The Sopranos*] also remember *Dragnet*, *Naked City*, *The Untouchables*, *The Fugitive*, *Police Story*, *Hill Street Blues*, or *NYPD Blue*? Equally significant, however, is a question such as this: What does it mean that these same viewers remember *Father Knows Best* or *Eight is Enough*, or, perhaps even more telling, *Roots* or *Dallas*?" (Newcomb, 2003: 139).

Similarly, Ien Ang also suggests that producers elaborate on what they already know about popular pleasures, so that the pleasures offered are not likely to be structurally new, experimental, and provocative (Ang, 1985: 23). Newcomb contends, however, that it is precisely this degree of familiarity with existing network series coupled with HBO's modification of the generic base of its programming that accounts for much of the appeal of *The Sopranos*.

In this sense, *The Sopranos* and other HBO series, like *Oz* are indicative of the pay-TV network's ambivalent relationship with network television. *Oz* borrows aesthetically, generically and thematically from its network predecessor, *Homicide,* as well as from other gritty dramas like *NYPD Blue* and *ER* (Dempsey and Williams, 1995: 5), but the show is set in a prison rather than a police station and focuses primarily on the inmates' points-of-view rather than the police officers'. *The Sopranos* mixes elements of the television drama (*Seventh Heaven, Picket Fences*) with the gangster film (*The Godfather Trilogy, Goodfellas*); blending genres from the two primary sources HBO has historically looked to for content, TV and film. Both series feature ensemble casts (*The Sopranos* has a more clearly defined "main character," but also myriad supporting players) involved in multiple story arcs that can unfold over the course of a single episode or can take an entire season or longer to develop. In this sense, both series are no different than *ER* or *NYPD Blue*. Like those shows, both *Oz* and *The Sopranos* can also be understood as workplace dramas, where romance and intrigue (or, in the case *of The Sopranos,* soccer matches and trips to the high school principal) intersect with the daily grind of prison and mafia life.

Still, both series take these conventions to new heights through their graphic depictions of violence and sexuality, their willingness to kill off major characters at the apex of their plot lines, their thematic focus on criminality and its incestuously familial intersections, and their ambiguously perverse repositioning of the villain as occasionally heroic, somewhat likeable, and often understandable. Thus, these series, like HBO, have positioned themselves in relation to network television. They are para-television. In so doing, they have borrowed and modified the existing "cops and docs" workplace drama genre that Tom Schatz identifies as central to network television, in an effort to offer potential subscribers both familiarity and "originality." Schatz argues that this quasi-serialized format has been one of the staples of network prime-time dramas like *Hill Street Blues* and *St. Elsewhere* and later, *ER* and *NYPD Blue*, since the early 1980s.

The generic adaptation of the work drama is also an effective strategy for increasing HBO's subscriber pool. This process involves a simultaneous need to attract new viewers while retaining old ones, with which the quasi-serialized and familiar (but not too familiar) nature of the work drama can assist at both ends. Mark C. Rogers, Michael Epstein, and Jimmie L. Reeves have argued that the HBO series, *The Sopranos*, combines serial and episodic elements, which "reward avid fans without alienating casual viewers." (Rogers, Epstein, and Reeves, 2001: 54) The use of the sequential series or episodic serial (Dolan, 1994: 36–60) assists HBO in retaining viewers through the incorporation of never-ending or continuing themes or plotlines within series that rely on self-contained episodes, which allow new subscribers to jump on at any given moment. HBO also strategically releases the previous season of a series on VHS and DVD just prior to a new season commencing, while also rerunning old episodes on most of its multiplex channels throughout the year. The advent of video-on-demand technology further increases the options available to new subscribers (and devoted fans) to catch up on old episodes.

Para-television always maintains a murky relationship with existing forms of television and traffics in ambiguous definitions of qualitative distinction. Whereas television seeks to attract a mass audience, para-television is designed to build coalition audiences. This, in turn, makes the semi-serialized, melo-dramatic genre appealing to HBO executives, precisely because its ambiguities can be marketed to multiple audiences, allowing the network to seek out new subscribers while maintaining their current audience base. Jim Collins has referred to this programming strategy as an attempt to build coalition audiences through series that contain interlocking appeals attractive to multiple audience segments (Collins, 1992: 342). Mary Celeste Kearney similarly asserts that "we must move beyond the problematic assumption that media texts featuring characters of a particular age are consumed primarily by viewers of that same age-spectatorial identifications cross the boundaries of sex, race, and sexuality" (Kearney, 2002: 23–68).

## What are viewers paying for?

What the previous two sections of this paper have argued is that HBO turned towards original programming out of a need to diversify and retain subscribers amidst industrial, legislative, and technological changes affecting the cable market, and in so doing, looked to network television for a working model. Moreover, HBO's programming differs from network fare primarily in terms of content, which is obfuscated by the fact that the pay station shoots a "clean" version of every episode that is suitable for network consumption. In fact, network television initially served as a viable syndication market for HBO fare, rather than a rival for ratings. It was only following the success of some of its early programming efforts that HBO moved to challenge the networks for a prime-time share of the audience. This involved a conscious duplication of network programming strategies and a modification of established genres resulting in the production of what I have termed para-television.

If this is the case, then why does HBO insist on differentiating itself from network television through its promotional catchphrase, "it's not TV, it's HBO"? Why not simply celebrate the fact that HBO can offer the best of both worlds in terms of feature films and original series? While partly this is a case of product differentiation through branding (even though the products have grown increasingly similar, and perhaps because of it), the rhetorical distinction is also vital to HBO's interpolation of an audience it believes is seeking "quality" programming and "exclusive" access that differ from free TV.

HBO first introduced the slogan "It's Not TV. It's HBO" in 1995. It was created by Richard Ellenson. Previously, HBO had utilized the slogans "Nobody Brings it Home like HBO" and "Simply the Best" in order to brand itself as the primary movie channel on television. HBO effected a branding change in the mid-1990s when it realized that it was already in the majority of pay cable subscriber homes and needed to focus on gaining new pay TV households. This shift put HBO in direct competition with network and basic cable television as opposed to other pay cable stations and required a branding strategy that would effectively convince potential subscribers that HBO offered something fundamentally different than what they could already get for free on other channels. As Eric Kessler, Executive Vice President of Marketing at HBO explains, "The consumer makes a purchase decision on our brand every single month, so we need to convince the consumer that our brand is different and it is worth paying for" (Bernstein, 2002: A9).

According to Deborah L. Jaramillo, branding in television is a matter of product differentiation, which establishes the brand's status in relation to other brands. Reaffirming HBO's intertwining relationship with the rest of television, Jaramillo suggests, "in the case of HBO's original programming branding strategies, the frame of reference for us is broadcast programming, and HBO is sure to incorporate that into its promotional slogan, 'It's not TV. It's HBO.' The implication is that TV is everything else" (Jaramillo, 2002: 59–75). Jaramillo further asserts that HBO has taken advantage of its particularly privileged position as a pay cable network to brand its programming with the "quality" label. Regarding *The Sopranos*, Jaramillo states that HBO executives repeatedly point to the "fundamental, if elusive, notion of 'quality'" (Jaramillo, 2002: 66) that separates the series from standard broadcast fare.

In *MTM: Quality Television*, Jane Feuer, Paul Kerr, and Tise Vahimagi suggest that television critics and industry people have often defined the term "quality" quite differently. Whereas the former have evoked the adjective "quality" to describe high production values, authorial style, and creative innovation that can be found within select television programming, the latter have conflated "quality" programming with "quality" demographics, essentially anointing any program capable of capturing the desired 18–49-year-old demographic as "quality" programming (Feuer, Kerr, and Vahimagi, 1984: 3). HBO appears to do a little of both. By applying the moniker of "quality" to its programming, HBO has attempted to distinguish what types of programs can be found on the pay network versus its broadcast counterparts as well as what type of audience HBO programming attracts. Similarly, Jaramillo argues that HBO executives regularly elide differences in regulation and financing between pay and broadcast TV, championing the uses of violence, vulgarity, and nudity on the former as appealing to a sophisticated viewership and derogating their tamed equivalents on the latter as pandering to the masses. "This pay cable chauvinism not only holds broadcast TV to a different standard but also implies that pay cable consumers can handle graphic language, sex, and violence in a more thoughtful and productive way than broadcast viewers" (Jamarillo, 2002: 66).

Still, many scholars continue to speak of HBO programming in terms that presume not only a discernable qualitative difference between the pay cable and its network counterparts, but also a continuation of the quality model associated with MTM productions. For instance, Rogers, Epstein, and Reeves identify HBO's *The Sopranos* as having "strong production values, [being] well written, and generally feature[ing] strong acting performances" while also stating that "HBO has cultivated and enabled the quality of the program by giving [producer David] Chase the creative freedom that only premium cable can offer" (Rogers, Epstein and Reeves, 2001: 53). While Jaramillo attempts to identify the regulatory and economic factors that have allowed *The Sopranos* to take the shape and tell the stories it has, there is still an underlying assumption that HBO's business model has given it access to "quality" programming strategies unavailable to network television. While scholarly interpretations of what makes HBO original series "quality" television might be open to debate, there can be little doubt that HBO has exploited the discursive ambiguities of defining "quality" programming in its marketing strategies.

In fact, it is precisely through its promotional efforts that the pay network has reconceptualized the term "quality." It no longer strictly conveys a sense of aesthetic criteria (though these are often lauded by critics and fans alike, suggesting that production values are still an important site of distinction for HBO series) nor does it identify a particular demographic (as HBO is interested in anybody willing to shell out the extra money per month to subscribe, regardless of age, gender, race, or class), but rather, "quality" now denotes a distinction between HBO and other television networks, which is primarily marked by the exclusive access and cultural capital subscribers receive, which in turn, separates them from the masses who must settle for "must see TV."[2] Or, as Lotz has stated, "HBO now brands its network with the strategic and contrary slogan, 'It's Not TV, It's HBO;' an attempt to differentiate the network's brand by distancing HBO content from stereotypic notions of television as a 'low art' form providing the 'least objectionable programming'— assumptions heavily weighted with cultural capital that affords assessments of higher quality to forms with less accessibility" (Lotz, 2003: 50).

Rogers et al. confirm that the apparent limitation of access to its programming is a significant aspect of HBO's branding strategies, when they state "it is the 'exclusivity' of its original programming that shapes HBO's identity" (Rogers, Epstein and Reeves, 2001: 51). Likewise, Jaramillo asserts that "the idea that subscribers can get products at HBO that they can get nowhere else has been a significant part of the channel's allure" (Jaramillo, 2002: 65). The exclusivity promised by HBO via subscription is one that supposedly grants paying viewers membership in a distinct community that clearly ranks above the riffraff who watch the standard broadcast and cable stations. Again, as Eric Kessler explained, "The consumer makes a purchase decision on our brand every single month, so we need to convince the consumer that our brand is different and it is worth paying for" (Goetz, 2002a: 37). Thus it may be argued that what HBO believes it is selling its subscribers is a form of cultural capital.

In *Distinction: A Social Critique of the Judgment of Taste*, Pierre Bourdieu argues that cultural capital grants its owners access and knowledge that enables them to distinguish themselves and gain elevated status in society. Cultural capital is also usually associated with an appreciation of high art, once again foregrounding discourses of aesthetic superiority found on HBO, and marking a (fuzzy) distinction between those who appreciate and those who consume. As Lotz suggests, "HBO thrives by defying program standards that appeal to the mass audience, and succeeds by exploiting limited access as the means to acceptance as high (or at least higher) elite art" (Lotz, 2003: 66). This distinction has an even more ambiguous relationship to television, a medium long derided for its lowbrow appeal to the greatest common denominator of viewers and for its imbrication in the proliferation of consumerism.

Lynne Joyrich asserts that television as a medium has historically been gendered feminine. Moreover, television reception has been marked by cultural critics and in popular discourse as an emasculating pastime and a feminizing preoccupation. This, Joyrich asserts, is particularly true of television's most dominant generic form, the melodrama. "The feminine connotations traditionally attached to melodrama – and to both consumerism and television viewing – are diffused onto a general audience, opening up contradictions of spectatorship and sexual differences" (Joyrich, 1996: 46). Thus it may be argued that HBO's branding and programming strategies position the pay network as the home for oppositional, non-televisual experiences. "It's Not TV. It's HBO" carries the implicit baggage of everything TV is (feminizing, consumerist, emasculating, massified), and by contrast, everything HBO supposedly is not. The discourse of "quality" that HBO stresses can also be understood as defensive posturing against the feminized assumptions made about television and its viewers, as HBO simultaneously seeks to distance itself and deny its own televisuality.

Joyrich claims that striving for the status of "quality" TV by creating proper spectator distance through the mimicking of cinematic conventions or by obsessively remarking the masculinity of a series thematics are key to warding off accusations of emasculation. HBO's marketing has continued to link the notion of quality to aesthetics, by emphasizing the high production values and cinematic influences found in its programming. Furthermore, HBO's series seem remarkably preoccupied with exploring white, middle-class male anxieties, whether they are Tony Sopranos' panic attacks over diminished standards or attorney Tobias Beecher's nightmarish experiences while incarcerated in the Oswald State Penitentiary or sheriff Seth Bullock's efforts to contain his savage rage in the face of the civilization of the town of Deadwood or the strain of married life and the lures of infidelity on *Mind of the Married Man* or the failures of commodified masculinity regularly put on display in *Sex and the City*, where men are consumed just as easily as clothing and food and always appear to be lacking despite the size of their bank accounts. It is possible that HBO's thematic emphasis deliberately situates it in opposition to the perceived feminization of the networks through the habitual "re-marking" of the masculinity of its series.

Rather than marketing itself to a male demographic, HBO utilizes masculinity as a site for distinguishing its quality brand and promoting the exclusivity it offers its clientele. If TV feminizes all who watch it, and feminization is linked to a loss of power and status brought about through the act of consumption, then HBO's brand offers to "re-mark" subscribers as "masculine," thus repositioning its audience as powerful bearers of cultural capital that is free from the commercialized trappings of regular television (after all, HBO does not pander to advertisers, but caters to subscribers). Of course, there are problems with this assumption. On the one hand, HBO's goal is to solicit as many subscribers as possible, which automatically renders the exclusivity it promises suspect. On the other hand, subscribers seeking a distinct televisual experience that rises above the base consumption of standard broadcast television must ignore both the transactional nature of the pay TV exchange and the real similarities between HBO programming and other forms of television in terms of genre, format, and style. Thus, at best, HBO and its subscribers share a series of anxious assumptions about what pay TV offers, since HBO can guarantee neither "quality" nor "exclusivity."

## The cultural conundrum

It is important, however, to state, that I am *not* asserting that HBO has purposely deceived its subscriber base; that it has, as Polan suggests, engaged in the "performance of distinction" (Polan, 2004: 1, 7).[3] Rather, I argue that HBO, and more precisely, those working for it, particularly at the upper management level, participate in a culture of production that allows them to believe in the distinctions they assert, even to the detriment of the company's long-range economic goals and institutional needs.

Whereas Barry Smart has asserted that production and consumption in contemporary societies continue to be determined by "capitalist rationality" (Smart, 2003: 81), my argument aligns more with the works of Paul Du Gay and Keith Negus, who each assert that cultural attitudes and beliefs shape production processes as much as they are shaped by them and that struggles over meaning and multiple interpretations of corporate goals often exist within production cultures, undercutting their supposedly mechanistic and rational functioning (Du Gay and Pryke, 2002: 1–9; Negus, 2000: 240–254). As Negus asserts, "what often appear to be fundamentally economic or commercial decisions... are based on a series of historically specific cultural values, beliefs, and prejudices" (Negus, 2002: 116). I contend that HBO executives have bought into notions of exclusivity and qualitative distinction from television to such an extent that these attitudes often supersede or interfere with other corporate goals, such as attracting greater numbers of subscribers and finding syndication outlets for their original series. This is, perhaps, less a contradiction as a shift in economic emphasis that is informed by cultural discourses that do not fully fit the rational profit generating model advocated by Smart. Similarly, Du Gay and Pryke argue that investigating the intersections of culture and economy requires "acting on the assumption that economics are performed and enacted by the very discourses of which they are supposedly the cause" (Du Gay and Pryke, 2002: 6).

While Du Gay and Pryke point to the increased "culturalization" of industry in the contemporary era as linked with efforts to improve organizational performance and contends that service-oriented industries (into which media industries in general fall, though somewhat uncomfortably, and HBO in particular fits precisely because of its direct marketing to subscribers) engage in a "contingent assemblage of practices" that are both economic and cultural, intended to increase sales and competitive advantage, they also wisely remind scholars that "corporate culturalism" does not unproblematically achieve what it sets out to accomplish, suggesting that the complex ways in which cultural attitudes inform economic decisions cannot be fully regulated by the profit principle (Du Gay and Pryke, 2002: 2). There is little doubt that HBO executives have absorbed the values they believe subscribers seek into their organizational philosophies. As Eric Kessler has repeatedly stated regarding the tagline "It's Not TV. It's HBO," "through the years, that line has articulated the basic positioning of the brand... But the important thing about that line is that it is *true*. What we're saying is that HBO is different from everything in the entire television landscape" (quoted in Bernstein, 2002: A9, italics added). The extent to which such beliefs fit with HBO's historical reliance on television as both a site for adaptation and syndication is where tensions begin to emerge. More specifically, HBO's belief in its own "non-televisuality" has led to programming and production decisions that adversely effect the company's stated syndication needs, their efforts to generate new subscribers, and their overall control over the production process.

As previously asserted, HBO's foray into original series production was largely predicated upon the opening up of syndication markets on network television. Due to rising production costs and subscriber growth either stalled or difficult to gauge in relation to programming efforts, HBO has aggressively sought out new revenue streams through DVD sales, theatrical film production, and syndication (Higgins, 2004: 1). With the explosion of cable channels throughout the 1990s (many owned by HBO's parent company, Time Warner Inc. [TWI]), it would initially appear that syndication options have grown exponentially for HBO. At first glance, HBO appears to have successfully syndicated its hit comedy, *Sex and the City*, selling rerun options first to 26 Chicago–Tribune owned independent stations for a combination of cash and free advertising time and then to TWI sister station TBS (Dempsey and Amdur, 2003: 1). *Sex and the City* has quickly become the highest rated prime-time program on TBS (Elliot, 2005: C7). Yet, press coverage of *Sex and the City* syndication is also quick to point out that HBO received far less than network equivalents *Seinfeld* and *The Cosby Show* got for their reruns, suggesting that the limited number of episodes produced, and their content, both crucial aspects of HBO's distinction from network television, diminished their value (Dempsey and Amdur, 2003: 1). Moreover, ratings success has not necessarily reduced advertiser skittishness, which led TBS to reconceptualize its marketing strategy in the wake of larger companies refusing to buy spots. Whether advertiser concerns affect future syndication deals for HBO remains to be seen. Similar comments have been made about the viability of syndicating *The Sopranos*. "As HBO moves ahead with plans to sell edited episodes of '*The Sopranos*' to a cable television network that runs commercials, the reaction of many advertisers asked to be sponsors will likely be 'Fuhgeddaboutit'" (Elliot, 2005: C7).[4] Thus, HBO's efforts to brand itself in opposition to television have potentially impacted on the pay station's efforts to syndicate its top series.

It is not merely in terms of limiting potential ancillary revenue streams that HBO's brand identity has seemingly undermined the economic bottom line, but it is also at the levels of series programming and subscriber accumulation that HBO's non-televisual philosophy proves potentially contentious. While other markets, including syndication, DVD sales, and product spin-offs (*Sopranos* cook-books, for instance) are becoming increasingly important to HBO's business model, subscribers remain the bread and butter of the pay service.

Original programming has served as a means of reducing churn and generating buzz in order to attract new viewers. In order to justify subscription rates, HBO has marketed itself as distinct from the rest of the televisual landscape by offering supposedly exclusive access to "quality" programming free of the mass-market appeals found on commercial television.

The Sopranos' appeal to exclusivity is often accompanied by anxious commentaries on what lies beyond such imaginary communities. In an interview in The Washington Post, creator David Chase is quoted as explaining Tony's motivations as, "his big goal in life is just to be left alone," to which the interviewer adds, "[this] is one of the things that make Tony so recognizable, so much the guy next door – albeit one who can have people beaten up or killed if he feels like it" (Shales, 2002: G1). In the same article, Tony's appeal is suggested to lie in his struggles against disruptive changes in the world, "a grimly familiar predicament" (Shales, 2002: G1). In other words, the reviewer believes the appeal of the series seemingly rests with identifying Tony as an everyman figure despite his enormous power and wealth. As Polan suggests, "such writings treat The Sopranos as a simulacrum of real-life issues the raising of which the writers claim accounts for the show's emotional and intellectual appeal" (Polan, 2004: 2). Polan also asserts that such appeals to ordinariness are often intertwined with discourses of quality television. In this manner, The Sopranos effectively negotiates HBO's need to market exclusivity to anyone willing and able to pay the cost of admission, leaving the pay cable door open to a wide range of potential subscribers, each seeking a reprieve from basic TV through identification with either Tony or the series as markers of quality and distinction.

Yet, as HBO's brand identity has continued to emphasize discourses of exclusivity that define the pay channel in opposition to television, series selection has moved away from this "everyman encumbered by the outside world" trope toward a greater thematic preoccupation with exposing the underbelly of the entertainment industry. This shift befits HBO's conceptualization of its audience as both seeking an elevated and insulated space from the rest of television. Still, while series such as Entourage, The Comeback, Unscripted, Project Greenlight, Extras, and Curb Your Enthusiasm each promote a type of insider status that allows viewers to simultaneously gain insight and feel superior to the shallow and fickle Hollywood lifestyles depicted (and their supposed correlation with the types of Hollywood product you see on network and basic cable television), they have also largely failed to generate the same type of popular appeal garnered by The Sopranos (with the possible exception of Curb your Enthusiasm, which has relied strongly on Larry David's distinctly televisual credentials as the creator of Seinfeld).

Previous programming choices sought to balance notions of exclusivity with the pay channel's need to attract as many subscribers as possible by emphasizing characters and situations with fairly broad or purposely ambiguous appeal in order to build coalition audiences among different constituencies. Current programming practices have largely been informed by discourses of cultural superiority that have a far narrower appeal. While it is certainly possible to feel superior to Tony and his crew, earlier HBO series often combined such elements with an underlying pathos toward their protagonists, depicting them as caught up in an unfulfilling world of their own making that they cannot escape from. In this vein, the character of Beecher on the series *Oz*, the white middle-class lawyer incarcerated for a hit and run killing while high on cocaine, has been described as the viewer's point of identification inside the prison, while the Fisher family on *Six Feet Under* seem trapped by familial obligations to remain in the funeral business despite how much misery it may bring them. Tony's brutality is mitigated by his unhappiness and consequent panic attacks.

Current series, however, which seem far more informed by the discourse of difference than the shows described above, generally lack empathy toward their protagonists, depicting them as vapid, neurotic, and willingly compromised. Viewers are encouraged to laugh at them, to feel superior to them, rather than empathize with them. Moreover, by setting these series within the entertainment industry, there is the implicit suggestion that viewers might also feel superior to the very media that they consume, since it is apparently created by such despicable figures. While this thematic preoccupation certainly fits with HBO's belief that what it sells to subscribers is exclusivity from commercial media, it has also limited the ways in which these series can be publicly discussed by downplaying their ambiguity in favor of reveling in their characters' shallow antics. Polan concurs that such "insider" shows might be "too caught-up in self-reflexivity to work with a broader audience" (Polan, 2004: 32). This, in turn, potentially hurts HBO's need to generate buzz in order to attract new subscribers and keep old ones.

While the above examples suggest how the categories of quality and exclusivity inform the actual content and form of HBO programming, they also reveal how HBO has bought into its brand identity in ways that require the pay channel to continuously innovate rather than try to repeat past successes. While this is encouraging from a critical perspective that habitually recognizes television's failure to push boundaries, it is a strategy that has led HBO down several failed paths in its attempts to continuously produce "groundbreaking, critically acclaimed, smash hits" that are distinct not only from the rest of television, but also from its own past successes. This is a tricky proposition given HBO's historical relationship with the rest of TV, not to mention the rest of television's efforts to diversify their programming in the face of increased deregulation and the success of cable programming found on channels like

HBO. As one reviewer succinctly states, "For years, HBO has gone with the tagline 'It's Not TV. It's HBO'. But recently, TV has become a lot more like HBO" (Goetz, 2002a: 63). Such pressures to keep up with (and ahead of) ever-changing standards of television, let alone, "Not" television, are even echoed in the comments made by HBO executives. Discussing the future of the pay channel, Chris Albrecht articulated HBO's anxious need to constantly adapt, stating, "there's no denying that '*Sex and the City*' and '*The Sopranos*' were huge hits... But if you set out to make those, you'll fail. We have to continue to do things, be things that other networks aren't" (Waxman, 2004: E1).

While the drive to innovate has produced series such as *Def Poetry Jam*, a rare focus on hip-hop as both a political and artistic endeavor, and led HBO to adapt series found on non-US television (*Da Ali G Show*) or found to be too controversial on network TV (*Real Time with Bill Maher*), failed HBO series' *K-Street*, *Mind of the Married Man* and *Carnivàle* were often seen as too unfamiliar for audiences judging HBO fare in relation to their other television experiences. *Carnivàle* was referred to by reviewers as "oblique," "infuriatingly dense," "impenetrable and distancing" and compared with another highly cherished yet unpopular network TV series that suffered similar accusations, *Twin Peaks* (Lowry, 2005: 44). The series was cancelled after 24 episodes. *K-Street*'s experimental fusion of reality TV and fiction set amidst the corridors of Washington's political elite probably drew inspiration from Altman's *Tanner 88*, but like that series, its appeal to a niche audience and general experimental narrative structure proved unpopular with HBO's substantially larger current subscriber pool. The series lasted only eight episodes. As one reviewer noted, *K-Street* was "thoroughly in keeping with HBO's reputation for cutting-edge programming, but conceivably of interest to a relatively select audience" (Shales, 2003: C3). *Mind of the Married Man* was perhaps the HBO original series that met with greatest resistance from subscribers. Described as "divisive" because of its desire to deviate from the standard sitcom format by featuring male protagonists actively pursuing extramarital affairs without moral condemnation, it was gone after 20 episodes (Dempsey, 2003: 6).

While *Carnivàle* received critical praise, it failed to generate the same level of attention as previous HBO series. As one reviewer succinctly states, "gazing beyond the show's conflict of good vs. evil, HBO has enjoyed an unusually laudable track record in the age-old war of good vs. mediocre. It's against that measuring stick, ultimately, that 'Carnivale' comes up short" (Lowry, 2005: 44). While HBO continues to assert that it does not measure the success of its original programming in terms of ratings, a clear mark of distinction between regular TV and itself, it is also apparent that the reliance upon buzz as a gauge of success repeatedly puts HBO at the mercy of reviewers comparing

its programming with other television series as well as HBO's own past successes. "For HBO, it's all about branding, and that requires a steady flow of
remarkable programming. But since the phenomenal success of '*The Sopranos*',
the network has not found a comparable series. '*Carnivàle*' was a disappointment, '*K Street*' was a pricey bust, and while the Western '*Deadwood*' garners
strong ratings, it has not been embraced as a cultural touchstone" (Waxman,
2004: E1). Polan further confirms this institutional pressure on HBO to continuously compete with its own programming history when he notes that "the
critical establishment sets out to judge each new series according to previously
established parameters of quality" creating, in essence, new "genre constraints"
every time HBO achieves some modicum of critical success (Polan, 2004: 8).

Rather than suggest that HBO's seeming lack of concern for ratings is
misguided, I concur with Du Gay and Pryke when they cite Michael Callon's
discussion of the cultural function of accounting tools for businesses,
"accounting tools...do not simply aid the measurement of economic activity,
they shape the reality they measure" (Du Gay and Pryke, 2002: 12). While the
inability to pinpoint the precise appeal of its programming to subscribers plays
well into HBO's branding efforts, which often stress the pay channel's lack of
concern for Neilsen ratings in measuring audiences, the reliance on a branding
strategy that denies the importance of audience measurement so essential to
the rest of television is also undoubtedly a source of tension amongst HBO
executives, who must justify mounting production and marketing expenses
without concrete evidence that branding efforts are responsible for subscriber
growth. "HBO has a particular challenge: Many of its series and movies have
generated accolades, and kept the nets suppliers enthusiastic. But it's nearly
impossible to bottom-line these successes—ie to prove how many subscribers
stay on thanks to '*Sex and the City*' or '61*'." (Dempsey, 2001: 1) An article
from *Daily Variety* on August 23, 2004, compares HBO's efforts to brand itself
via original programming like *The Sopranos* to "more alchemy than science"
(Lowry, 2004: A1).

Finally, HBO's corporate culture seeks to assure series producers creative
freedom, which, in turn, is promoted as a means of distancing HBO from both
the supposed lack of creativity and economic bottom-line found on regular TV.
David Hesmondhalgh convincingly argues though that the greater degree of
creative freedom the culture industries offer to talent often leads to contradictory texts that do not always reflect the corporate bottom line. "Yet because
original and distinctive symbolic creativity is at a premium, the cultural industries can never quite control it. Owners and executives are forced to make
concessions to symbol creators by granting them far more autonomy than they
would to most other workers" (Hesmondhalgh, 2002: 6).

While HBO has successfully absorbed such creative freedoms as part of its

"Not TV" image, the emphasis has also raised concern over the sustainability of its most popular programs. *The Sopranos* executive producer, David Chase, has repeatedly suggested that the series might be nearing the end of its run despite its popularity. "HBO has talked to me about another season after next year's. . . but I just don't think I can do it" (Carter, 2002: C1). There have also been lengthy delays between seasons as Chase develops new story arcs. This certainly generates anticipation, but it also contributes to the sense that HBO's success is fleeting. While the logic that subscribers should get on board before the HBO ship sets sail might actually be an effective (if pressure-filled) marketing tactic, it is one that relies on maintaining a constant sense of imminent danger that contradicts the safe-harbor HBO promises subscribers as an exclusive site of cultural capital unobtainable on network television.

Moreover, creative freedom occasionally fails to conform with HBO's stated goals of producing groundbreaking para-television, as evidenced by recent production stoppages on the set of the upcoming series *Rome*. Unhappy with the early footage they were seeing and the already overextended budget, HBO executives intervened to replace producer Stan Wlodkowski and director Michael Apted. This obviously contradicts HBO's edict of creative freedom and indicates the extent to which economics and conceptions of audience play into programming and production decisions. Still, HBO's solution was not to slash production values, but actually to increase the budget in an effort to produce the highest quality series possible. "We said, 'We love most of what we're seeing, but OK, OK, hold on, we need to put more money in here, revamp this thing'" (Waxman, 2004: E1).

The concern stemmed from the fact that the series seemed too much like television. Yet, this example is also an exception that proves the rule regarding HBO's corporate culture. While the immediate impact of HBO's intervention on the set of *Rome* is unknown, there is already great speculation that this uncharacteristic move will have a ripple effect and constrain HBO's future creative partnerships. "The chaotic start represented an uncharacteristic stumble on the part of a network that prides itself on doing things first class. And there is little question that the chapter led to bruised feelings in the close-knit entertainment world, where HBO relies on a stable of proven talent" (Waxman, 2004: E1).

The above example suggests that HBO's corporate culture is quite complex, willing to reign in creative freedom whenever it fails to meet production values that sufficiently distinguish HBO series from regular television, but also willing to squander economic resources in search of those marks of distinction.

## Conclusion

To conclude, this essay has attempted to complicate understandings of HBO's production and programming practices vis-à-vis television, asserting that, on the one hand, HBO engages in a purposeful strategy of creating para-television, and, on the other, that HBO's institutional culture and assumptions about its subscriber base have led it to absorb particular notions of exclusivity and quality that guide production and programming decisions in ways that occasionally contradict the pay channel's economic goals. In so doing, it has been my double aim to move discussions of HBO away from a focus on whether or not it is television and from a tendency to assume institutional practices are always guided by economic rationality. While I have elaborated upon how HBO's brand identity emerged and how it intersects with particular institutional goals or practices, there is still much to be written on how HBO's self-image, put forward through advertising, interviews, ancillary products, and, of course, actual programming, is understood by those judging HBO's claims to non-televisuality and distinction.

## Notes

1 HBO has also relied upon a steady stream of known film entities for their original productions, ranging from Ron Howard's executive producing the short-lived *Maximum Security* in 1984, a prison drama precursor to *Oz*, to Robert Altman's *Tanner 88* to Steven Spielberg and Tom Hanks' *Band of Brothers* (2003), Mike Nichols' *Wit* (2002), and *Angels in America* (2003), Steven Soderbergh and George Clooney's *K-Street* (2004) and *Unscripted* (2005), and Mark Wahlberg's *Entourage* (2004–) to name but a few. This further confirms HBO's reliance on known and established professionals for their programming needs, but it also explicitly connects many of HBO's production choices with a distinctly filmic sensibility.

2 HBO regularly releases entire series' seasons on VHS and DVD that can either be purchased (for the equivalent cost of a six-month subscription) or rented at your local video store. This is largely a strategy to increase subscribers by releasing one season on DVD just prior to the commencement of a new season on the pay network, but it is also a recognition that the likelihood of syndicating their series on network TV is slim at best. A third argument could be made that by releasing entire seasons on DVD, HBO is following the trend set by Hollywood movies, thus strengthening the comparisons of its product with the high art status bestowed on the cinema. Nevertheless, the strategy directly counteracts the sense of exclusivity that is central to HBO's discursive appeal, since it makes exclusive products available for general consumption and potentially attracts new subscribers who further dilute the special status bestowed upon earlier members. Perhaps this explains the discursive emphasis placed on the limited and ephemeral nature of HBO products, which are either singled out for their shortened seasons (most HBO series average 13 episodes per season), the extended delays between seasons (*The Sopranos* is a prime example) or the finite number of episodes that any series will inevitably produce (*The Sopranos* was originally envisioned as a single season series, but was then extended to three, four, and now six seasons). I am less interested in the actuality of when any of HBO's series will end, but

in the discourse that repeatedly emphasizes that the end—of a season, or of a series—may be close at hand.

3  While Polan does go on to argue that HBO executives have absorbed "a philosophy of meaningfulness as the sign of distinction," he largely situates this corporate philosophy within a rational business model that, to my mind, affords the pay channel too much control over its own image.

4  Since this chapter was originally written, HBO has successfully syndicated *The Sopranos* to A&E for $1.8 million dollars per episode, suggesting that basic cable might be a viable site for future deals, but articles covering the sale once again hinted at concerns about attracting advertisers that might mark these current sales successes for HBO as short-term experimentations for other cable stations, if suitable advertising dollars cannot be found. Equally as telling, reviews of edited episodes of *Sex and the City* appearing on TBS have reinforced anxieties over distinguishing HBO fare from other television. Rather than comment on how episodes devoid of swearing, nudity, and other "raunchy" content detract from the series, one reviewer says that these changes merely constitute a change in emphasis, not quality. Comments like these capture the core contradiction that exists between HBO's economic needs and brand identity. HBO needs to be able to syndicate its programming to meet rising production costs and subscriber stagnation. If HBO's programming were truly "Not TV" syndication would either be impossible or a colossal failure. If syndication succeeds, as it appears to have done with *Sex and the City*, then HBO's claims to non-televisuality are once again opened to scrutiny.

## Works cited

Ang, I. (1985) *Watching Dallas: Soap Opera and the Melodramatic Imagination*. New York: Routledge.

Bernstein, P. (2002, November 4–10) 'Branding Bolsters Expectations', *Variety*. A9.

'Bigelow Spells Out HBO's MO' (1988, November 14) *Broadcasting*. 115: 20, 64.

Blumenthal, H. J. & Goodenough, O.R. (1988) *This Business of Television*. Hillsdale, NJ: Lawrence Erlbaum Associates.

Bourdieu, P. (1984) *Distinction: A Social Critique of the Judgment of Taste*. Cambridge: Harvard University Press.

Brown, M. (1984, June 10) 'HBO in Transition: Slowing of Growth Worries Industry; Questions Raised about Future of Cable and Pay TV Business', *Washington Post*. G1.

Carter, B. (2002, December 23) '*Friends* Coup May Put Focus on *The Sopranos*', *New York Times*. C1.

Cerone, D. (1992, June 19) 'A New Kind of Networking Going On', *Los Angeles Times*. 8.

Cerone, D. (1994, January 22) 'Toned-Down *Tales from the Crypt* Starts on Fox Tonight', *Los Angeles Times*. 2.

Coe, S. (1990) '*Dream On* could be HBO Sleeper', *Broadcasting* 119:11.

Collins, J. (1992; 2nd edn) 'Television and Postmodernism', pp 327–353 in R.C. Allen (ed.) *Channels of Discourse, Reassembled: Television and Contemporary Criticism*. Chapel Hill: University of North Carolina Press.

Dempsey, J. (2001, September 10–15) 'It's Lonely at the Top', *Variety*. 1.

Dempsey, J. (2003, January 16) 'HBO Is Out of Its *Mind*', *Daily Variety*. 6.

Dempsey, J. and Amdur, M. (2003, September 11) 'Tribune Spices HBO's *Sex* Life', *Daily Variety*. 1.

Dempsey, J. & Williams, M. (1995, October 9) 'Hour Drama in HBO Plan', *Daily Variety*. 5.

Dolan, M. (1994) 'The Peaks and Valleys of Serial Creativity: What Happened to/on Twin Peaks', pp 36–60 in D. Lavery & R. Wilcox (eds) *Full of Secrets: Critical Approaches to Twin Peaks*. Detroit: Wayne State University Press.

Du Gay, P. & Pryke, M. (2002) 'Introduction', pp 1–20 in P. Du Gay & M. Pryke (eds), *Cultural Economy: Cultural Analysis and Commercial Life*. London: Sage Publications.

Elliott, S. (2005, January 11) 'Would a Cleaned-Up Version of *The Sopranos* Still be Too Naughty for Most Sponsors?', *New York Times*. C7.

Feuer, J., Kerr, P., & Vahimagi, T. (1984) *MTM: Quality Television*. London: British Film Institute.

Gatesward, F.K. (1997; 2nd edn) 'Home Box Office', pp 783–784 in H. Newcomb (ed.), *The Encyclopedia of Television*, vol. II, Chicago: Fitzroy Dearborn Publishers.

Goetz, D. (2002a, March 18) 'The Biz: Taking Cue from Cable, Gingerly', *Advertising Age*. 63.

Greenstein, J. (1991, May 13) 'HBO: Three Channels are Better Than One', *Multichannel News*. 12: 19, 1.

Hesmondhalgh, D. (2002) *The Cultural Industries*. London: Sage Publications.

Higgins, J. M. (2004, February 9) 'Premium Networks Take a Hit', *Broadcasting and Cable*. 1.

Hilmes, M. (1990) 'Pay Television: Breaking the Broadcast Bottleneck', pp 297–318 in T. Balio (ed.), *Hollywood in the Age of Television*. Boston: Unwin Hyman.

Jaramillo, D. L. (2002) 'The Family Racket: AOL-Time Warner, HBO, *The Sopranos*, and the Construction of a Quality Brand', *Journal of Communication Inquiry* 26 (1): 59–75.

Joyrich, L. (1996) *Re-Viewing Reception: Television, Gender, and Postmodern Culture*. Bloomington: Indiana University Press.

Kearney, M. C. (2002) 'The Changing Face of Teen Television, or Why We all Love Buffy', Unpublished manuscript. 23–68.

Lippman, J. (1990, December 9) 'The Changing Landscape of Pay Television', *Los Angeles Times*. 1.

Lotz, A. (2003) 'Why Isn't it TV? Post-Network Television Economics and Evaluating HBO Texts', pp 49–70 in S. Carr, W. Metz, & J. Tankel (eds), *It's Not TV, It's HBO: Home Box Office, Pay Cable and the Transformation of Quality Television*. Unpublished manuscript.

Lowry, B. (1994, October 21) 'Fox Takes *Dream On*', *Daily Variety*. 3.

Lowry, B. (1999, May 15) 'At HBO, Life After *Larry* Ain't So Bad', *Los Angeles Times*. 1.

Lowry, B. (2004, August 23) 'Jersey Beginnings, Infinite Rewards', *Daily Variety*. A1.

Lowry, B. (2005, January 7) '*Carnivale*', *Daily Variety*. 44.

Margulies, L. (1985, March 15) 'HBO Orders More Episodes of 3 Shows, Plus New Series', *Los Angeles Times*. 6.

Miller, S. (1994, May 20) 'HBO Rates Top Billing', *Daily Variety*. 1.

Mitchell, K. (1990, October 1) 'HBO Sets Up Unit to Produce Programs for Broadcasters', *Multichannel News*. 11:40.

Modderno, C. (1987, May 16) 'HBO Banks on Its Own *Conspiracy*', *Los Angeles Times*. 1.

Morgan, T. (1986, November 1) 'HBO Increasing Production of Its Own Cable TV Films', *New York Times*. 50.

Negus, K. (2000) 'Identities and Industries: The Cultural Formation of Aesthetic

Economics', pp 240–254 in J. Curran (ed.), *Media Organisations in Society*, London: Arnold.

Newcomb, H. (2003) '"This is Not Al Dente": *The Sopranos* and the New Meaning of "Television"', pp 137–166 in S. Carr, W. Metz, & J. Tankel (eds), *It's Not TV, It's HBO: Home Box Office, Pay Cable and the Transformation of Quality Television*. Unpublished manuscript.

Polan, D. (2004) 'Cable Watching: HBO, *The Sopranos*, and Discourses of Distinction', Unpublished manuscript. 1–37.

Richmond, R. (1997, May 15) 'HBO Makes "11th Hour" Decision', *Daily Variety*. 5.

Rogers, M.C., Epstein, M., & Reeves, J.L. (2002) '*The Sopranos* as HBO Brand Equity: The Art of Commerce in the Age of Digital Reproduction', pp 42–59 in D. Lavery (ed.), *This Thing of Ours: Investigating The Sopranos*. New York: Columbia University Press.

Schatz, T. (1997; 2nd edn) 'Workplace Programs', pp 1869–1873 in H. Newcomb (ed.), *The Museum of Broadcast Communications Encyclopedia of Television*, vol. III, Chicago: Fitzroy Dearborn Publishers.

Shales, T. (1983, April 13) 'The Cable Giant: Branching Out, Raking It In; HBO', *Washington Post*. L1.

Shales, T. (2002, September 15) '*The Sopranos*: Crooks Who Still Steal Your Heart', *Washington Post*. G1.

Shales, T. (2003, September 15) 'HBO's *K Street* in Uncharted Territory', *Washington Post*. C3.

Smart, B. (2003) *Economy, Culture and Society: A Sociological Critique of Neo-Liberalism*. Philadelphia: Open University Press.

Stilson, J. (1991, May 27) 'In a First, HBO Cops Two Fox Series Deals', *Multichannel News*. 12:21, 14.

Streeter, T. (1987) 'The Cable Fable Revisited: Discourse, Policy, and the Making of Cable Television', *Critical Studies in Mass Communication* 4 (2): 174–200.

Strover, S. (1997; 2nd edn) 'United States: Cable Television', pp 1721–1727 in H. Newcomb (ed.), *The Encyclopedia of Television*, vol. III, Chicago: Fitzroy Dearborn Publishers.

Waxman, S. (2004, October 21) 'New Big-Budget Series Generates High Hopes and Some Bruised Feelings', *New York Times*. E1.

# Chapter 2

# And now no word from our sponsor

## How HBO puts the risk back into television

*Tony Kelso*

"*Friends* spin-off sitcom *Joey* has been permanently cancelled by US TV broadcaster NBC after being labeled a catastrophic ratings failure," the World Entertainment News Network reported on May 16, 2006. After only two seasons, the offshoot of the phenomenally popular *Friends*, which had enjoyed a prodigious 10-year run, simply vanished into the ether. Regarded as, perhaps, "the one sure comedy hit this fall" (Hughes, 2004) when it was launched, *Joey*, after opening with sizeable ratings, quickly saw its numbers tumble, and was eventually moved from NBC's prominent Thursday night position, and then was finally terminated altogether.

Yet the cancellation of *Joey* should not be seen as a surprise. The truth is, most television shows fail and hits are few and far between. The television business, like most, if not all, media businesses, is deeply rooted in insecurity. To minimize this anxiety, commercial network executives typically follow certain routines and conventions, which have a significant influence on what ultimately winds up on TV screens across the nation. One industry maxim can be summed up in two words: avoid risk. The result, too often, is a lack of innovation and highly original programming (Butsch, 2003). Yet amidst this symbolic ocean of sameness stands HBO. As the pay TV network puts it (and as this book aptly appropriates it for its title), "It's not TV, it's HBO." Drawing primarily from a political economic perspective, this chapter will explore how HBO's structural advantages facilitate the production of programming that distinguishes the premium channel from commercial television. I argue that subscriber-backed HBO has generally had the capacity to show greater respect for its audience than advertising-supported networks by more often not merely giving viewers what they are *willing* to watch (Magder, 2004), but what they really *want* to watch. Yet this chapter also examines the likelihood that HBO will be able to continue to separate itself from its commercial counterparts as we enter the "post-television" age. Adapting to quickly changing conditions, will HBO still live up to its slogan or see the phrase become fodder for mockery? Then again, maybe HBO will mutate into a considerably different vehicle of entertainment.

## Commercial television: risk as a four-letter word

In his groundbreaking book that investigates the mechanisms behind decision-making at commercial networks, Todd Gitlin (1985: 14) describes the "problem of uncertainty and the industry's attempts to overcome it." Operating within a profit-driven environment, commercial television executives are not only pressured to generate high ratings to secure more dollars from advertisers, but to provide an "advertising friendly" context that does not alienate their corporate sponsors as well. In an atmosphere monitored by fidgety sponsors, risk usually takes a back seat. Indeed, the television industry learned this lesson early on. The television historian Erik Barnouw (1990) explains that when television was in its infancy in the United States, programs often featured contentious themes and scenarios that highlighted social issues such as racism and working-class struggles. Given that some of these shows garnered significant ratings, one might assume they would have been deemed "successful." Yet their run was short-lived because there was one institution that viewed these offerings as problematic: the advertising industry. Gleaming white-toothed smiles and sales pitches for sugary breakfast cereals appeared absurdly superficial when placed directly after a dramatic scene of a family worrying about where its next meal would come from. Once broadcasters realized programs that evoked disturbing emotions in the audience or triggered thoughts that challenged deep-seated cultural assumptions could result in a loss of advertising revenue, they inevitably came to terms with the need to create relatively "safe" programming. The pattern, in general, has been followed ever since. In short, great ratings do not suffice; the content of the show itself must be conducive to selling the brands that corporations are eager to build.

Yet advertising has an impact on the content of programs in other ways. Shows must be written with commercial interruptions in mind, yielding "mini-narratives" designed to reach a climax before the breaks, which, arguably, impose on scriptwriters' creativity (Levinson, 2002: 30). From an ideological perspective and somewhat cynically, then, commercial television programs partially function as the bait to lure viewers into watching commercials and position the needs of advertisers ahead of the desires of audiences for quality entertainment, promoting a worldview predicated on consumption along the way. David Chase, the creator of HBO's hugely successful *The Sopranos*, alluded to this in discussing why he "couldn't take it anymore" and welcomed the opportunity to move to HBO from the commercial networks:

I think the first priority is to push a lifestyle. I think there's something they're trying to sell all the time . . . I think what they're trying to sell is that everything's OK all the time, that this is just a great nation and a wonderful society, and everything's OK and it's OK to buy stuff. . . . There's some indefinable image of America that they're constantly trying to push as opposed to actually being entertaining (Fresh Air, 2004).

The influence of advertising on non-advertising media content is typically addressed through argument or qualitative measures. But in an intriguing quantitative study, Keith Brown, of the Federal Communications Commission,[1] and Roberto Cavazos (2005: 33) come to the same conclusions. Evaluating data on programming and rates charged for advertising placement, while controlling for other variables, they affirm that one "market failure is the distortion of programming stemming from advertisers' preferences. Advertisers prefer programming content that best 'frames' their advertising. Such content tends to be light and 'unchallenging.' Viewers who prefer darker and more challenging content will go under-served."

Yet responding to the sway of advertisers is not the only impetus for adhering to a kind of "logic of safety." Because the demand to achieve and maximize ratings is so severe, commercial television executives try to lessen their insecurity by heeding the guideline, "nothing succeeds like success" (Gitlin, 1985). In other words, the television industry is a copycat business (Magder, 2004). *Survivor* begot *Risk Factor*, *The Jerry Springer Show* begot *The Ricki Lake Show*, *CSI* begot *CSI: Miami* and *CSI: NY*, and so on. As noted above, hits emerge only infrequently; when they occur, nervous producers leap to emulate them. Predicting success is always a leap in the dark—despite over 50 years of accumulated knowledge and mounds of consumer research, television professionals can never really know what will work. Just ask Matt LeBlanc, the actor who played Joey.

## HBO: risk as embedded in the corporate culture

Judging from its list of accomplishments and accolades, HBO indeed appears to occupy a different space than commercial network television. In 2004, for instance, according to *USA Today* (September 28, 2004: D1), it collected more Emmys than the four major broadcast networks combined. Praise from the critics has bordered on redundancy. In a comment that epitomizes this tendency and takes the discourse to a hyperbolic level, *The New York Times* once hailed *The Sopranos* as "the greatest achievement in American pop culture in the last quarter-century." Not only has HBO evoked acclaim for its quality programming, however, it has also stirred considerable analysis from scholars. David Lavery

(2002) writes, for instance, that *The Sopranos* is "heavy" with significance, even to the extent that it has spawned the sub-field of "*Soprano* studies" (Lavery, 2006: 6). In a book on feminism in popular culture, Joanne Hollows and Rachel Moseley (2006) offer a summary of the debates surrounding feminism in the "post-feminist" *Sex and the City*. This program, too, has triggered lively scholarship (see Akass & McCabe, 2004, for one notable example of an entire book devoted to academic work on *Sex and the City*). Nor is the "buzz" associated with HBO confined to the halls of academia and offices of journalists. *The Sopranos* and *Sex and the City*, for example, have signified full-fledged cultural phenomena. Maurice Yacowar (2002) notes that on Sundays, when a new episode of *The Sopranos* was telecast, restaurant business in some areas declined because people stayed home to view the characters' latest ventures. Lavery (2002: xii) describes a lexicographer predicting that the next edition of the *Oxford English Dictionary* will include *Sopranos* citations. Meanwhile, *Sex and the City* was "discussed around countless water-coolers across America" and appeared on the cover of *Time*, a rare happening for a sitcom (McCabe & Akass, 2004: 2). Aside from all this buzz, HBO translates into economic success—in 2001 it generated more profit than any other network (Peterson, 2002). What can account for such symbolic and monetary triumph? Part of the answer, as this chapter suggests, lies in HBO's political economic structure and business model.

The traditional argument on how HBO stands apart from the rest goes like the following: Based on the evidence, as demonstrated above, there is a quality divide between pay TV in general (and HBO in particular) and commercial television. Because HBO is dependent on subscribers rather than advertisers for its main source of revenue, it can take risks without fear of upsetting sponsors (C. Anderson, 2005; K. Anderson, 2005; Auster, 2005; Weinman, 2006). Not only does HBO not have to worry about offending corporate backers, it can also produce plots that develop slowly instead of building toward mini-climaxes before commercial interruptions. Furthermore, as a pay service, HBO does not have to contend with government censorship violations or the public service requirements that other networks, at least in theory, must fulfill (Auster, 2005; Rogers et al., 2002; Weinman, 2006). Nudity, utterly profane language, and especially violent representations are fair game for HBO. But there is still more to it than freedom from advertisers and censors. The network, in a sense, is *forced* to take risks. If it relies on millions of everyday viewers to relinquish a few extra dollars each month for the opportunity to view programming they cannot get on commercial TV, then HBO simply must continuously distinguish itself from broadcast and basic cable stations if it hopes to remain viable. Consequently, HBO, through both marketing efforts—including its slogan, of course—and program creation, has attempted to focus on "counter-programming" and resisting the commercial networks' formulaic approach as illustrated earlier (Auster, 2005; *Broadcasting & Cable* [Supplement], November 2002: 6; Friend, 2001; McCabe & Akass, 2004). Because it is guided by "first-order commodity relations" (Rogers et al., 2002), that is, in direct transaction with audiences rather than in a relationship centered on selling their attention spans to advertisers, HBO has not generally obsessed over ratings (K. Anderson, 2005; Peyser, 2006; Rogers et al., 2002). "We don't care how many people watch our shows," one HBO insider once declared in *The Economist* (November 21, 1998: 95). "We just want people to decide at the end of the month that it's worth renewing their subscription." HBO can ignore individual ratings because all it needs to ensure is that it delivers to each subscriber *something* worth paying for. This means, therefore, that the network must explicitly attend to audience satisfaction based not on quantitative data, but qualitative measures, and evaluate its *total* programming schedule. No wonder, then, HBO has been remarkably recognized for producing some of the most novel television programming of the past two decades. In addition, as already implied, the premium station is not timid about tackling socially demanding subjects, such as third-wave feminism (*Sex and the City*), drug addiction (*The Corner*), and (egad!) death (*Six Feet Under*). Despite taking such chances (or perhaps *because* of them), each of these programs resonated with large audiences. Again, unlike the commercial networks, which appear to be steered by the notion that TV viewing is not something one seeks out but a habitual activity, HBO is able to furnish programming that people really want to see rather than simply settle for (Magder, 2004).

The buzz that HBO must incite to mark itself from commercial networks, however, does not simply happen through programming choices and "organic" means. The pay channel, as mentioned earlier, also engages in intense promotional and branding efforts designed to buttress the perception that it is somehow unique. Apprehending its need to convince people to increase the size of their cable bills, HBO began spending heavily on promotion from the start (Albiniak, 2003); building a brand identity has been essential (McCabe & Akass, 2004; Rogers et al., 2002). Moreover, unlike commercial outlets that come aggregated through standard cable packages, HBO is a brand that can actually be *bought* (Ross, 1999). Similar to the manner in which a manufacturer of an everyday consumable uses branding to symbolically connote that its bottled water, deodorant, or lip balm is different from the rest (even though the dissimilarities are in fact negligible), HBO adopts the same tactic (although in this case, HBO, in general, has seemingly been able to live up to its claim of distinction). The network's challenge is particularly fierce because brand loyalty is tough to achieve. "Churn," or the tendency for a portion of subscribers to forego HBO each month, is endemic. Building a strong brand identity is one method for minimizing churn, which is intended to not only create the impression that HBO is truly one-of-a-kind and therefore worth paying for, but also that those who opt into HBO's lineup belong to a special set of viewers who thereby acquire "consumer capital" (see Santo's chapter in this book). In this sense, direct marketing endeavors and programming go hand in hand—the shows function, in part, as devices or product placements that augment HBO's brand (Epstein et al., 2006; McCabe & Akass, 2004; Rogers et al., 2002). The premium service's promotional energies have appeared to pay off, at least until recently (more about this later). One qualitative study published in 2000 noted that HBO was one of the four most recognized and remembered cable networks, an especially remarkable finding given that it serves far fewer homes than the other three, each of which resides in the realm of basic cable (Bellamy & Traudt, 2000).

In a word, as alluded to on previous occasions, it boils down to "quality." Instilling its programs with contradictions and complexity generally unseen on commercial networks, HBO can disseminate "real adult drama" (Lavery, 2002; Willis, 2002; Yacowar, 2002). Accordingly, partially due to its political economic structure, HBO can also emphasize creative freedom, which, ostensibly, only a first-order commodity station can offer (Rogers et al., 2002: 53). Moreover, the network appears to have internalized this ethic into its very corporate culture (Auster, 2005; Friend, 2001; McCabe & Akass, 2004). It comes as no shock, then, that so many artists known for their considerable creative talents are attracted to the prospect of working for HBO (Auster, 2005: 227). A number of industry insiders have revealed the relief that follows from escaping the inhibiting commercial networks to bask in the relative liberty that comes with a stint at the network. When David Chase, quoted above, originally sought a taker to his *The Sopranos*, he was turned down by several commercial outlets (although FOX showed initial interest it eventually pulled out; Lavery, 2006; Lavery & Thompson, 2002; Peyser & Gordon, 2001). Discussing his move from the commercial networks to HBO, he states: "I had just had it up to here with all the niceties of network television. . . . I don't mean language and I don't mean violence. I just mean storytelling, inventiveness, something that really could entertain and surprise people" (Fresh Air, 2004). Alan Ball, writer for *Six Feet Under*, echoes the theme that commercial networks do not appreciate the audience enough to believe it can comprehend sophisticated plots. "The difference between working for a network and for HBO is night and day," he says. At ABC, Ball was admonished to "articulate the subtext" and "spoon feed" information (Weinraub, 2000). The creator of HBO's provocative prison drama *Oz*, Tom Fontana, complains about how commercial television tends to resort to copycat formulas. "The networks go with the prevailing wind. If a show works on one network, they want one just like it" (Peyser & Gordon, 2001).

## Delving deeper into HBO's institutional advantages

Much has already been stated about the traditional reasons given for why HBO has the capacity to enact a more innovative stance toward programming. In this section, additional institutional advantages will be highlighted, and then tendencies that *contradict* the idea that the pay service is free from customary economic constraints will be elucidated.

Without doubt, in striving to ensure quality programming, HBO frequently establishes considerably larger production budgets than its commercial counterparts. It can devote such enormous resources, in part, because it neither produces many original shows (far more of its schedule is still devoted to second-run Hollywood films), nor, most of the time, creates as many programs per season for its series as the big broadcast corporations develop. "The reality is," states Nick Davatzes, former President and CEO of A&E Television Networks, that HBO functions less as a network than as "a movie studio almost" (Chunovic, 2002). Further, because it depends on subscribers rather than ratings, HBO can allow its series to slowly accumulate a large audience (Auster, 2005; Friend, 2001; McConville, 1999; Rogers et al., 2002). A commercial show, under the surveillance of advertisers, must immediately post strong results in Nielsen's charts or likely wind up on the chopping block before viewers even have a chance to find the new program in their television listings. HBO, conversely, handling its content as fine wine, has the luxury of waiting for buzz to kick in as more and more people discover its distinctive offerings. Neither *The Sopranos* or *Sex and the City*, for example, had they been accepted by commercial networks to begin with, might have had the opportunity to reach the status of cultural phenomena because their ratings performances during their respective first seasons were not particularly sparkling. Having fewer scheduling restraints, which enables it to target certain evenings for maximum buzz (for instance, Sunday nights were used to premiere new *Sex and the City* and *The Sopranos* episodes) and repeat shows throughout the week, also contributes to HBO's advantage in cultivating an audience over time.

Despite the fact that HBO does not follow a commercial sponsor business model, it must be clearly grasped that the pay station is not utterly free of advertising. It may not place 30-second spots between segments of programming, but HBO indeed engages in product placement transactions. *Sex and the City*, for instance, is notorious for drawing attention toward designer labels, especially for shoes. In fairness, however, the implicit plugs often appear to work within the spirit of the show and add to its feeling of authenticity—*Sex and the City's* main characters, after all, love to shop. Moreover, HBO, as a rule, does not accept direct payment for its placements (Atkinson, 2003; Edwards, 2004). On the other hand, by inserting freely provided products into the texture of its programs, the network benefits by lowering its sizeable production costs. Consequently, its placements are not always particularly subtle. In one episode of *The Sopranos*, for example, Tony asks the character Johnny Sack about his Maserati: "Kinda draws attention, no?" The conversation continues:

TONY: Absolutely. And in a Guinea gray, looks fantastic.
JOHNNY: Tops out at 176 miles per hour. Standing quarter, 13 and change.

This is hardly the stuff of "seamless" integration. Obviously, HBO is not above overtly plugging a brand to offset costs. A larger issue to consider, then, is to what extent the premium service challenges the consumer ideology that commercial networks relentlessly circulate. The tendency to promote a worldview centered on buying things, though, is probably not as pronounced in the case of HBO—arguably, even more so than its commercial rivals, it disseminates polysemic messages that both affirm and undermine dominant capitalist ideology. This theme will be touched on again later in the chapter. Ultimately, though, HBO is still located within a commercial structure. As noted above, marketing is a fundamental component of its enterprise. HBO might be different, but not *so* different. Though, of course, "It's sort of not TV. It's HBO" would not resonate as a tagline.

At the same time, HBO is not immune from corporate influence. It is, for sure, part of the Time Warner empire. If its business model were to yield diminished returns, it is hardly likely that its parent company would simply endorse the cause of producing quality programming for quality's sake and that HBO would not hear from the suits at headquarters. In addition, as a member of the extended family, HBO's programs serve as commodities for other Time Warner enterprises (Bignell, 2004). Yet overall, in spite of its economic constraints, when placed side-by-side with the commercial networks, HBO's structure and philosophy seem to promote an environment in which creative individuals can collectively express their talent and inventiveness can flourish.

## HBO's distinction from its pay-TV rivals

Until now, a number of factors have been cited to demonstrate why HBO has earned a reputation of offering more quality fare than its commercial competitors. Yet HBO is not alone in the pay-TV universe. If other premium services adhere to a similar political economic structure, then why have they not achieved the same cachet as HBO? To answer the question would require a case-by-case examination beyond the scope of this chapter. Yet one comparison will be attempted: HBO vs. Showtime. The choice deserves special attention because the latter represents the former's most long-standing rivalry.

Over the course of its run, Showtime has indeed enjoyed moderate success. By 1999, the boom in direct-satellite subscriptions had given a boost to the channel (Kafka, 1999). As of this writing, *the L word* is in its third season and signifies Showtime, too, places a premium on risk—the program is the first one in American television history to concentrate its action on the lives of a group of mostly lesbian women (Sedgwick, 2006). Robert Greenblatt, Showtime's president of programming, admitted he was committed to "making some noise" with the series. His wish appeared to be materializing, as the drama, early on, generated a 300 percent larger audience in primetime than other Showtime originals (Anderson-Minshall, 2006: 13). *The L word* followed on the heels of another show based on explicitly homosexual themes, *Queer as Folk*, which was modeled after a UK series of the same name. Together, these two programs have helped gay programming more fully enter "mainstream" commercial distribution. Furthermore, in 2005, Showtime drew its own share of critical acclaim, garnering an uncharacteristically significant number of Emmy nominations (Hill, 2005). Historically somewhat content to reside in the shadows of HBO, so it seems, Showtime has lately shifted course and implemented an increasingly vigorous effort to directly compete with its nemesis (Frutkin, 2004; Rutenberg & Carter, 2003; Weinraub, 2000). The network, in fact, had hired Greenblatt in 2003 to revamp its corporate climate and take a more aggressive stance toward HBO.

Despite the similarities between HBO and Showtime—the focus on risk and quality, "edgy" programming; and the production of content that sparks lively debate among journalists and academics alike—there are differences as well. These points of distinction illuminate why, in part, HBO has secured far greater profits and significantly more critical commendation than Showtime. For starters, HBO has a much larger financial base on which to operate. But how did such fortune transpire to begin with? HBO's head start accounts for one reason. As Greenblatt mentions, "they [HBO] got into the series business way before we did, so they've had a long time to gain momentum and try shows that didn't work and ultimately find their way into shows like *The Sopranos*" (Lafayette, 2005a). "They became a generic for cable TV," Matthew C. Blank, Showtime's chairman, adds (Frutkin, 1999). Showtime, consequently, has been playing catch-up ever since its beginnings. Accordingly, HBO has the resources to dedicate to expansive marketing campaigns and, not surprisingly, has been considerably more adept at the process (Frutkin, 1999). Moreover, HBO has an advantage in procuring inclusion in cable packages, given that its owner, Time Warner, owns a huge stable of cable systems (Frutkin, 1999; Kafka, 1999).

Still, HBO's economic structural factors cannot entirely account for why it has towered over Showtime. Corporate agency probably provides much of the answer as well. Put simply, HBO is plainly better at executing the same recipe than its competitor. As Greenblatt concedes, the gap between the two networks is a result of HBO "being at the top of their game . . . and doing it as well or better than anybody else does it" (Frutkin, 2004). Showtime, for years, utilized a niche programming strategy (Frutkin, 2004). But this tactic appears to be changing as the network seeks to expand its reach. *Weeds*, a suburban comedy ("dramady"? [Goodman, 2006]) *a la Desperate Housewives*, yet one in which marijuana plays a key role (ah, there's the risk!), has been generating the ever-elusive buzz. Besides receiving critical attention, it has also captured the fascination of audiences—after one season it became the most highly rated program on Showtime (Pope, 2006). With *The Sopranos* nearing completion and HBO's *Deadwood* and *Big Love* serving as poor substitutes in cultivating a large following, Showtime could finally be mounting a serious threat to HBO's preeminence. Yet with only about half the number of subscribers as HBO (Pope, 2006), Showtime faces an uphill climb. In the post-television age, circumstances change quickly. Stay tuned.

## What have you done for me lately?

As just indicated, HBO could be in the midst of a serious slump, a possibility that many critics have recently suggested (for example, see K. Anderson, 2005; Berman, 2006; Epstein et al., 2006; Flint, 2005; Goldstein, 2005; Hill, 2005; *USA Today*, September 28, 2004: D1; Weinman, 2006). HBO's business model, although grounded on structural advantages, is not necessarily foolproof and, consequently, the pay service could be in the middle of a transformation as it endeavors to maintain or increase profits in a mutating climate featuring the potential for anything, anywhere, anytime television.

The loss of hit shows, of course, has put HBO under increased pressure. In short, HBO faces a serious challenge: How does it continue to raise the bar and retain the momentum it has already established? HBO's success could be its worst enemy. "How have you shifted the paradigm lately?" asks journalist Kurt Anderson (2005). Can HBO find a new way to be edgy now that its formula has become mainstream (Weinman, 2006)? The critics, once falling over themselves in praise of HBO, are currently questioning its hegemony. Where's the buzz?

Part of the problem is that the underside of HBO's business practices is coming into view. Yes, producing fewer series with shorter seasons supplies the network with the space to exercise creativity and allows it to spend heaps of cash per episode. But its minimalist approach to programming, creating large gaps in its schedule, can also lessen enthusiasm and alienate viewers (K. Anderson, 2005; Berman, 2004). A long delay before the start of a new season can raise expectations beyond reason, making it nearly impossible to deliver the goods to audiences hungry for larger servings of quality-TV nourishment. "And when you piss off a fan," writes Marc Berman (2006) with respect to HBO's ostensibly haphazard scheduling, "the results in the long run can negatively impact the entire network."

Uncontrollable external factors are impinging upon HBO as well. General cable and satellite subscription sales have reached the saturation point (*USA Today*, September 28, 2004: D1), making it a tougher task for HBO to build its subscriber base amid inexhaustible churn, which only intensifies once a series run completes (Auster, 2005). At the same time, cable companies themselves are not promoting HBO as diligently as they did previously. Recognizing the prospective windfall associated with broadband and incipient telephony services, these providers no longer place a premium on HBO—over a 20-year period, revenue from the network diminished from 35 percent of their total cash flows to less than 5 percent (Atkinson, 2005).

Yet perhaps the single-most threat to HBO, with the potential to undermine everything the network supposedly embodies, is the gaining capacity of commercial networks to compete with HBO at its own game (see, for instance, K. Anderson, 2005; Epstein et al., 2006; Goetzl & Halliday, 2002; Goldstein, 2005; Stanley, 2004; *USA Today*, September 28, 2004: D1; Weinman, 2006; Worrell, 2002). As much as it would like to claim otherwise, HBO does not "own" edginess, quality, and originality. Other outlets are quickly catching on. For years, HBO has influenced its commercial competitors, stirring them to not only mimic its accent on fresh programming, but also loosen their "moral" standards by showcasing more profanity and bare flesh (K. Anderson, 2005; Chunovic, 2002; Flint, 2000; Goetzl & Halliday, 2002; Haley & Knight, 2002; Peyser & Gordon, 2001; Yacowar, 2002). Some networks are parroting HBO in other ways. For example, FX has experimented with limiting the number of episodes it produces so it can spend more money per unit to render, it hopes, well-crafted, provocative shows (Berman, 2004). With highly acclaimed and rated programming, including *Nip/Tuck*, *The Shield*, and *Rescue Me*, the tactic may be paying dividends. FX, despite its advertising support, has been usurping some of the aura once monopolized by HBO (Chunovic, 2002; Epstein et al., 2006; Goetzl & Halliday, 2002; Haley & Knight, 2002; *USA Today*, September 28, 2004: D1; Weinman, 2006), which is aptly captured in two recent business magazine headlines: "FX Aims for HBO's Cachet" (Goldstein, 2005) and "Cutting-Edge FX hailed as Next HBO" (Stanley, 2004). Even launching branding campaigns to forge unique identities has extended into commercial channels (Rogers et al., 2002). Suddenly, HBO does not seem so special anymore.

But how can a commercial network, such as FX, create risky programming, given the political economic constraints spelled out in this chapter? It turns out that funding from advertisers also has its flip side, in this case, one that benefits basic cable and broadcast stations. After all, strong advertising support yields another means of generating revenue that can be shoveled into high-end productions. The problem, then, reduces to this: can a commercial network secure payment from sponsors without their accompanying meddling influence on content and the softened edges that generally result? Some advertisers have indeed demonstrated hesitancy in aligning themselves with FX's somewhat controversial offerings. "There is still a bit of skittishness because of content," Shari Anne Brill, an executive for a media buying firm, concedes (Stanley, 2004). On the other hand, as certain media-savvy audiences acclimate to more "dangerous" fare, a number of advertisers are indeed willing to take the chance. Alcoholic beverage manufacturers, carmakers, and movie studios are particularly prone to view "adult" content as suitable for their branding efforts (Elliot, 2005; Goetzl & Halliday, 2002). Concurrently, several television executives have been known to replace antsy sponsors rather than water down their productions (Goetzl & Halliday, 2002). Furthermore, FX has notably upped the ante by flirting with commercial-free, single-sponsor episodes of *Rescue Me* and *Nip/Tuck*. If the practice were to become widespread, with no need to build toward commercial interruptions, FX, arguably, could even more closely resemble HBO.

But this development seems highly improbable. When Sony became sole sponsor of the third-season premiere of *Nip/Tuck*, for instance, it was still allotted 11 minutes of commercial time for trailers promoting its movies (Lafayette, 2005b). In addition, spot-free cablecasts have occurred only rarely on the network. Consequently, the same limitations that apply to traditionally advertising-funded programming persist—at least in part. Mini-episodes in between commercial pods are not likely to vanish. Nor could one anticipate that advertisers will stand by patiently and wait for a new program on FX or any other station to build an audience slowly—the need to engender immediate ratings success will almost certainly remain. If so, producing quality shows in the vein of pay-TV networks will pose a constant struggle, more the exception than the norm.

Yet looking at the big picture, the trend is clear: HBO is confronted with far greater competition today—including, as mentioned earlier, living up to the very standards the network itself set. Still, HBO's "decline" should not be overstated and how a situation forever in flux plays out can only be surmised. For now, HBO's standing is hardly bleak. Ratings may be down (which, as already pointed out, is merely a secondary concern for HBO), but its subscriber numbers (what really count) continue to impress and its profits could stir the envy of just about any television executive (Flint, 2005).

## It's not TV: It's DVDs and other forms of distribution

To keep its revenue soaring and adjust to transmuting conditions, HBO, since at least 1999, has been revising its business model by expanding its reach through other distribution venues (Epstein et al., 2006; Flint 2004, 2005; Haley & Knight, 2002; McConville, 1999; Rogers et al., 2002; *USA Today*, September 28, 2004: D1). Although the subject has been adeptly discussed elsewhere (see especially Rogers et al., 2002), to provide context and better understand this moment in time, a brief historical overview is merited here.

By the 1950s, cable was introduced to merely bring television into homes unable to receive broadcast signals. It was not until the 1970s and 1980s that the industry actually began channeling significant energy into developing original programming (Levinson, 2002: 26). A major turning point for HBO, in particular, was the release of the VCR. Until then, HBO earned its bread and butter through televising Hollywood films after their initial run in theaters; now that people could easily bypass HBO by renting movies (and choosing from a much greater selection), HBO realized it had to venture into the production of original content (Edwards, 2004).

Rogers et al. (2002: 43–44) present a novel theoretical perspective on broadcast and cable television history that is broken into three divisions, fittingly named, TVI, TVII, and TVIII. TVI describes the oligopoly of the "big three" networks, ABC, CBS, and NBC, and their focus on so-called lowest common denominator programming, once portrayed by former FCC chair Newton Minow as a "vast wasteland." TVII witnessed the precipitous weakening of broadcast dominance and the elevation of "niche marketing," as cable penetrated the symbolic landscape and the television audience became increasingly fragmented with a much larger number of channels from which to pick. The authors contend this period was characterized by cult programming that inspired an "avid fanship" (44–5). Breaking up the "bottleneck" of limited distribution options, TVIII foregrounds the ability of viewers to access programming through diverse formats and sources on demand (46–7). Thus, branding is now more crucial than ever if a media distributor expects to drive viewers to its content, whether by satellite, traditional cable, on-demand cable, TIVO, DVDs, Internet downloads, podcasts, and so on. For years, HBO cultivated considerable brand equity through its production of quality programming. But this approach, no doubt, will not be enough to sustain it into the future. So currently the pay network (a term that is perhaps outmoded in relationship to HBO—it presently transcends such a narrow distinction) is employing various strategies to extend its brand, a chief trait of the TVIII age. By the time its buzz had apparently peaked in 2005, HBO was already contemplating additional revenue streams. "The new script: DVD sales, syndi-cation, international growth, and even investing in theatrical movies," explains reporter Joe Flint (2004). At the time of his article, HBO's non-subscriber profit had already grown from 5 to 20 percent. It is no longer simply a matter of gaining additional subscribers for the traditional station but of building the overall brand; in this sense, HBO is evolving into more of an owner-syndicator than a network (Epstein et al., 2006: 19–20). Spin-offs and merchandizing represent a salient part of the story. *The Sopranos*, for example, has spawned a cottage industry, featuring T-shirts, baseball jerseys, gourmet foods, the *Soprano's Family Cookbook*, and a *Sopranos* poker set. A movie based on the series is not out of the question (Epstein et al., 2006: 23–4). What Epstein et al. argue, however, is that expanding the brand will dilute it and undermine HBO's claim to exclusivity, which could eventually diminish its established channel's luster and HBO's capacity to create high-quality content as business decisions trump creative integrity. Indeed, they conclude, "it is just a matter of time before channels such as HBO become a relic of the past, replaced with new technologies of distribution like on-demand program streaming or on-line video file sharing" (25). HBO as a brand, they claim, will supersede its import-ance as a premium channel. Whether or not these authors are inflating the account will be taken up shortly.

## Maybe HBO is not completely different, but it's different enough

As it labors to at least somewhat redefine itself, HBO will inevitably deepen its interactions with the very commercial networks from which it has spent years symbolically distancing itself. In his contribution to this book, Avi Santo argues that HBO's relationship with other networks has always been more ambivalent than the pay service would have the audience believe. According to Santo's reasoning, HBO has not fundamentally changed television as much as paral-leled its rivals' strategies and tweaked their standard genres to produce "better" content. But now, the author maintains, by executing a more serious attempt to live up to its tagline in response to the need to retain the buzz it has already instituted, HBO is failing because of its structural reliance on its commercial competitors.

Without question, HBO has not revolutionized television. Appropriated from the commercial networks, the series format itself, David Chase asserts, can stifle creativity—although limiting a show's run in advance can reduce the tendency for a program to lose its edge over time (Lavery & Thompson, 2002: 23–4; Rogers et al., 2002: 54). And now the symbiotic flow between the commercial outlets and HBO goes in both directions. Not long ago, a branch of

HBO, HBO Independent Productions, agreed to assist ABC in developing new programs (Chunovic, 2002; Peterson, 2002). Moreover, as Santo points out, since early on, HBO has turned to its competitors as a syndication market for its original shows—a trend, it appears, that will only intensify. HBO, for sure, has for years produced episodes with syndication in mind, shooting alternate, sanitized scenes (obviously to please advertisers rather than viewers) for use down the line (Elliott, 2003, 2005; Heuton, 1994; Peyser & Gordon, 2001). One might conjecture that if the premium service ever places syndication interests above others it could result in more conventional fare and undercut HBO's emphasis on quality. Can the especially risky programs of late find success in syndication? Maybe yes. *Sex and the City* is already in syndication with TBS and the safer version seems to have escaped utter rebuke from television critics (see Poniewozik, 2004, for example). At the same time, it has triumphed in securing a large audience, becoming the top show among adults of 18–49 on any advertising-supported cable station (Epstein et al., 2006: 23). Meanwhile, *The Sopranos* began its launch on A&E in 2006. It could be that once commercial TV executives perceive a show as a proven commodity, it no longer signifies unbearable risk.

But to counter Santo, it is not as though the executives at HBO truly believe the pay service is essentially different than the commercial networks; they realize they are merely following conventions, albeit, in a manner, they hope, that results in better interpretations of the formulas. "It's a tagline," blurted Richard Piepler, an HBO executive vice-president, after Tad Friend (2001), writing for *The New Yorker*, said Leslie Moonves, CEO of CBS Television, had carped that if HBO is not TV, then it should not be winning Emmy Awards but something else. "Get a life. Jesus." "Does he think we have legally disqualified ourselves?" HBO chair Jeffry Bewkes added. "Tell Les," he continued, "that we were trying to create a vague idea that we were different from regular TV." Just as a professional symphony orchestra will do greater justice to Beethoven's Fifth than its high-school counterpart down the street, HBO has demonstrated that it can be more consistent in producing superior content than its commercial competitors. There is no solid evidence to suggest that HBO has abandoned its commitment to creating high-quality fare, a criterion it is arguably still dependent on for its overall profitability. What is more, in rebuttal to Epstein et al., a case could be made that HBO as a network is not going away. Instead, it will play a critical role in extending the brand into other areas because its buzz-making shows will drive success in these other venues. "No hit shows also means no big DVD or rerun sales," Joe Flint (2005) posits. Even as it cultivates additional revenue streams, HBO's first priority is holding onto subscribers, which still account for the lion's share of the pay service's income, in the midst of churn (Flint, 2004). Risk will remain a central ingredient in the recipe and, in spite of the threats from the commercial networks and its adaptation to the post-television era, HBO yet partially holds both the structural and corporate-cultural advantages that have been depicted throughout this chapter.

Interestingly, Kurt Andersen (2005) suggests that HBO, in a sense, has evolved into what PBS was intended to be. But, I would suggest, while PBS strove to insert "educational value" into its "quality" offerings, HBO took a less paternalistic approach. Audiences have made it clear which option they prefer: entertainment rules the day. But who is to say that viewers are not learning something as they watch Tony struggle to be a good family man in the face of remarkably stressful "workplace" conditions? A rigorous critical textual analysis would probably indicate that HBO does not systematically challenge capitalist American ideologies or dominant myths regarding race, gender, sexual orientation, or other identity issues (Hermes, 2006). Evaluated from this vantage point, HBO is *not* so unlike its commercial competitors. Still, as illustrated above, the premium brand tends to deliver multilayered content that invites diverse readings. Ultimately, the audience will decide what HBO means and whether or not it will remain the benchmark for provocative programming.

## Note

1   Brown notes, "The views in this paper are my own and do not represent the views of the Federal Communications Commission, its Commissioners, or its staff" (Brown & Cavazos, 2005: 17).

## Works cited

Akass, K. & McCabe, J. (eds) (2004) *Reading Sex and the City*. London: I.B. Tauris.

Albiniak, P. (2003, June 23) "Sex And Marketing: HBO Has Long Been Known For Heavy Promo Spending", *Broadcasting & Cable*. 18.

Anderson, C. (2005) "Television Networks and the Uses of Drama", in G.R. Edgerton & B.G. Rose (eds) *Thinking Outside the Box: A Contemporary Television Genre Reader*. Lexington: University Press of Kentucky.

Anderson, K. (2005, August 1) "I Want My HBO", *New York*. 18.

Anderson-Minshall, D. (2006) "Sex and the Clittie", in K. Akass & J. McCabe (eds) *Reading The L Word: Outing Contemporary Television*. London: I.B. Tauris.

Atkinson, C. (2003, August 4) "Absolut Nabs Sexy HBO Role: 'Sex and the City' Features Fake Ad", *Advertising Age*. 6.

Atkinson, C. (2005, February 28) "HBO's Playbook: Playing Hard to Get", *Advertising Age*. 3.

Auster, A. (2005) "HBO's Approach to Generic Transformation", in G.R. Edgerton & B.G. Rose (eds) *Thinking Outside the Box: A Contemporary Television Genre Reader*. Lexington: University Press of Kentucky.

Barnouw, E. (1990) *Tube of Plenty: The Evolution of American Television, 2nd edition*. Oxford: Oxford University Press.

Bellamy, R.V., Jr. & Traudt, P.J. (2000) "Television Branding as Promotion", in S. Eastman (ed.) *Research in Media Promotion*. Mahwah, NJ: Lawrence Erlbaum.

Berman, M. (2004, February 23) "A Pity About City", *MediaWeek*. 38.

Berman, M. (2006, June 12) "HBO's Midlife Crisis", *MediaWeek*. 38.

Bignell, J. (2004) "Sex, Confession and Witness", in K. Akass & J. McCabe (eds) *Reading Sex and the City*. London: I.B. Tauris.

Brown, K. & Cavazos, R. (2005) "Why is this Show So Dumb? Advertising Revenue and Program Content of Network Television", *Review of Industrial Organization* 27: 17–34.

Butsch, R. (2003) "Ralph, Fred, Archie, and Homer: Why Television Keeps Re-creating the White Male Working-class Buffoon", in G. Dines & J.M. Humez (eds) *Gender, Race, and Class in Media, 2nd edition*. Thousand Oaks: Sage.

Chunovic, L. (2002, October 28) "Broadcast Feels HBO's Influence: 'Kingpin' Drama is NBC's Answer to 'The Sopranos' ", *Electronic Media*. 15.

Edwards, J. (2004, January 23) "HBO's 'No Ads' Attitude Keeps Top Programmes Out of Reach", *Campaign*. 17.

Elliott, S. (2003, October 10) "Stuart Elliott in America", *Campaign*. 14.

Elliott, S. (2005, January 11) "Would a Cleaned-Up Version of 'The Sopranos' Still Be Too Naughty for Most Sponsors?", *The New York Times*, http://select.nytimes.com/search/restricted/article?res=F30A14F9345D0C728DDDA80894DD404482. Retrieved August 3, 2006.

Epstein, M.M., Reeves, J.L. & Rogers, M.C. (2006) "Surviving 'The Hit': Will *The Sopranos* Still Sing for HBO?", pp 15–25 in D. Lavery (ed.) *Reading The Sopranos: Hit TV from HBO*. London: I.B. Tauris.

Flint, J. (2000, April 7) "With Eyes on Cable, Networks Permit Racier Plots, Unprint-able Dialogue—Success of HBO's 'Sopranos' is Impetus, as is a Nation Inured to Sex Scandals", *The Wall Street Journal*, Eastern Edition. B1.

Flint, J. (2004, January 5) "HBO's Next Business Model; Theatrical Films, Syndication and DVDs Supply Revenue, Supplementing Subscriber Fees", *The Wall Street Journal*, Eastern Edition. B1.

Flint, J. (2005, June 8) "As Critics Carp, HBO Confronts Ratings Decline", *The Wall Street Journal*, Eastern Edition. B1.

"Fresh Air: 'The Sopranos' Writer and Director David Chase" (2004, March 2) Radio Program, National Public Radio, Washington DC.

Friend, T. (2001, May 14) "The Next Big Bet: Is a Family of Depressed Morticians HBO's Best Hope for Life After 'The Sopranos'?" *The New Yorker*. 80.

Frutkin, A.J. (1999, November) "Searching for Buzz: Despite a Renewed Commitment to Original Programming, Showtime Remains in the Shadow of HBO", *Media-Week*. 38.

Frutkin, A.J. (2004, October 18) "Analyze This: Robert Greenblatt is Helping Show-time Find its Inner Self by Enlisting A-level Hollywood Talent", *MediaWeek*. 18.

Gitlin, T. (1985) *Inside Prime Time*. New York: Pantheon Books.

Goetzl, D. & Halliday, J. (2002, March 18) "Taking Cue from Cable, Gingerly", *Advertising Age*. 63.

Goldstein, D. (2005, September 19) "FX Aims for HBO's Cachet: Higher-Brow Original Programming is Grabbing Audiences and Advertisers", *Business Week*. 90.

Goodman, T. (2006, August 11) "Greatness of 'Weeds' Could Make Showtime Must-Pay-for-Television", *The San Francisco Chronicle*, Final Edition. E1.

Haley, K. & Knight, B. (2002, November) "Rocking the Industry: HBO has Redefined Excellence in TV Entertainment. What's Next?", *Broadcasting & Cable*. 3.

Hermes, J. (2006) " 'Ally McBeal,' 'Sex and the City' and the Tragic Success of Feminism", in J. Hollows & R. Moseley (eds) *Feminism in Popular Culture*. Oxford: Berg.

Heuton, C. (1994, May 30) "Is There Life After Pay Cable?" *MediaWeek*. 14.

Hill, L.A. (2005, August 15) "Broadcast Brings Back the Buzz: Newcomers, Network Resurgence Provide Compelling Plot for this Year's Contest", *Television Week*. 29.

Hollows, J. & Moseley, R. (2006) "Popularity Contests: The Meanings of Popular Feminism", in J. Hollows & R. Moseley (eds) *Feminism in Popular Culture*. Oxford: Berg.

Hughes, M. (2004, August 24) "Highly Anticipated 'Joey' May Be Best Comedy on TV This Fall", *Gannett News Service*. http://web.lexis-nexis.com/universe/document?_m=5c3c2f44b5a2269b8b79670c0c8e7e68&_docnum=1&wchp=dGLbVlb- zSkVb&_md5=3a0f8ffc5b37d8c9bc4cc2a3c7557a2f. Retrieved August 8, 2006.

Kafka, P. (1999, August 9) "Win, Place, Showtime", *Forbes*. 52.

Lafayette, J. (2005a, January 3) "It's Showtime for 'Hate' Pilot: One Pay Cable Drama Project's Journey from Development to Delivery", *Television Week*. 1.

Lafayette, J. (2005b, August 22) "Sony to Solo on 'Nip' Preem; FX's Single-Sponsor 'Launch Nights' Enable Advertisers to Stand Out", *Television Week*. 1.

Lavery, D. (2002) " 'Coming Heavy': The Significance of *The Sopranos*", pp xi–xviii in D. Lavery (ed.) *This Thing of Ours: Investigating The Sopranos*. New York: Columbia University Press.

Lavery, D. (2006) "Introduction: Can this Be the End of Tony Soprano?" pp 1–14 in D. Lavery (ed.) *Reading The Sopranos: Hit TV from HBO*. London: I.B. Tauris.

Lavery, D. & Thompson, R.J. (2002) "David Chase, *The Sopranos*, and Television Creativity, pp 18–25 in D. Lavery (ed.) *This Thing of Ours: Investigating The Sopranos*. New York: Columbia University Press.

Levinson, P. (2002) "Naked Bodies, Three Showings a Week, and No Commercials: *The Sopranos* as a Nuts-and-Bolts Triumph of Non-Network TV", pp 26–31 in D. Lavery (ed.) *This Thing of Ours: Investigating The Sopranos*. New York: Columbia University Press.

Magder, T. (2004) "The End of TV 101: Reality Programs, Formats, and the New Business of Television", in S. Murray & L. Ouellette (eds) *Reality TV: Remaking Television Culture*. New York: New York University Press.

McCabe, J. with Akass, K. (2004) "Introduction: Welcome to the Age of Un-Innocence", in K. Akass & J. McCabe (eds) *Reading Sex and the City*. London: I.B. Tauris.

McConville, J. (1999, October 25) "Competition Driving HBO: Merges Film Units to Maintain Momentum", *Electronic Media*. 1.

Peterson, T. (2002, August 20) "The Secrets of HBO's Success", *Business Week Online*, http://web.ebscohost.com/ehost/detail?vid=4&hid=9&sid=d9dfc13e-1cf7-4e0c-8e22-09e127661341%40SRCSM1. Retrieved August 2, 2006.

Peyser, M. (2006, May 1) " 'Sopranos' Takes a Hit", *Newsweek*. 15.

Peyser, M. & Gordon, D. (2001, April 2) "Why the Sopranos Sing: Nothing Else on TV Can Touch HBO's Mob Hit—That's Got the Network Suits Watching Their Backs. Will 'The Sopranos' Change the Face of Television?" *Newsweek*. 48.

Poniewozik, J. (2004, June 21) "S_x and the Scissors", *Time*. 22.

Pope, K. (2006, August 6) "For Showtime, Suburban Angst is Fast Becoming a Ratings Delight", *The New York Times*, Final Edition. B26.

Rogers, M.C., Epstein, M., & Reeves, J.L. (2002) "*The Sopranos* as HBO Brand Equity: The Art of Commerce in the Age of Digital Reproduction", pp 42–57 in D. Lavery (ed.) *This Thing of Ours: Investigating The Sopranos*. New York: Columbia University Press.

Ross, C. (1999, December 6) "Funny About HBO . . . It Works", *Advertising Age*. 20.

Rutenberg, J. & Carter, B. (2003, June 30) "Sex and Death Just Like HBO, but Showtime Gets No Love", *The New York Times*, Late East Coast Edition. C1.

Sedgwick, E.K. (2006) "Foreword: The Letter L", in K. Akass & J. McCabe (eds) *Reading The L Word: Outing Contemporary Television*. London: I.B. Tauris.

Stanley, T.L. (2004, October 11) "Cutting-Edge FX Hailed as Next HBO", *Advertising Age*. 3.

Weinman, J.J. (2006, April 3) "Is it Time to Declare HBOver? It Used to Be the Only Place to Go for Daring Unconventional Shows. Not Anymore", *Maclean's*. 54.

Weinraub, B. (2000, November 20) "Cable TV Shatters Another Taboo; A New Show-time Series Will Focus on Gay Sexuality", *The New York Times*, http://select.nytimes.com/search/restricted/article?res=F10F14F9355F0C738ED-DA80994D8404482. Retrieved August 3, 2006.

Willis, E. (2002) "Our Mobsters, Ourselves," pp 2–9 in D. Lavery (ed.) *This Thing of Ours: Investigating The Sopranos*. New York: Columbia University Press.

Worrell, N. (2002, October 28) "Quick Takes: What Can Commercial Television Do to Compete with the Crop of Popular Shows on HBO?" *Electronic Media*. 8.

Yacowar, M. (2002) *The Sopranos on the Couch: Analyzing Television's Greatest Series*. New York: Continuum.

# Chapter 3

# Will Yingshuiji buzz help HBO Asia?

*Shawn McIntosh*

The question of whether yingshuiji (literal translation: "drinking-water machine") buzz will help HBO Asia comes with as much cultural baggage as American tourists eager to discover the "real Asia" on their one-week, five-country tour. The question is loaded with cultural baggage because it glosses over the myriad complexities that make up the Asia-Pacific market and media landscape, and it assumes in that totalizing American way that people are, basically, the same everywhere and therefore the same marketing techniques will work everywhere in the world.

This chapter will attempt to unpack much of that cultural baggage. It will show how HBO Asia has, for the most part, been savvy enough to leave the air-conditioned, dark-tinted windows of the tourist bus and trudge through the sweaty, tangled jungles of changing telecommunications and media regulations, protectionist government policies, disruptive media technologies, growing domestic media competition, and rampant piracy in a market so culturally and linguistically diverse that it makes the other international HBO divisions in Latin America and Central Europe look practically homogenous.

In exploring how HBO Asia has developed as a packager of quality programming and as a brand, the Asia-Pacific region provides an excellent example of the myriad factors that must be unpacked from the entity "HBO Asia" and the success or failure of particular shows. Especially for cultural content producers like HBO, issues of technology, regulations, marketing, and branding—all closely connected to the larger concept of globalization and tensions that have come between developing and industrialized nations—are fundamental to better understanding how modern media companies like HBO operate internationally (Curtin, 2005). Whether one calls this era post-modern, post-traditional, or from a media-centric perspective post-television or the TV III era (Rogers et al., 2002), all these factors have greatly affected the ability of HBO Asia to enter the Asia-Pacific market and gain subscribers.

However, just because a tourist is willing to venture into a steamy Southeast

Asian marketplace with unfamiliar sights, sounds and smells, does not mean they will return to the hotel unscathed. HBO Asia has made some business decisions, like showing commercials on its channels in some countries and heavily censoring content to fit cultural norms, which may perhaps harm the HBO brand in the region in the long run. Similarly, technological changes that alter media consumption habits and widespread cable and satellite TV piracy could be factors that could dramatically change business models and that are largely beyond HBO's ability to control. This chapter will provide a snapshot of these forces and the roles they have played and continue to play in the development of HBO Asia and the chances of success for its programming, especially its original programming.

## Development of HBO Asia

In the early 1990s, Asia-Pacific was widely acknowledged as being in its infancy regarding cable and satellite TV, and HBO had hopes of counteracting the slowed growth of its maturing domestic subscription market (Goad, 1993). HBO Asia launched an English-language, 18-hour-a-day movie service in Asia through Singapore's SCV channel in 1992, using Indonesia's Palapa satellite for distribution (HBO Asia, 2007b). A joint venture of Paramount Films, Sony Pictures Entertainment, Time Warner Entertainment, and Universal Studios (HBO Asia, 2007c), today HBO Asia promotes itself as bringing "the best of Hollywood to Asia first" and a "24-hour subscription movie channel that offers viewers in Asia the latest and biggest blockbuster movies," as well as promising "quality original movies and series that are produced by HBO, exclusively for viewers of the HBO channel" (HBO Asia, 2007a, c).

In 1993, HBO Asia opened its regional headquarters in New Tech Park, an industrial park in Singapore, and became available in Thailand and the Philippines. Singapore was a likely choice for a regional headquarters, partly because of its location and role as an important transportation hub more or less in the center of the vast Asia-Pacific region and partly because Singapore was also trying to establish itself as a media hub for the region (McDaniel, 2002; Goad, 1993). By 1994, HBO became a 24-hour movie channel and added Taiwan, one of the most highly developed cable markets in Asia (Oba and Chan-Olmsted, 2005), and Indonesia to its markets. By the time of HBO Asia's fifth anniversary in 1997, HBO Asia distributed programming to 18 countries in the region, including from 1995 three-star and above hotels and foreign housing compounds in China, becoming the first movie channel to be distributed to residential homes on CCTV in China in 2004 (HBO Asia, 2007b).

HBO now distributes five channels of programming to the following 22 territories in Asia-Pacific: Bangladesh, Brunei, Cambodia, China, Hong Kong,

India, Indonesia, Macau, Malaysia, Maldives, Mongolia, Nepal, Pakistan, Palau, Papua New Guinea, Philippines, Singapore, South Korea, Sri Lanka, Taiwan, Thailand, and Vietnam. The five channels are HBO, HBO Signature, HBO Hits, HBO Family, and Cinemax, in addition to video-on-demand services from 2007 in Hong Kong (HBO Asia, 2007c). Some countries receive programming with closed-captioning native-language subtitles. HBO Asia reaches the most countries compared to its two other international divisions, HBO Latin America and HBO Central Europe, and with an estimated one-third of the world's population in India and China alone, the region makes an attractive potential market for new subscribers. However, the Asia-Pacific region is made up of an incredibly complex mix of ethnic groups, languages, cultural norms, and religions. Almost all the countries that are part of HBO Asia had been colonized in whole or in part by Western countries, and the effects of their various colonial powers are often still felt in everything from infrastructure and the economy, to laws and customs. The region's diversity shows in the dominant religions, which include Catholic, Muslim, Buddhist, and Hindu (often with sizeable minorities of these religions within nations). Governments likewise are equally diverse, covering parliamentary democracies, republics, parliamentary republics (sometimes in name only), constitutional monarchies, and communism (World Factbook, 2007).

In addition to all these complexities and the cultural baggage that HBO, as part of transnational media conglomerate Time Warner, brought in setting up shop in Asia-Pacific, there were the additional difficulties of the vastly varied levels of telecommunications and television transmission development in Asia, along with all the regulatory and legal issues involved with that development. In order to begin to understand the level of complexity that HBO Asia faced as it launched in Singapore in 1992, it is important to have a basic sense of the television and telecommunications environment in Asia-Pacific then and now.

## TV development in Asia-Pacific

Like in the U.S., satellites play a crucial role in distributing programming to local cable operating systems (Vogel, 1998). HBO led the way in 1975 in the U.S. in using satellite communications to deliver programming, which led to two significant developments (Gershon, 2005). First, it gave HBO an efficient distribution network for its programming to cable operators; and second, the satellite/cable interface showed other cable programmers such as WTBS, ESPN, CNN, and MTV that they could do the same thing, ushering in a new era of cable networks. For a variety of economic, political, technological, and industry reasons cable and direct broadcast satellite (DBS) television did not become important in most countries in Asia-Pacific until the 1990s, even though the technology was available from the 1970s (McDaniel, 2002; Cheng, 2005).

There are no direct measures such as GDP per capita or length of time of a country having cable or satellite services that can be clearly correlated with the development and current state of cable and satellite TV in various Asia-Pacific countries. A case in point is Indonesia, which launched its own satellite network, Palapa, in 1976 with the help of U.S. technology from American space industries and NASA, allowing Televisi Republik Indonesia (TVRI) to reach the entire archipelago of 17,000 islands that stretch from the edge of the Pacific Ocean to the Indian Ocean (McDaniel, 2002). According to a study done by Oba and Chan-Olmsted of the penetration of cable TV in 10 Asia-Pacific countries (nine of which are part of HBO Asia), Indonesia was categorized as an undeveloped market along with the Philippines, Malaysia, and Thailand and ranked 10th out of the countries studied, with cable penetration of only 0.3% (Oba and Chan-Olmsted, 2005). Although some of the low penetration of cable could be attributed to Indonesia's island geography, making laying undersea cable and constructing local microwave transmitters time-consuming and expensive (McDaniel, 2002), Indonesia has a similarly low satellite TV penetration rate of 1.1%, above that of the Philippines (0.4%) and comparable to Thailand (1.6%), but far below that of Malaysia (21.2%) (Oba and Chan-Olmsted, 2005).

The industrial organization (IO) model provides a good framework from which to better understand the complex factors involved in the adoption and success of cable and satellite in different Asia-Pacific countries where HBO Asia offers programming. The IO approach states that industry factors and external, home country factors each play roles and interact with each other in influencing the success of a company within a given industry (Hitt et al., 2004). Industry characteristics include industry structure, industry conduct, and industry performance, while for East Asian cable markets six country-specific environmental factors can be considered: economic factors, regulation/policy factors, technology factors, consumer factors, supporting factors, and substitution factors (Oba and Chan-Olmsted, 2005).

HBO Asia does not build cable or satellite telecommunications systems, so the success or failure of HBO Asia's strategy lies only tangentially in the various factors outlined in the IO model regarding cable TV and satellite development in the region. However, several parallels can be made with the cable TV and satellite industry and what HBO Asia had to heed when creating its business strategy in the region. For example, Oba and Chan-Olmsted claim that the economic environment in which an industry operates is probably the most direct factor in determining the structure, conduct and shape of a business (Oba and Chan-Olmsted, 2005). Issues having to do not only with modernization, but with liberalization policies and gradual partial privatization of state-owned media monopolies all have direct influences not only on the technical infrastructure but on the abilities of HBO Asia to enter and succeed in a media market. Similarly, it can be seen how regulatory and policy factors regarding allowing multiple ownership or partial foreign ownership of networks would have an important influence on HBO Asia's business decisions.

Consumer buying power likewise plays a major role for HBO Asia, as there has to be enough of a middle class and elite audience in each country to afford the hardware such as a TV and a satellite dish, as well as subscriptions. Unlike HBO in the U.S., HBO Asia runs commercials on some of its networks, such as HBO South Asia, partly because Indian subscribers do not pay extra for HBO service and partly because, like in much of Asia, set-top decoder boxes are not available (Flagg, 1999). Running commercials on HBO may seem like sacrilege to U.S. viewers, where at least part of the allure of the tagline "It's Not TV" is that the consumer can afford to pay to not watch commercials. The potential ramifications of HBO's decision to run commercials on some of its networks and how that may affect its brand will be discussed later in this chapter.

Pent-up consumer demand among Asian audiences for televised entertainment has been a driving force not only for transnational media companies (TNCs) entering the Asia-Pacific media markets, but has given incentives for the growth of local cable operators as well (Gershon, 2005; Rao, 2005). For many years, state-run media in many of the countries in Asia-Pacific offered limited channels and programming that emphasized development or education rather than entertainment, and private commercial channels were often forbidden or had severe restrictions because of government policies to control broadcasting (McDaniel, 2002).

It has been argued that although state-run media industries in countries like India and China have used three main rationales to protect themselves from transnational media entering the countries and from domestic commercial competitive pressures, they have in fact acted as "state capitalists" regarding their state-run media (Pashupati et al., 2003). Despite the differences in their governments and economic growth in the latter half of the twentieth century, the three main rationales both China and India used for the protection of CCTV and Doordarshan, the state-owned television networks in each country, respectively, was the role they played in development communication, nation-building, and as protectors of cultural imperialism (Pashupati et al., 2003). However, the costs associated with running large media industries eventually led both countries to allow advertising in their state-run media to offset expenses. Doordarshan started running advertisements in the mid-1980s, while Shanghai TV was the first to allow advertisements in China in 1979, with most other networks following suit by the late 1980s (Pashupati et al., 2003). These commercial pressures had a role in changing not only programming, but in how the mission of state-run media was perceived in each of the countries.

Many Asia-Pacific countries have shown explosive growth of cable and satellite TV audiences from the early 1990s, partly because of increased liberalization of markets and the commercial pressures mentioned above (McDaniel, 2002). In India, the Gulf War was a major impetus for Indians to get cable TV so they could better follow the news, as many had relatives working in the Gulf region (Indian Television, n.a.). Doordarshan faced increasing competition from a growing number of international and domestic private networks, and added more channels to its programming to remain competitive. According to one study, cable penetration in India rose from 412,000 households in January 1992 to 1.2 million in November 1992, increasing to 3.3 million in 1993 and 11.8 million by the end of 1994 (Rao, 2005). By 1999, 22 million households were estimated to have cable and satellite connections, with many more believed to be connected through ad hoc neighborhood connections.

China, in 2002 already the world's largest cable TV market with 100 million subscribers and a TV penetration rate of 94 percent (China Daily, 2002), showed similarly rapid growth. In 1983, there were only 52 TV stations in the country. But by 2001, China had 357 TV stations and 2,194 channels (Cheng, 2005). This rapid growth was partly due to changes in government structure of TV stations, launching of satellite and cable TV services from the mid-1980s, and a conscious effort on the part of the government to place more importance on the media industries as important cultural producers and viable businesses rather than solely as propaganda vehicles (Bin, 1999). By 2001, 39 percent of the programming in China was entertainment (SARFT, 2002).

It was this kind of rapid growth that attracted transnational media companies such as News Corp., Viacom and Time Warner to the Asia-Pacific market in the early 1990s. However, these companies not only faced an unfamiliar and complex market, but were considered as prime symbols of cultural imperialism. Worries over cultural imperialism by Asia-Pacific leaders and government ministries responsible for granting national broadcast rights placed these transnational companies (with HBO arguably at the forefront, with its emphasis on showing primarily Hollywood movies) at the heart of a long-standing debate about globalization and cultural production and concerns of destroying local customs and ways of life at the expense of consumerism.

## Globalization and cultural production

Globalization is a multifaceted concept and its effects are a hotly debated topic (Held and McGrew, 2003: 4). A general definition of globalization can be given as follows:

Simply put, globalization denotes the expanding scale, growing magnitude, speeding up and deepening impact of interregional flows and patterns of social interaction. It refers to a shift or transformation in the scale of human social organization that links distant communities and expands the reach of power relations across the world's major regions and continents.

One can see globalization in the flow of international trade of goods and services and how unrest or unemployment in one region (for example, the Middle East) can greatly affect people in another region (people in India and the Philippines who rely on funds being sent by their relatives who are employed as construction workers or domestic help in the Middle East). Because of the reach and speed of global communications, news of events in one place can be learned about very quickly in another. This compression of time and space, or time-space distanciation, has had profound effects on our social relations and our lives (Giddens, 1990, 1984).

The issue of globalization becomes more complicated when dealing with media and cultural production. As many authoritarian governments have learned, in today's global communication environment it is nearly impossible to completely control the information and media a particular nation's people receive. This is especially true in a region like Asia-Pacific in which several countries border each other. The "footprint" of satellite beams does not distinguish between national borders, and the citizens of countries like Indonesia soon realized they could receive programming from neighboring countries if they had satellite dishes, which entrepreneurs quickly made available at reasonable prices. Nations have attempted to deal with this in various ways, including making private ownership of satellite dishes illegal, such as in Malaysia (McDaniel, 2002).

Critics of globalization regarding media markets state that an influx of foreign, primarily American, shows will swamp locally produced programming in terms of the number of shows available, production quality, and marketing and promotion, imparting American consumerist values and destroying local cultural values in the process (Ritzer, 2002; Schiller, 1976, 1969). One study done on several islands in rural Indonesia after satellite TV became widely available found a range of social and cultural changes after the communities got satellite access (Chu et al., 1991). These included positive effects, such as greater knowledge of development programs and education on topics such as family planning and modern healthcare, and negative effects that included a created demand for foreign consumer goods, such as soft drinks. Although some of the study's findings were later criticized for placing too much emphasis on the role of media exposure to such social and cultural changes, Indonesian policymakers nevertheless tried to devise ways to mitigate the negative effects and accentuate the positive effects (McDaniel, 2002).

Other critics of the role of TNC media organizations penetrating foreign media markets, while acknowledging potential detrimental effects, have more nuanced analyses in that they recognize there is nothing inherently "American" about the forces of globalization and that foreign media can at times have a beneficially radical effect on a country's media's policies, especially in countries that have had a history of strong censorship or restrictive controls on the types of content its citizens can receive (McChesney, 1999). Still others question how much influence media by itself actually has in changing cultural attitudes and local social practices (Lull, 2000; Thompson, J. B., 1995).

Nevertheless, the perception of the damaging effects of cultural imperialism remains firmly embedded among Asian policymakers and in anti-globalization social movements (Curtin, 2005; Yingshi, 2002; Zhu, 2001). It is now used as an important rationale for keeping restrictions on foreign media from entering national television markets as Asia-Pacific countries moved from developing countries to newly industrialized countries (NICs) as the other two rationales of development and nation-building become less important than they were 20 or 30 years ago (Pashupati et al., 2003).

Despite the charges of cultural imperialism and worries that local cultures throughout the Asia-Pacific region would be transformed under a tsunami of American television shows and consumerism, it has turned out that the competition of foreign shows has actually spurred local production of television shows in many countries (McDaniel, 2002). In addition, it has been shown that audiences tend to favor programs in their native languages over subtitled foreign-language programs, and prefer locally produced programs over imports, even when the imports are dubbed into the local language (Flagg, 2000; Hua, 2003). This means that on the one hand transnational media companies face charges of cultural imperialism even as their entry into national markets creates greater competition and can help spur the development of better locally produced television programs that tend to be preferred by the national audiences.

HBO, arguably an example par excellence of a global media empire as a wholly owned subsidiary of Time Warner, faced not only the various technical, regulatory, and market hurdles in expanding into Asia-Pacific, but the various cultural barriers as well even as its primary product, Hollywood movies, is also one of the most successful American cultural exports. Along with its Hollywood movies, HBO also imported its own high-quality original programming and the all-important "buzz" that came with some shows from the mid- to late-1990s.

## *Sex and the City* does **Bangkok, or brand strategy and the buzz factor**

Although HBO original programming only accounts for 30 to 40 percent of its total programming, much of HBO's brand equity in the U.S. as a channel of high-quality programming has been inextricably linked to its original shows and original series, especially from the late 1990s (see McCabe and Akass, this collection) (Rogers et al., 2002). Shows like *Sex and the City* and *The Sopranos* created the much ballyhooed water cooler "buzz" that helped vault them to ratings that regularly beat network shows scheduled in their Sunday evening time slots. With *Sex and the City* ending in 2004 and *The Sopranos* in 2007, news articles about HBO often fretted about which new HBO original series could capture the same kind of viewer loyalty, excitement, and generate the buzz that these shows were able to do (Blum, 2004; de Moraes, 2005; Goodale, 2005; Thompson, K. D., 2005). To date, none of their new series have been able to meet these lofty expectations, even though many continue to receive critical acclaim and *Entourage* has been touted by former HBO chief Chris Albrecht as a "water cooler" show (de Moraes, 2005).

The notion of "buzz" means essentially word-of-mouth marketing (WOMM)—or, more accurately, successful WOMM. Fortunately for the entertainment industry, people like to talk about creative goods (Caves, 2000). People value nonpurposive conversation, and "creative goods and the cultural consumption capital that surrounds them provide what is likely the most suitable grist" (Caves, 2000). According to Mark Hughes, author of *Buzzmarketing*, "To put it simply: Buzz starts conversations" (Hughes, 2005). He lists "six buttons of buzz" that will drive conversations between people: the taboo (sex, lies, bathroom humor), the unusual, the outrageous, the hilarious, the remarkable, the secrets (both kept and revealed) (Hughes, 2005). It is easy to see how many of HBO's highly touted original series have some—and often all—of these factors.

If commercials are essentially commodifying an audience's viewing time and attention and selling that to advertisers, then buzz is enlisting that audience to do the marketing work for free for the product. Buzz, of course, is not new. What is new, however, thanks largely to the Internet, is the ability for viewers not only to talk with each other in numbers far greater than any single corporate water cooler could ever accommodate, but also to reflexively monitor their conversations across time and space. This high degree of reflexivity and "stretching" of time, or what Giddens calls time-space distanciation, is an essential characteristic of what some call the postmodern society but what Giddens calls late modernity, or "post-traditional" society (Giddens, 1990). Just as electronic communication plays a vital role in globalization's effects of local events having repercussions in regions far removed from where they occur, it has an equally important effect on the ability of audiences to learn what others are saying about a program they like and to *easily join the conversation* through online forums, email lists, chat rooms, and recently in social networking sites. It is widely recognized that digital media has greatly reduced the cost of producing and distributing media content. What should be realized is that it has also greatly reduced the cost of producing and distributing (often nonpurposive) conversation.

Buzz has become important as a marketing tool, not because it never existed before, but because there was no space allowed for it in the models of industrial media production and promotion used by corporations. Although industrial media production is still prevalent, especially in capital-intensive media such as film or TV production (Benkler, 2006), promotion has been partially decoupled from that process due to the marketing work that audiences can now do for creative goods in the form of buzz. In the past, roughly corresponding to the eras of TV I and TV II that Rogers, et al. discuss (Rogers et al., 2002), audiences could only be heard through crude ratings measurements, surveys and other research methods, or very limited "upstream" channels of communication such as letters to the editor or focus groups. Production and promotion were both highly vertical, top-down processes to an audience that was perceived as passive when in fact they were primarily mute. Consider the number of heavily promoted shows that flopped, and the lamented shows of quality that were cancelled because they did poorly in the ratings, as well as the surprise hits that became popular even when they were not heavily promoted by the networks.

What marketers trying to "get people to talk about their stuff" often overlook is the role that conversations play in how we make sense of our world and how we shape our identities. Even people who recognize the power of WOMM often slip into the mode of thinking of the transmission model of communication, as seen in statements like "word-of-mouth is a far more powerful transmitter of information on creative goods than on goods that lack their cachet as a social catalyst" (Caves, 2000). Word-of-mouth is not primarily about simply "transmitting information," but about discursively creating and sharing meanings to create our social milieu and our very identities in a process more emblematic of Carey's ritual model of communication than that of sending and receiving information (Carey, 1992).

The notion of water cooler buzz, with its imagery of white collar workers in comfortable, air-conditioned offices excitedly discussing last night's show, reinforces the image of exclusivity that the HBO brand promotes even as it underplays the complex cycle of marketing, media promotion, and mediated audience conversations across online networks that make up our current media landscape. HBO creates their own "water cooler" spaces online in the form of interactive websites for each of their shows, complete with episode descriptions, information on the actors and characters, back stories, behind-the-scenes clips or interviews, discussion forums, and of course items to buy (Rogers et al., 2002). Further, the mainstream press often taps these resources, as well as fan-created forums when doing stories on shows that have buzz, which plays a crucial role as a feedback loop and in informing an even larger audience in a classic agenda-setting function.

Closely tied to this complex mix of media, mediated discourses and identity formation, and playing an increasingly important, some say revolutionary role in all facets of business, is the concept of branding and brand equity (Hart and Murphy, 1997). Brand equity has been defined as "a set of brand assets and liabilities linked to a brand, its name and symbol that add to or subtract from the value provided by a product or service to a firm and/or to that firm's customers" (Aaker, 1991:15). Brands of certain companies, such as McDonald's and Coca-Cola, are estimated to account for 70 percent and 50 percent, respectively, of their companies' total shareholder value (Lindemann, 2003). Managing a corporation's identity through its brand and maintaining brand equity have become important areas of corporate strategy, and in many service-related industries "branding activities are almost synonymous with corporate-identity activities" (Schmitt and Pan, 1994: 35). A similar argument could be made for companies that sell creative goods, such as HBO.

Its expansion of channels throughout the region connects not only to the rise in channel capacity available as delivery technologies get better, but can also be seen as integrally tied to its branding strategy, as channels like HBO Signature, HBO Hits, and HBO Family were brought to Singapore, Hong Kong and other select Asian markets in 2005 and bundled with HBO Asia and Cinemax (Osborne, 2006; Television News, 2005).

Quality is an important aspect of good brand recognition and awareness, and is especially important for Asian consumers (Schmitt and Pan, 1994). For several years in a row from 2000, HBO Asia was recognized as the best cable and satellite TV channel by regional cable TV and satellite operators, being named as leader in several categories such as "Best Programming Quality," "Best Sales and Marketing," "Best On-Air Promotions," "Most Popular Channel and Best Viewer Feedback," and "Best Value for Money" (BusinessWorld, 2003).

The numerous industry and customer satisfaction awards HBO Asia has won shows that it has established itself as a brand of high-quality programming, although from an Asian perspective how much of this can be attributed to HBO's original series and how much to the licensed Hollywood fare that they promote heavily and that makes up the majority of their programming is difficult to determine.

HBO has helped promote itself as a supporter of high-quality entertainment through efforts like sponsoring the Hong Kong International Film Festival in 2006, in which it used the opportunity to screen six of its original features in select theaters in Hong Kong (Television News, 2006). It has also been involved in various cross-marketing promotion events with retailers like Samsung and Johnson & Johnson, in which popular shows like *Sex and the City* were shown and were used with fashion shows, invitation-only cocktail parties, and events like "Shoes in the City" to promote the show and products in upscale malls in the Philippines and Thailand (Prystay and Narkvichien, 2002).

The popularity of *Sex and the City* among young female viewers was surprising to many, as the show's racy (though for Asian viewers, often edited) content seemed at odds with conservative Asian social values (Prystay and Narkvichien, 2002). However, the show seemed to resonate with young professional women. "The series speaks for everything that is in the minds of most women," a single, 30-year-old Thai public-relations consultant told the *Wall Street Journal* (ibid).

Popular shows like *Sex and the City* and the fan base they have attracted speaks to the growth of a consumer category known as the "cosmopolitan consumer." The cosmopolitan consumer is "a consumer whose orientation transcends any particular culture or setting" (Cannon and Yaprak, 2002: 30). Although this may appear to be an example of exactly the kind of cultural imperialism and inculcating of Western, consumerist values that Asia-Pacific policymakers have long feared, in fact the notion is far more complex in reality (Cannon and Yaprak, 2002). Despite a growing middle-class throughout Asia and the ability of people in that class to emulate certain aspects of consumerism or consumerist values, local culture still plays a crucial role as a kind of "blueprint" in guiding social interactions (Craig et al., 2005). This makes trying to calculate which shows may resonate with Asian audiences very difficult, as cultural and linguistic assumptions, as well as comedy, are often hard to accurately translate to foreign audiences (Flagg, 2000). Even with shows that do prove popular among Asian audiences, HBO Asia faces several other hurdles in making sure that popularity translates into profits, which has been a difficult task.

### *Et tu* globalization and the bad side of buzz

If entering the Asia-Pacific market was uncharted territory for HBO, they successfully navigated several large hurdles regarding licensing of movies on the other side of the Pacific. Prior to HBO Asia, movie studios negotiated licensing deals individually with each country in Asia-Pacific, but HBO was able to negotiate pan-Asian rights for content from a number of key studios, thanks in part to being a joint venture of three key studios, and because they arranged exclusive licensing deals with several independent studios such as Castle Rock, Focus Features, Morgan Creek, and New Line, among several others (HBO Asia, 2007a). This makes it easier not only for the movie studios involved in the licensing deals, but also gives HBO an important advantage in providing movies first to the Asia-Pacific cable TV market.

Despite HBO Asia's success in obtaining complex licensing deals with movie studios, getting distribution in nearly all of the cable TV markets in the region, and being recognized among regional cable operators as a high-quality channel, the media has reported disappointing growth in subscribers (Flagg, 2000). HBO Asia's subscriptions rose from 600,000 in 1995 to 1.1 million by 1996 and 3.5 million in 1999 (HBO Asia, 2007b). Growth has slowed since then, however, with parent company Time Warner claiming about 4 million sub-scribers in March 2005 (Time Warner, 2005) and an executive vice president of HBO Asia claiming 4.5 million in July 2005 (The Nation, 2005).

The numbers are small given the overall size of the region's cable TV market. There are a number of factors that can help explain the rate of growth of HBO Asia subscriptions. These include cable TV penetration rates still below 50 percent in many of the region's countries, new technologies that compete with television for consumers' time and money, competition from local cable TV networks, which are free, and cable TV piracy. Any single one of these is detrimental, but taken in combination it creates a cyclone of potential trouble for the bottom line.

Despite great strides in development throughout the region, there are still large gaps in development levels between the rural poor and urban poor, and even larger gaps between the poor and growing middle class. It can be easy for Western executives to myopically equate the locals in the professional class they do business and socialize with (generally in English) in urban areas as representative of the country, when in fact they still are a relatively small percentage and represent either the elite or the new middle class. In most of the countries of the region, with the exceptions of Singapore, Hong Kong, Macau, Taiwan, and South Korea, one does not have to search hard to find sporadic or no electricity, underdeveloped sanitation and health services, and other reminders of the developing world.

At the other end of the development spectrum, technologies such as DVDs, video-on-demand, mobile phones, and broadband Internet connections are rapidly changing the communications and entertainment landscape (McDaniel, 2002; Vogel, 1998; Wallenstein, 2005). Consumers are able to access enter-tainment through a wider variety of means besides the standard television set, and the proliferation of cheap entertainment options competes directly with the cable TV business model of paying subscribers sitting down in front of the television to watch commercial-free movies they cannot get elsewhere (Wallenstein, 2005).

HBO Asia has had to follow its cable competitors in allowing commercials on some of its channels in three of its markets, India, The Maldives, and Taiwan (Flagg, 1999). Asian viewers are accustomed to seeing commercials, even on state-run channels, so the practice has not seemed to hurt it in the eyes of Asian viewers, although Western brand managers have expressed concern that it may ultimately hurt HBO's brand of exclusivity in the long run and make it especially hard to enforce a pay-TV model (Flagg, 1999). Despite early outlooks that emphasized the huge potential in the region and tended to downplay the number of difficulties HBO would face (Goad, 1993; Warner, 1996), HBO executives later claimed they were well aware of the problems they would encounter in Asia-Pacific and that although their penetration was lower than that in the U.S., they claimed that their "reach is certainly far greater" (Murrell, 2000).

One big reason HBO's reach and penetration may be greater than the official numbers show is because of rampant cable and satellite TV piracy throughout Asia-Pacific, which is particularly damaging in the two potentially largest markets, China and India (Amnatcharoenrit, 2005; Fowler and McBride, 2005). In 2006, the Cable and Satellite Broadcasting Association of Asia (CASBAA) released its fourth annual study on cable TV piracy costs in the region that claimed the costs of cable TV piracy had risen from $1.06 billion in 2005 to $1.13 billion, continuing a rise in piracy costs since they began the study (CASBAA, 2006). Not all the countries covered by HBO Asia were in the study, but even with casting a skeptical eye on the figures because of the interests of the study's sponsors, it does give some idea of how rampant piracy is. Macau provides a good example, as it was included in the 2006 study for the first time. It was estimated that for every one legitimate subscriber there were 10 illegal cable subscriptions. Macau had the second highest ratio for piracy, after Vietnam (one legitimate for 15 illegal subscriptions) (CASBAA, 2006). CASBAA estimated that the number of illegal connections had risen 20 percent across the region in 2006, to 5.2 million. "Pay-TV piracy is possibly the number one issue facing the entire industry in the Asia Pacific," said Simon Twiston Davies, chief executive officer of CASBAA (CASBAA, 2006).

Piracy is also prevalent because of underreporting of "last-mile" connections to individual households from local MSOs, who pocket the profits directly and fail to report their actual subscribers (Groves, 2001). "Undeclaring subs in the Philippines is running at worse than 50 percent," Rik Dovey, managing director of ESPN Star Sports, told *Variety* in 2001. "In China, it's about 30 percent under. In India, there are 31 million homes connected to cable and just 10 million legal decoders." HBO Asia tried various digital technologies to ID programming and determine where the illegal decoders were coming from and would shut down signals to offending local operators, but learned—in an ironic twist to the transnational interactions taking place in globalization— that decoders sold in one country were also being shipped to a neighboring country (Groves, 2001). The problem of piracy had only gotten worse by 2006, with India in particular being singled out in the CASBAA study for its underreporting.

Piracy has taken an additional high-tech twist in China, where it has become a leading exporter of pirated cable TV content sent over peer-to-peer (P2P) broadband Internet networks, exactly like how music files had been shared worldwide for the past several years (Fowler and McBride, 2005). Media companies worry that this could catch on in the U.S. as more people get broadband connections, hurting the revenues of cable TV and satellite TV providers (Fowler and McBride, 2005). Of course part of the reason piracy is so rampant, and why HBO is a victim of it, is because of the popularity of its programming. It could be argued that HBO would be facing much bigger problems if nobody wanted to pirate its programming.

## Branding, buzz, and buying: The future for HBO Asia

Despite disappointing subscriber numbers and the various technological hurdles HBO faces, it does seem to have positioned itself well in Asia-Pacific as a provider of high-quality programming. It is likely that further success will entail the kinds of cross-marketing events it has done in recent years with retailers or other media companies, and providing support to local media productions—perhaps some that may even be developed with an eye to the U.S. market—could be another way to further build its brand equity. It would not be hard to envisage an HBO joint production with a Chinese production company or even state-run media entity like CCTV of an historical series similar to what was done with the BBC and the series *Rome*. China's rich cultural history, desire to promote its culture industry and itself to increase its soft power (Qin, 2006; Xue, 2007), and the large numbers of overseas Chinese throughout Southeast Asia would mean not only fertile ground for historical drama content, but provide a ready audience.

Although cable TV piracy no doubt will continue to hurt HBO Asia's income from subscriptions, it also has a growing number of revenue-generating sources that HBO is actively focused on developing, such as video-on-demand, DVD sales, and syndication deals (Wallenstein, 2005). Similarly, the growing affluence of the NICs in the region works in HBO's favor, not only in terms of getting paid subscriptions, but in terms of finding audiences that can identify easier with its original programming. Further liberalization of national media markets and developments in channel capacity and technologies likewise help HBO Asia cement its position as a brand leader in the region and shut down cable pirates. Like everything in Asia, nothing is as simple as it seems, and the future for HBO Asia and the success of its brand as "not TV" in Asia-Pacific will prove to be . . . interesting.

## Works cited

Aaker, D. (1991) *Managing Brand Equity*. New York: Free Press.

Amnatcharoenrit, B. (2005, July 28) "HBO to Show More Movies, Fight Piracy", *Bangkok Post*.

Benkler, Y. (2006) *Wealth of Networks: How Social Production Transforms Markets and Freedom*. New Haven: Yale University Press.

Bin, Y. (1999) "Mouthpiece or Money-Spinner? The Double Life of Chinese Television in the Late 1990s", *International Journal of Cultural Studies* 2 (3): 291–305.

Blum, D. (2004, November 16) "How HBO Lost Its Groove", *The New York Sun*.

Businessworld (2003, August 12) "HBO Rules for Three Years in a Row", *BusinessWorld*.

Cannon, H. & Yaprak, A. (2002) "Will the Real-World Citizen Please Stand Up! The Many Faces of Cosmopolitan Consumer Behavior", *Journal of International Marketing* 10 (4): 30–52.

Carey, J.W. (1992) *Communication as Culture: Essays on Media and Society*. New York: Routledge.

CASBAA. (2006) "CASBAA study highlights deterioration in 2006 piracy level", http://www.casbaa.com/press_releases/press_content.asp?press_id=161. Retrieved August 23, 2007.

Caves, R.E. (2000) *From Creative Industries: Contracts Between Art and Commerce*. Cambridge: Harvard University Press.

Cheng, H. (2005) "China", in A. Cooper-Chen (ed.) *Global Entertainment Media: Content, Audiences, Issues*. Mahwah: Lawrence Erlbaum.

China Daily (2002, August 22) "Huge Potential in Broadcasting Market—Forum", *China Daily*. http://www.chinadaily.com.cn/en/doc/2002-08/22/content_133178.htm. Retrieved August 22, 2007.

Chu, G., Alfian, C., & Schramm, W. (1991) *Social Impact of Satellite Television in Rural Indonesia*. Singapore: AMIC.

Craig, C.S., Greene, W.H., & Douglas, S.P. (2005) "Culture Matters: Consumer Acceptance of U.S. Films in Foreign Markets", *Journal of International Marketing* 13 (4): 80–103.

Curtin, M. (2005) "Murdoch's Dilemma, or 'What's the Price of TV in China?' ", *Media, Culture and Society* 27 (2): 155–175.

de Moraes, L. (2005, July 17) "At HBO, A Series of Disappointments", *Washington Post*.

Flagg, M. (1999, December 20) "HBO May Come to India . . . With Commercials", *Wall Street Journal*, Eastern Edition.

Flagg, M. (2000, August 23) "Asia Proves Unexpectedly Tough Terrain for HBO,

Cinemax Channels—National Censors Dictate Cuts, Ban Some Films Altogether; Neutered 'Sex and the City' ", *Wall Street Journal*, Eastern Edition.

Fowler, G.A. & McBride, S. (2005, September 2) "Newest Export From China: Pirated Pay TV", *Wall Street Journal*, Eastern Edition.

Gershon, R.A. (2005) "The Transnationals: Media Corporations, International TV Trade and Entertainment Flows", in A. Cooper-Chen (ed.) *Global Entertainment Media: Content, Audiences, Issues*. Mahwah: Lawrence Erlbaum.

Giddens, A. (1984) *The Constitution of Society*. Cambridge: Polity.

Giddens, A. (1990) *The Consequences of Modernity*. Stanford: Stanford University Press.

Goad, G.P. (1993, February 2) "HBO Is Drawn To Vast Size Of Asian Market", *The Asian Wall Street Journal*.

Goodale, G. (2005, August 21) "Once-Edgy HBO Strives to Remain Water Cooler-Worthy", *Chicago Sun-Times*.

Groves, D. (2001, April 23–29) "Catching the Cable Cheats", *Variety*.

Hart, S. & Murphy, J.M. (eds) (1997) *Brands: The New Wealth Creators*. New York: New York University Press.

HBO Asia. (2007a) "About HBO", http://www.hboasia.com/hbo/about_channel. Retrieved August 15, 2007.

HBO Asia. (2007b) "Milestones", http://www.hboasia.com/hbo/milestones. Retrieved August 15, 2007.

HBO Asia. (2007c) "Who We Are", http://www.hboasia.com/hbo/who_we_are, Retrieved August 15, 2007.

Held, D. & McGrew, A. (2003) "The Great Globalization Debate: An Introduction", pp 1–49 in D. Held & A. McGrew (eds) *The Global Transformations Reader: An Introduction to the Globalization Debate*. Cambridge: Polity.

Hitt, M.A., Ireland, R.D., & Hoskisson, R.E. (2004) *Strategic Management: Competitiveness and Globalization*. Cincinnati: South-Western College Publishers.

Hua, H. (2003, August 26) "Culture Looking to Capture Leading Role", *China Daily*.

Hughes, M. (2005) *Buzzmarketing: Get People to Talk About Your Stuff*. New York: Portfolio.

Indian Television. (n.d.) "India's Television History", http://www.indiantelevision.com/indianbrodcast/history/historyoftele.htm. Retrieved August 21, 2007.

Lindemann, J. (2003) "Brand Valuation", in R. Clifton & J. Simmons (eds) *Brands and Branding*. Princeton: Bloomberg Press.

Lull, J. (2000) *Media, Communications, Culture: A Global Approach*. Cambridge: Polity.

McChesney, R.W. (1999) *Rich Media, Poor Democracy: Communication Politics in Dubious Times*. New York: The New Press.

McDaniel, D. (2002) *Electronic Tigers of Southeast Asia: The Politics of Media, Technology, and National Development*. Ames: Iowa State University Press.

Murrell, D. (2000, September 26) "Letters to the Editor: Its Venture in Asia a Success, HBO Says", *Wall Street Journal*, Eastern Edition.

Oba, G. & Chan-Olmsted, S.M. (2005) "The Development of Cable Television in East Asian Countries: A Comparative Analysis of Determinants", *Gazette: The International Journal for Communication Studies* 67 (3): 211–237.

Osborne, M. (2006, March 14) "HBO Asia to Launch Nets", *Variety* 53.

Pashupati, K., Sun, H.L., & McDowell, S.D. (2003) "Guardians of Culture, Development Communicators, or State Capitalists?: A Comparative Analysis of Indian and Chinese Policy Responses to Broadcast, Cable, and Satellite Television", *Gazette: The International Journal for Communication Studies* 65 (3): 251–271.

Prystay, C. & Narkvichien, M. (2002, August 9) " 'Sex and the City' is a Hit in Asia—Single, Working Women Follow Show, Spawning A Cross-Marketing Boom", *Wall Street Journal*, Eastern Edition.

Qin, X. (2006, September 16) "Nurture Creativity to Propel Culture Industry", *China Daily*.

Rao, S. (2005) "India", in A. Cooper-Chen (ed.) *Global Entertainment Media: Content, Audiences, Issues*. Mahwah: Lawrence Erlbaum.

Ritzer, G. (ed.) (2002) *McDonaldization*. Thousand Oaks: Pine Forge.

Rogers, M.C., Epstein, M., & Reeves, J.L. (2002) "The Sopranos as Brand Equity: The Art of Commerce in the Age of Digital Reproduction", in D. Lavery (ed.) *This Thing of Ours: Investigating The Sopranos*. New York: Columbia University Press.

SARFT (2002) "Development of Radio and TV in China", http://www.sarft.gov.cn/manage/publishfile/51/1095.html. Retrieved August 22, 2007.

Schiller, H.I. (1969) *Mass Communication and American Empire*. New York: Augustus M. Kelley.

Schiller, H.I. (1976) *Communication and Cultural Domination*. New York: International Arts and Science Press.

Schmitt, B.H. & Pan, Y. (1994) "Managing Corporate and Brand Identities in the Asia-Pacific Region", *California Management Review* 36 (4): 32–48.

Television News (2005) "Expand and deliver", *Television News*.

Television News (2006) "HBO is the Official Sponsor of Hong Kong International Film Festival", *Television News*.

The Nation (2005, July 28) "HBO Targets Premium Market with New Signature Channel", *The Nation (Thailand)*.

Thompson, J.B. (1995) *The Media and Modernity: A Social Theory of the Media*. Stanford: Stanford University Press.

Thompson, K.D. (2005, June 4) "Sans Hits, It's a Buzz-Light Year at HBO", *Palm Beach Post*.

Time Warner (2005) "HBO Asia Announces Launch of Additional HBO Channels", http://www.timewarner.com/corp/newsroom/pr/0,20812,1056034,00.html. Retrieved August 22, 2007.

Vogel, H.L. (1998) *Entertainment Industry Economics: A Guide for Financial Analysis*. Cambridge: Cambridge University Press.

Wallenstein, A. (2005, August 26) "Success for HBO Goes Beyond State of 'Rome' ", *Hollywood Reporter*.

Warner, F. (1996, March 11) "HBO Asia is Negotiating an Agreement for Movie Channel Tailored to China", *Wall Street Journal*, Eastern Edition.

World Factbook (2007) "The World Factbook", http://www.cia.gov/library/publications/the-world-factbook/. Retrieved August 30, 2007.

Xue, C. (2007, July 27) "Culture Seen as Key to Soft Power", *China Daily*.

Yingshi, Y. (2002, October 30) "Preserving Culture in the Face of Globalization", *China Daily*.

Zhu, W. (2001) "International Political Economy from a Chinese Angle", *Journal of Contemporary China* 10 (26): 45–54.

# Chapter 4

# It's not TV, it's HBO's original programming

## Producing quality TV

### Janet McCabe and Kim Akass

> *HBO is more than a place; it's an idea . . . I've even thought about this: In certain cases, it's like the Medicis, like we're patrons of the arts.*
> Chris Albrecht, ex HBO Chairman-CEO (Carter, 2002b: 11)

Robert J. Thompson provocatively claimed in 1996 that "Quality TV is best defined by what it is not. It is not 'regular' TV" (13). Identifying a new kind of program that had first appeared on American screens in 1981, which was "better, more sophisticated, and more artistic than the usual network fare" (12), he initiated a debate for defining quality at the very moment HBO was in the process of rebranding its original series as "not TV." Since then, and as the cable channel ever more relied on its original programming to entice subscribers, "no institution across the range of the entertainment industry—in films, television, music or books—has been more talked about, written about, imitated and emulated than HBO" (Carter, 2002a: C1). The premier cable subscription channel has in fact come to define and *make visible* a new era of quality TV; and how it institutionalized that discourse of quality will be the subject of this chapter.

## Instituting original programming: HBO and the post-1996 television era

Long has HBO been known as a pioneer for its uncut theatrical releases and original series like *Dream On* and *The Larry Sanders Show*. But with its rebranded original programming the pay-TV service had by 2002 "eclipsed its cable competitors and broadcast rivals as the gold standard in television, if not all of entertainment" (Grego, 2002: A2). Starting with *Oz* in 1997, and maturing in 1999 with *The Sopranos*, its stable of high-performance originals renewed the channel and sealed its reputation as a "groundbreaking leader in programming"

(Grego, 2002: A2). "There is a feeling about HBO [Ray Solley, head of cable program development consultants the Solley Group, says] that when that name goes on a program, you at least know that it's going to be—whatever genre—the top of its line" (Grego, 2002: A2).

Original programming like *The Sopranos, Sex and the City, Deadwood, Curb Your Enthusiasm* and *Six Feet Under* have not only proved highly profitable for the company in terms of revenue and industry awards, but also in "intangible factors such as prestige, cultural influence and public awareness" (Carter, 2002a: C1). But why is HBO so widely discussed in this way, and why do critics and commentators repeatedly enthuse over the channel's original programming? For HBO has surely not invented any new markers for defining quality, and it has doubtless not discovered any new ones. But it has, nonetheless, defined new rules for talking about, and understanding what we mean by, quality TV in the post-1996, post-network era. To this end HBO has imposed itself as a model for producing quality TV, enforcing those ideals, and spawning new forms of television culture and subjectivity, new opportunities for transformation in creative practices and business strategies. So successful in fact has the channel been in its rebranding exercise that it has become synonymous with quality in the contemporary television landscape.

Original programming does more than merely strengthen HBO's status as a purveyor of quality. Subscription is key. Unlike the networks that sell "viewers to advertisers" HBO is in the "business of selling programs to viewers" (Friend, 2001: 82). With 50–60 percent of its business subject to churn, as people cancel subscriptions (either because they move home or fail to renew) the company must offer viewers a reason to keep watching. HBO cannot take for granted customer loyalty; instead, a fundamental business principle must provide value for money for its subscriber base. Consumer satisfaction is high on the agenda. Its commercial logic for investing in its programs is that while "only four million people want to watch . . . they want to watch it so badly they will pay to do so" (Bradberry, 2002: 8). "As the marketplace became more competitive," Chris Albrecht has said, "we had to go from being an occasional-use medium to something people use on a regular basis in order for people to justify paying for us . . . original programming became a tool for doing that" (Grego, 2002: A4).

Original programming was thus, according to Albrecht, a pragmatic business decision. And it was one taken at a time when broadcasters were coming to terms with, and responding to, transformations taking place elsewhere in the industry. 1996 saw the ratification of the Telecommunications Act in Congress. Its passing, argues Michele Hilmes (2003: 66), paved the way for industry deregulation and "sparked a tsunami of corporate mergers." Through legislation, the federal government intended to provide as much economic latitude and content freedom for the industry as possible (Rowland, 2003: 135). Increasingly, the American television business, with support from Washington, emphasized diversification and competition. In so doing it made possible the recent TVIII era driven by among other things brand equity, consumer demand and customer satisfaction (Rogers, Epstein, & Reeves, 2002: 42–57; Epstein, Reeves, & Rogers, 2006: 15–25). Principles of competition, advertising, branding and customer choice, facilitated by legislation, come into view through HBO's business strategy. Its approach to original programming is rooted in this legislative change, emerging at the very moment the Act comes into effect.

Advertising itself with the audacious marketing claim, "It's Not TV. It's HBO," the channel brands itself as something worth paying for. In fact HBO has made much capital from cultural snobbery around television as it sets out to appeal to the college-educated audience who supposedly do not watch TV. Its niche marketing gently pokes fun at its discerning consumer base, such as the 2004 campaign, where those working in the watercooler business thank HBO for its smart programming. Why? Because the channel has contributed to a revival of its fortunes as employees up and down the country start congregating around watercoolers to talk about HBO's original programs (Stevenson, 2004). Campaigns like this enable HBO to create a "buzz" about itself. It trades on the fact that they are offering something unique, something audiences cannot get elsewhere and something that everybody is talking about.

1999 saw famed photographer Annie Leibovitz shoot the cast of *The Sopranos* (including creator David Chase) for *Vanity Fair*. Imitating Leonardo da Vinci's "The Last Supper" (1498) with Tony Soprano (James Gandolfini) at the center, and winning the Alfred Eisenstaedt Award in 2000, the image that has the cast positioned as apostles cost $60,000 to produce and took a week to prepare. 2002 and HBO hired Leibovitz. This time she conceived and shot the promotional image of the Sopranos crammed into an Italian restaurant; and in 2004 she was responsible for the season 5 "Hell Hath No Fury Like The Family" campaign (Goodman, 2004). Another homage, possibly referencing Theodore Gericault's "The Raft of the Medusa" (1819) that focused on Algerian immigrant survivors from a shipwreck in 1816, has the Soprano family overseeing tormented bodies washed up on the dark and muddy New Jersey shore. Matching the original in size, it is a dramatic presentation of a television event on a huge canvas; and its presentation on public billboards confirms the epic-ness of *The Sopranos* narrative— the sublime and the terrible. Referencing artworks that signaled new directions in art to advertise a television show is telling, however. Evoking da Vinci and Gericault who made art that changed art, Leibovitz makes clear, in these photo-spreads, that *The Sopranos* is television that is changing television.

Arguably original programs are produced in and through an institutional discourse that works hard to tell us that HBO's original programming stands as a beacon in a highly competitive marketplace. HBO has long made a virtue of its autonomy from the constraints and restrictions that limit network television. But let us be cautious. HBO is not, writes Tad Friend, "a band of artistic guerrillas who occasionally hijack the airwaves but an elite alternative to the parent company's mass-market brands" (2001: 89). HBO may set itself apart from network channels, but it is embedded in the very working practices and business strategies that it sets itself against. Furthermore it needs network television, and a comprehensive working knowledge of it, in order to justify its "Not TV" label. HBO's corporate parent is in fact the Time Warner empire, owner of, among other media enterprises, Warner Bros. Television, producer of *E.R.* and *The West Wing*. HBO original programs may only attract a sixth of the audience that *The West Wing* enjoyed, and Chris Albrecht may say, "At least when *West Wing* creams us, it'll all be in the family" (Friend, 2001: 89), but HBO's original programs function within the parent company as a select product designed to appeal to a lucrative demographic.

For a company that prides itself on its original programs, there is an awful lot of regular television within its schedules. The presence of the *Real Sex* documentary series covering topics from Kama Sutra workshops to a penile puppet troupe, *Taxicab Confessions* and *G-String Divas*, for example, does not have the HBO team waxing lyrical in the same way as it does about its signature shows *Sex and the City*, *Six Feet Under* and *The Sopranos*. The channel's top-rated programs may include boxing and the *Real Sex* documentaries, but as Friend (2001: 90) reports "nobody at HBO ever started a discussion with me about boxing or blowup dolls . . . HBO executives would rather discuss its riskier, artier ventures, emphasizing just how different it is—some of the time any-way." Discretion shrouds institutional practice, circumspection rules. Internal regulation is cautious in handling the salacious and gratuitous, and absorbs the illicit into the serious business of making original groundbreaking programs.

## Instituting quality: Authorship and controversy

Implanted in its original programming philosophy, and made intelligible in each original series, HBO to a certain extent disturbs established rules while voicing their determination to change television fiction and how it is made. Yet to utter a new direction is no easy matter; and what the subscription channel did with its original programming proved sufficiently groundbreaking that at first HBO had to account for its existence and take charge of what made it unique as something to be inserted into a system of values, institutionally managed and regulated. Evoking ideas of quality in terms of creative risk-taking and artistic integrity are cited as a way of distinguishing what makes HBO's programs exceptional within the television landscape. Celebrating authorial freedom and managing controversy in particular are crucial tools used to distinguish HBO's original programs from other network dramas—nothing new perhaps. But it is the way the channel uses these to make sense of what it is doing—justifying it as quality to make acceptable—that intrigues.

Veteran television writer David Chase, the maestro behind *The Sopranos*, never fails to vocalize his frustrations with the networks and underscore that the mobster hit series could have *only* achieved success on a channel like HBO: "I had just had it up to here with all the niceties of network television . . . I don't mean language and I don't mean violence. I just mean storytelling, inventiveness, something that really could entertain and surprise people" (Longworth, 2000: 34). What Chase is saying is that the freedom granted at HBO goes beyond writing brutal violence and lurid language. "It [is]," says Chase, "being able to tell the story in an unconventional way" (Monroe, 1999: 3). Latitude to tell stories differently, creative personnel given the autonomy to work with minimal interference and without having to compromise, has become the HBO trademark—how they endlessly speak about and sell themselves, how the media talks about them, and how their customers have come to understand what they are paying for.

Reliance on an authorial vision driving the project finds HBO placing a high premium on the kind of authorship more commonly associated with traditional art forms carrying high cultural kudos: theater, international art cinema, and literature (Lavery & Thompson, 2002: 18–25; Millichap, 2005: 101–114; Feuer, 2007: 145–157). Brutal violence on *The Sopranos*, for example, is enclosed within a discourse of quality and its existence justified by the "intensely personal vision" of Chase (Carter, 2000b: E1). Repeated apocryphal tales of his refusal to compromise or apologize "for the way Tony's 'violent line of work' is depicted" (Holston, 2002: B10), the incessant emphasis placed on Chase's outsider status, his dislike of network television and admiration for independent filmmakers he credits with reinventing cinema, his personal control over script revisions and participation in the editing process, and HBO's willingness to wait patiently for him to deliver, sees an idea of authorship emerge as about someone with vision enough to take risks and not afraid to buck convention. Free from the usual preoccupations engrossing broadcast networks like ratings and advertising revenue may explain why HBO can afford to be patient about extended breaks between seasons (Grego, 2002: A2). But it also institutionally justifies the decision to allow Chase time to develop his "addictive storytelling" (James, 2001a: E1). The cable network may have been nervous (or so reported) about the now-celebrated first-season episode "College" where, taking his daughter Meadow (Jamie-Lynn Sigler) to look at colleges in Maine, Tony executes with his bare hands a loathed former colleague who turned state's evidence. But authorial vision prevailed—and the episode eventually picked up the Emmy for Outstanding Writing for a Drama Series in 1999. Murder may be committed out of professional necessity, in a business where those entering know the deadly (generic) rules, but how extreme violence crafts the morally complex and utterly compelling New Jersey mob boss Tony Soprano reveals how decisively those creative and institutional freedoms are used at HBO.

Each HBO series—such as *The Sopranos*, *Sex and the City*, *Deadwood*, *Six Feet Under*—strives to create a distinctive and highly unique visual style. Each original may have a coherent authorial vision behind it, but those with established reputations are often enlisted to help its realization. The hideously beautiful visual referencing of *Deadwood*, for example, combines a nostalgic haze with a coarse realism in its sepia tones and gritty *mise-en-scène*, replicating the verisimilitude of nineteenth-century photography as well as modernist interpretations of the genre—not too surprising given that Walter Hill, director of *The Long Riders* (1980), took the helm for the pilot. With *Six Feet Under*, series creator Alan Ball wanted a cinematographer who would bring "a cinematic sensibility to TV, and who would strive to create a visual palette that would not only tell the story of the Fisher and Sons funeral home but also comment on it" (Magid, 2002: 71–72). Director of photography, Alan Caso, worked with him to come up with what Ball calls "an anti-TV language." Describing it as "a combination of very painterly, motivated, natural lighting, desaturated colors and lots of depth" (Magid, 2002: 71–72), Caso avoided "the kinetic, almost chaotic movement style of network TV." Instead he explains, "we don't move the camera a lot unless there is a reason to move it, motivated by the emotional intent of the scene. We do a lot of very formal shots where you let things play out in a proscenium, treating the frame almost like it's a stage" (Press, 2003: 55). What is clear from the above is how the search for a quality TV aesthetic plunders already established "high-end" media—theater, European art cinema and painting—to determine and legitimize the new. But, and more importantly, HBO intensifies speech around such a debate as it institutes aesthetic difference. Never more attention has been focused on explaining and dissecting the new—verbalized within DVD commentaries, in feature-length interviews for newspapers, magazines, and specialist media journals.

Viewers and TV journalists have long come to expect controversy, provocative content, and thought-provoking television from HBO. Contentious subject matter and edgy scripts containing adult themes is predicated on a risk-taking that strains broadcasting limits. Constantly reasserted, through incessant self-promotion and the brand equity, and waged in aggressive marketing campaigns,

is the perceived cachet of HBO—and in particular its original programming—
as a haven for creative integrity, initiating diversity and bucking convention
that breaks the rules in terms of language, content and representation. Repeatedly writers, producers and directors talk about the creative freedoms enjoyed
at HBO. "Primarily I wanted to do a comedy about sex, and I knew that
couldn't happen on network television," Darren Star, creator of *Sex and The
City*, has said (Bradberry, 2002: 8). "On network TV it would have been
substantially different," says Scott Buck, writer for *Six Feet Under*. "We couldn't
show a dysfunctional family without trying to solve all their problems. Some
episodes perhaps could play on the networks because they're not filled with
'fucks' and such—*but that's not the difference really*" (Bradberry, 2002: 8;
emphasis ours). Arguably the channel takes control of the illicit and encloses it
within its institutional discourse of quality—implied as an original tele-literary
product that places emphasis on smart writing, compelling stories told in an
innovative way, high production values and a unique creative vision behind each
project.

The solemnity with which HBO tells us about how it is challenging cultural
taboos while asserting the importance of the creative contribution that they
believe they are making to modern television drama is crucial. Take, for
example, HBO's high profile original drama *Deadwood* and how the series
raised the level of TV violence and profanity in an unprecedented way. Series
creator David Milch cites "scholarly fidelity" and "historical rationale" as justifying the incessant cursing, "a much closer approximation of the language of the
real West" (Martel, 2004: 34). Alluding every time to the meticulous research
he undertook for the project, Milch constantly reasserts that "the one thing
upon which everyone agrees was that the profanity and obscenity was astound-
ing" (Holston, 2004: C19). Whether or not the language is historically accurate
(and several dispute Milch's claim) is less important than how it serves to
support HBO's institutional policy for sponsoring original drama, as well as
how it functions as modern television dramaturgy. *Deadwood*'s linguistic use of
the profane, the obscene, the indecent, emerges as a convention of tele-literary
achievement: primitive expletives mixed with ornate rhetoric, "often verging
on Shakespearian verse or Victorian prose" (Millichap, 2006: 106); and vulgarity spoken with poetic cadence or possibly as Jacobean oratory. Enclosing the
profane in a discourse of historical verisimilitude and saturating it in literary
respectability and highly valued performative traditions promises to liberate
television fiction from the laws governing established creative practices and
writing styles.

## Instituting quality: Interpretive communities

Named "a contemporary American masterpiece" (Monroe, 1999: 2) and cited as "maybe the greatest work of American popular culture of the last quarter century" (Holden, 1999: 23), *The Sopranos* exists enclosed in a sustained critical discourse ensuring the series is widely discussed and its bloodshed explained. Some of the most shocking violence committed by Tony may ambiguously weave unremorseful brutality with a strict moral code, but in many ways it is how the interpretative community takes charge of that meaning and makes it acceptable that contributes further to how HBO's originals become defined as quality.

Deciphering explicit violence as not merely some "ratings stunt" but "the only way to remain true to the complex reality of Tony's life" (James, 2001b: E6), Caryn James, along with other TV critics, cultural commentators and academics, legitimizes graphic scenes and puts into discourse a cultural agenda for talking about such matters. James cites "a piece of capicola as Tony's Proustian madeleine, evoking memories of his boyhood introduction to violence;" (2001a: E1) and Stephen Holden describes the accumulated conflicts as having "the force of Greek tragedy. Or is it a Chekhov comedy replayed in the profanity littered argot of New Jersey hoodlums?" (1999: S2, 23). Claudia Rosett describes the "intricately well-written . . . superbly acted . . . mobster story" as defying the usual television labels likening it instead to "a Greek drama adapted with all its gore and insight into the modern world—Oedipus with semi-automatics; the House of Atreus on Prozac" (2002: A13). Reading the interpretations of *The Sopranos* as using "extreme violence to a profound artistic end" (James, 2001b: E6) leads us to wonder if not evoking valorized literary and dramatic forms in order to give the violence respectable affiliations, and set it apart from the "increased violence [that] has crept into network shows" (James, 2001b: E6), does not bear traces of the same old snobbishness? As if those reputable associations are essential before a discourse of what constitutes originality in television drama can be articulated and/or accepted. HBO may tell us that *The Sopranos*, for example, is not TV, but critical discourse classifies exactly what that might mean.

Original programming has long been sold to those who do not watch (regular) TV. The notion that this is television for those not interested in the medium gives additional meaning to the channel's slogan "It's Not TV. It's HBO." Strategies for defining and regulating television have long been guided by assumptions about those who are imagined to be watching; and HBO is no exception. Endlessly it talks about (and, in turn, flatters) its audience for original programming as professional, college-educated and discerning. "In a recent *New York Times* feature," reports Grace Bradberry for *The Observer*, "sophisticated New Yorkers boasted about how they packed the kids off to bed each Sunday night for a session of 'guilt TV', this being the night when the channel shows its flagship programmes" (2002: 8). An obsessive preoccupation with an elite, intellectual niche audience with high expectations, willing to pay a premium price for the subscription service, has the effect in fact of shifting attention away from regulative activities onto sanctioning and protecting the right of HBO to take creative risks in the first place. If traditional values coalition groups evoke fears about the exceptional vulnerability of certain television viewers to moral corruption, then HBO draws into this public debate another social grouping not so easily corruptible because, educated and sophisticated, they want something "distinctive, high-quality [and] edgy" (Carter, 2002b: S3, 11), something challenging, different from the usual television fare, and are prepared to pay for it. Justifying the latitude granted him in terms of the viewers, David Chase talks of trusting the audience over the vicissitudes of broadcasting dictates: "We all have the freedom to let the audience figure out what's going on rather than telling them what's going on" (quoted in Lavery, 2006: 5). Suggested here is that the HBO audience authorize the new, and safeguard institutional freedoms to defy established broadcasting regulations, lift prohibitions, and reinvigorate television fiction in the process.

## Conclusion: Instituting quality television

"HBO is now the gold standard of television programming, mentioned by innumerable producers and even network programmers as what they would like to aspire to," wrote Bill Carter in 2002 (2002a: C2). But HBO has started to lose ground to other cable companies like FX (*Nip/Tuck*, *The Shield*, *Rescue Me* and *!huff*) and Showtime (*Queer As Folk*, *The L Word* and *Weeds*) who, absorbing the lessons, are producing dramas that are as risqué and taboo-busting as anything HBO can offer. More recently, network companies like ABC have, with *Desperate Housewives* and *Lost*, translated the "quality" formula for the mainstream. *Desperate Housewives* may have been rejected by HBO for not being risqué enough, but without the success of *Sex and the City* would the ladies of Wisteria Lane have ever made it to our screens?

Collaborations between HBO and the BBC, with its international reputation for producing quality programming, may ensure an international outlet, but it also serves to consolidate HBO's market position through association with another producer of quality. Long has this relationship existed with award-winning high-profile miniseries like *Band of Brothers* and *The Gathering Storm*. But, more recently this has extended to a collaborative working relationship on the original series *Rome*—*I Claudius* meets *The Sopranos*—as the show fuses reputations: British theatrical acting credentials with HBO's rule-book. But its failure to revive HBO's fortunes reveals how the channel is playing it safe with its established quality markers, an inevitable consequence of its market leadership.

But television is changing.

Despite attempts to replicate the earlier successes of signature shows like *The Sopranos, Sex and the City*, and *Six Feet Under*, the difficulties HBO are having may say more about how the television market is shifting rather than their failure to find the next television hit. But what it has done with its original programming will be felt throughout the industry for years to come. Argued here is that HBO purposefully liberated television fiction from established rules and determined different industrial and creative approaches in the post-network, post-1996 era: authorship as brand label, the illicit as a marker of quality, high-production values, creative risk-taking and artistic integrity, the viewer as consumer, customer satisfaction, and value for money. "We've raised the bar," Chris Albrecht has boldly claimed (Bart, 2003: 8). Maybe so, but HBO's original programming has instituted a norm of quality that has entered the lexicon. It is still HBO, but television has caught up.

## Works cited

Bart, P. (2003, January 13) "The Hunt For Hits". *Variety*. 8.

Bradberry, G. (2002, October 20) "Swearing, Sex and Brilliance", *The Observer*. 8.

Carter, B. (2002a, 20 July) "If Media Is Really AOL's Oyster, Its Biggest Pearl is Clearly HBO", *The New York Times*. C1, C2.

Carter, B. (2002b, December 29) "He Lit Up HBO. Now He Must Run It." *The New York Times*. S3, 1, 10, 11.

Epstein, M.M., Reeves, J.L. & Rogers, M.C. (2006) "Surviving 'The Hit': Will *The Sopranos* Still Sing for HBO?" pp 15–25 in D. Lavery (ed.) *Reading The Sopranos: Hit TV from HBO*. London: I.B. Tauris.

Feuer, J. (2007) "HBO and the Concept of Quality", pp 145–157 in J. McCabe and K. Akass (eds.) *Quality TV: Contemporary American Television and Beyond*. London: I.B. Tauris.

Friend, T. (2001, May 14) "The Next Big Bet", *The New Yorker*. 80–91.

Goodman, T. (2004, May 5) "It's Back and Ready to Shatter Your Idea of What TV Should Be. Season Five of 'The Sopranos' Proves its Genius is Intact", *San Francisco Chronicle*. D1.

Grego, M. (2002, November 4) "Feared Yet Respected". *Variety* (Special on HBO at 30). A1–A2, A5.

Hilmes, M. (2003) "US Television in the Multichannel Age (Protectionism, Deregulation and The Telecommunications Act of 1996)", pp 62–67 in M. Hilmes (ed.) *The Television History Book*. London: BFI Publishing.

Holden, S. (1999, June 6) "Sympathetic Brutes in a Pop Masterpiece", *The New York Times*. S2, 23.

Holston, N. (2002, September 13) "For Show's Creator, An Unexpected Run", *Newsday*. B10.

Holston, N. (2004, March 21) "A Six-Gun Saga in 4-Letter Words", *Newsday*. C19.

James, C. (2001a, March 2) "*Sopranos*: Blood, Bullets and Proust", *The New York Times*. E1, E30.

James, C. (2001b, May 22) "*The Sopranos*: Brutally Honest", *The New York Times*. f E1, E6.

Lavery, D. (2006) "Introduction: Can this Be the End of Tony Soprano?" pp 1–14 in D. Lavery (ed.) *Reading The Sopranos: Hit TV from HBO*. London: I.B. Tauris.

Lavery, D. & Thompson, R.J. (2002) "David Chase, *The Sopranos*, and Television Creativity, pp 18–25 in D. Lavery (ed.) *This Thing of Ours: Investigating The Sopranos*. New York: Columbia University Press.

Longworth, J.L. (2000) "David Chase 'Hit' Man", pp 22–36 in *TV Creators: Conversations with America's Top Producers of Television Drama*. Syracuse: Syracuse University Press.

Magid, R. (2002) "Family Plots", *American Cinematographer* 83 (11): 71–72.

Martel, N. (2004, March 21) "Resurrecting the Western To Save the Crime Drama", *The New York Times*. 34.

Millichap, J. (2006) "Robert Penn Warren, David Milch, and the Literary Contexts of *Deadwood*", pp 101–113 in D. Lavery (ed.) *Reading Deadwood: A Western to Swear By*. London: I.B. Tauris.

Monroe, J. (1999, June 6) "Voice of a Nation". *The Observer*. 2–3.

Press, J. (2003, March 19–25) "Exquisite Corpses," *Village Voice*. 55.

Rogers, M.C., Epstein, M., & Reeves, J.L. (2002) "*The Sopranos* as HBO Brand Equity: The Art of Commerce in the Age of Digital Reproduction", pp 42–57 in D. Lavery (ed.) *This Thing of Ours: Investigating The Sopranos*. New York: Columbia University Press.

Rosett, C. (2002, January 28) "TV: Much More Than A Mob Story", *The Wall Street Journal*. A13.

Rowland Jr., W.D. (2003) "The V-Chip", pp 135 in M. Hilmes (ed.) *The Television History Book*. London: BFI Publishing.

Stevenson, S. (2004, June 15) "The Oscars of the Ad World", http://slate.msn.com/id/2102442.

Thompson, R.J. (1996) *Television's Second Golden Age: From Hill Street Blues to ER*. New York: Continuum.

# Part II

# Texts and contexts

# Introduction: The not TV text

*Brian L. Ott*

The term *text* is simultaneously one of the most commonly utilized and least frequently defined concepts in media studies. A word that initially referred to Holy Scripture and later to any written or printed message with clearly demarcated boundaries has—since the "linguistic turn" in mid-twentieth century philosophy—been expanded to describe any message or set of signs that can be subject to interpretation and assessment (Threadgold, 2005: 345). Today, media scholars refer to songs, films, internet sites, video games, and television shows all as texts. In media studies, then, a text is a structured set of discursive codes comprised of visual and/or linguistic signs that is potentially meaningful and pleasurable for an audience. As this definition suggests, any cultural commodity produced, distributed, and circulated by the entertainment industry can be approached as a text. Operating from this perspective, each of the four chapters in this section addresses, in one way or another, the question: "What, if anything, is distinctive about and characteristic of the texts on HBO?"

HBO has long marketed its programming under the moniker "original," suggesting that it is both unique and innovative. To understand how the essays in this section affirm, revise, and sometimes challenge this claim, it is useful, first, to reflect briefly on the textual dynamics of commercial network programming. Network TV is, by all accounts, a medium that traffics in what Todd Gitlin (1983) calls *recombinancy*, or the endless recycling of well-worn (and profit-proven) formulas and genres. Conforming to a logic of safety, commercial network TV is risk-adverse, a practice that has generated an array of easily recognizable and popular genres such as soap operas, daytime talk shows, game shows, situation comedies, hour long dramas, and reality programming. The appeal of commercial network TV lies, at least in large part, in the comfort and security offered by its predictability and reproduction of prevailing cultural norms and values. Network television texts are in a word *conservative*, not in a political sense so much as in an aesthetic sense. Their well-rehearsed visual conventions and banal narrative tropes function rhetorically to create and fulfill audience appetites in a manner that pacifies and placates, rather than shocks and unsettles.

In his chapter about the short-lived series *Carnivàle*, David Marc explores the limits of genre breaking and nonconventional story-telling on HBO. For Marc, the quick cancellation of *Carnivàle* highlights that though HBO is willing to push the aesthetic envelope from time to time, if the audience does not sufficiently bite, then HBO will swiftly retreat to more familiar and thus palatable fare. *Carnivàle*, Marc contends, was a long-shot from the beginning not just because it broke with familiar generic and narrative conventions, but also because it demanded an intertextual literacy and activeness not typical of television viewers. Whereas most commercial network television is relatively self-contained, requiring little viewer knowledge beyond the pop culture of the moment, *Carnivàle*—to be satisfyingly appreciated—required an uncommon historical and literary competence. Ironically, then, the very (inter)textual properties of *Carnivàle* that made it unique and thus reflective of the HBO "Not TV" tagline were also the properties that sealed its fate. The failure of *Carnivàle* does not automatically necessitate a wholesale rejection of HBO's claim to originality, however.

As Lisa Williamson demonstrates in her chapter on *The Larry Sanders Show, Curb Your Enthusiasm*, and *The Comeback*, HBO's reworking of the traditional network situation comedy into a hyperconscious, hybridized televisual form has been highly successful. Like *Carnivàle*, HBO's more comedy-based series pushed network television's traditional genre and narrative boundaries. But it did so in a less threatening way than *Carnivàle* had done by utilizing the stylistic devices of pastiche and self-reflexivity. Whereas *Carnivàle* had largely thumbed its nose at genre altogether, series like *Curb Your Enthusiasm* and *The Larry Sanders Show* creatively recombined the aesthetic conventions of several popular television genres, resulting in a look that while different was not entirely unfamiliar. A pastiche of sitcoms, reality programming, and late night talk shows, HBO's comedy series relied upon viewers' knowledge of television's formulas and formats to create inside jokes, which along with self-referential gestures and knowing winks, resulted in television that knew it was television. Like fine art that reflexively comments on its status as art, the comedy series on HBO simultaneously distinguished themselves from network sitcoms and fostered the appearance of "smart" television.

HBO's "It's Not TV" advertising mantra was almost certainly designed to evoke (perhaps even consciously) the very response to its programming Williamson describes. Undoubtedly, HBO actively tries to position itself as an elite brand that offers "quality" entertainment. But, as Marc Leverette so deftly illustrates in his chapter, what most distinguishes HBO from network programming is its explicit language, violence, and sex—what he refers to as its "cocksucker, motherfucker, tits" brand of programming. Engaging HBO's comedy specials, boxing, and late night sex-related docudramas, Leverette demonstrates that HBO serves up a platter of salacious programming that does not, indeed legally cannot be, found on network TV's more "family-friendly" menu of choices. Unregulated by the FCC, HBO programs are by prevailing standards of taste (i.e. FCC regulations) decidedly transgressive. For Leverette, the transgressive character of HBO programs appeals to the collective uncon-scious of its viewers allowing them, in effect, to take pleasure in an array of culturally repressed desires, all in the name of "quality television." Whereas Leverette examines the numerous social transgressions that occur *within* HBO texts, the final chapter in this section raises questions about HBO texts *as* transgressions.

Blake Ethridge begins his chapter by examining what he terms the "tragic moralism" of *The Wire*. Although the show may, on first glance, appear to be a cop drama typical of those seen on commercial network television, Ethridge argues that, based on the show's structural form, it is better classified as a modern-day Greek tragedy. As his chapter unfolds, however, it becomes clear that *The Wire* is not simply a modern-day Greek tragedy, but also a *real life* Greek tragedy. Reading Ethridge's chapter, it is clear that the show's central character is the city of Baltimore (and to a lesser extent Baltimoreans), for the social and political realities of the actual city are employed to undertake a critique of the American dream. Interestingly, the show's title operates on multiple levels, referring not just to the ongoing wiretap case that animates the serial plot, but also to the thin line separating fact from fiction and politics from entertainment. *The Wire*, then, is more than just a representation of politics in the U.S., though it certainly is that as well; it *is* politics (and very public politics at that) in the U.S. In important ways, *The Wire* erases the line between text and context, for its images do not have an external referent. Perhaps more clearly than any show on network television, *The Wire* articulates what it means to live in a postmodern society of simulations in which image and reality have imploded. As with other HBO programs such as *K-Street*, for instance, *The Wire* makes entertainment political and politics entertaining.

Collectively, the four chapters in this section resist a simple (and singular) response to the question, "What, if anything, is distinctive about and character-istic of the texts on HBO?" What the chapters do agree upon is that HBO compares itself to and measures itself against the content and programming of network television. Interestingly, this discourse functions both rhetorically and ideologically to normalize the codes and conventions of network television as natural, rather than arbitrary. Consequently, the "originality" of HBO's own programming is constrained by what HBO blindly accepts as "television." As long as HBO continues to react to and against network TV (i.e. to define itself in relation to network TV), the range of aesthetics and ideas available and acceptable to it will be significantly limited. In the meantime, viewers can reliably count on HBO to continue to deliver its "unique" *version* of hyper-conscious, genre-blurring, spectacle-laden, and simulated "TV."

## Works cited

Gitlin, T. (1983) *Inside Prime Time*. New York: Pantheon.
Threadgold, T. (2005). "Text", pp 345–347 in T. Bennett, L. Grossberg, & M. Morris (eds) *New Keywords: A Revised Vocabulary of Culture and Society*. Malden: Blackwell.

# Chapter 5

# *Carnivàle*

## TV drama without TV genre

## David Marc

Viewers who believe *Carnivàle* is the best of the HBO original hour-long drama series will have to argue that question of taste with partisans of *Oz*, *The Sopranos*, *Deadwood*, *The Wire*, and other formidable candidates from what is already being bracketed as the "the golden age of HBO drama." But there is a good case to be made that Daniel Knauf's bizarre and short-lived tale of the eternal Manichean struggle playing itself out in the trans-Mississippi West during the 1930s can lay good claim to being the most innovative of the lot. *Carnivàle* differs from the other HBO dramas in that it lacks an obvious place among existing popular story-telling genres. This is rare wherever it occurs in the narrative arts. When it happens in big-money American popular culture, one can only wonder how it got past the gatekeepers. It is possible that HBO launched *Carnivàle* as a probe to see just how far a premium cable series could push the aesthetic envelope. If so, its early death, considered in the context of the cancellations of *Deadwood* and *The Wire* that followed, may be read as the cooldown following a hot creative period at the company. The off-premium syndication bonanzas delivered by *The Sopranos* and *Sex and the City* may have moved Time Warner execs to repeat one of broadcast television's oldest mantras: "Can you give me more like that?" The 2006 premiere and renewal of *Big Love*, a cookie-cutter job on *The Sopranos'* recipe, substituting polygamy for the mob as the fly in the suburban ointment, might be evidence that, advertising slogans notwithstanding, HBO *is*, after all, TV.

Although "genre" is a French word that few Americans can pronounce and fewer yet can define, the concept it embodies is generally considered crucial to a work's success in the American entertainment industry. John Cawelti, perhaps the leading theoretician of popular culture criticism during the second half of the twentieth century, believed genre development was a driving force throughout the commercial mass-culture process.[1] At the gatekeeping stage, associations with popular genres give proposed properties quantified track records that provide necessary reference points for rationally predicting audience size to investors and sponsors. In the production phase, a genre's history offers models for factoring audience expectations into crucial casting and plotting decisions. At the distribution or retail level, genre identity provides guidelines for effectively promoting a work to likely consumers and for reaching out to less likely audiences, which is what makes a hit. Leonard Goldenson, who headed the American Broadcasting Company for more than 30 years, put it this way: "Without a well-known format to count on for a new series, a television producer is flying blind—with other people's money" (Kuney, 1998).

Cawelti described genres as the sum results of continuing interactions between two essential elements: conventions ("set-ups" familiar to audiences) and inventions (unexpected twists designed to invigorate familiarity). As successions of works sharing similar conventions try out new inventions, the variations that are successful with viewers are inevitably reused, either in spin-offs by their originators or in imitations by competing production houses until they, in turn, become conventions of the genre, begging reinvigoration with new inventions. As long as the process repeats itself, the genre survives. Tom Schatz (1981), in a study of film genres, likens the role of genre in popular culture to a contract between artist and consumer brokered by a distributor, who then promotes generic features of the work to the public. An action picture "promises" chase scenes; a sitcom—one-liners; a soap opera—rocky romances, and so on. Consumers expect these things and feel cheated if a work fails to deliver.

In the traditional fine arts, or "high culture," genres develop in a similar way, but critics, who exert far greater influence here than in popular culture, tend to value inventions more than conventions. James Joyce's *Ulysses*, for example, is often appreciated as a great novel precisely because it is like no other novel; it transcends the conventions of genre. In pop culture, *I Love Lucy* is appreciated as a great sitcom because it established conventional features for dramatic comedy on television that became operative for hundreds of works that followed.

Placing *Carnivàle* in a familiar popular genre is a difficult, perhaps impossible task. Exotic music and close-up images of tarot cards in the opening of the credits signature gestures the viewer toward the occult, but quickly reverses direction as a painted image turns to documentary footage invoking the 1930s: the hungry lining up at a soup kitchen, a zeppelin floating above the water, Mussolini on the balcony. So, what have we got here? *The Outer Limits* or *The American Experience*? Sci-Fi Channel or PBS? The fact that such a question needs asking portends a basic failure in the entertainment-industrial process. *Carnivàle's* problems are further compounded by two more strikes against it: (1) the cast lacks a star of the magnitude that would allow for effective promotion in lieu of genre identity; and (2) even if a viewer can be persuaded to watch an episode or two, the mystery of what kind of show is on television is not likely to be solved because the story is told in visual language bearing little resemblance to the naturalistic techniques that dominate the narrative genres of American television and film.

The same cannot be said of other HBO original series. Tom Fontana's *Oz* (1997–2003) adapts an old film chestnut for TV, the prison story, and revital-izes it with a psycho-realist dynamism not felt in the genre since *I Am a Fugitive from a Chain Gang* (1932). Taking advantage of HBO's relaxed language restric-tions, *Oz* penetrates the setting's inherent homoeroticism, a topic previously reserved for porno novels. David Chase's *The Sopranos* (1999–2007), the most popular of the HBO drama weeklies, televisualizes the social mythology developed by Mario Puzo and Francis Ford Coppola for the post-60s gangster film. In true TV style, the Corleones' epic rise in novel and film from the urban-peasant ghetto of Lower Manhattan to a baronial estate on Lake Tahoe becomes a trip measurable in turnpike exits, grounding *la famiglia* in a McMansion on a New Jersey cul-de-sac. In *Deadwood* (2004–2006), David Milch takes on the Western, the most popular American story-telling genre for more than a century in print, film, radio, and television. Unfortunately, he has time to do little more than remind HBO subscribers that every other word from a pioneer's mouth was "fuck" because sidewinders from back East unceremoniously cancelled his ass.

A year earlier, *Carnivàle* (2003–2005) had met with a quicker end than purely good viewing would have dictated. In a press release announcing the decision to end production, HBO Entertainment president Carolyn Strauss is quoted as saying, "We feel the two seasons we had on the air told the story very well and we are proud of what everyone associated with the show has accom-plished" (Carnivàle, 2005).[2] Strauss's phrase, "told the story very well," is curious language to describe a drama whose narrative technique—especially its unencumbered flow across conventional boundaries dividing fiction and his-tory—is more suggestive of a Borges short story or a Buñuel feature film than just about anything presented on television, with the possible exceptions of *Twin Peaks* and *The Fairly Odd Parents*.

By the standards usually applied to almost any kind of drama, not much of any kind had happened in *Carnivàle*'s 22 one-hour episodes: no protagonist met death due to a tragic flaw; no young couple was happily integrated into society through mutual discovery of their capacity to love; not even a moment of modernist relief through illumination of a shared human identity while staring at the void. The protocols of cancellation being what they are, it would have been less than reasonable to expect Strauss to say, "We are canceling *Carnivàle* because most people who saw it couldn't figure out what in the world was going on—so they changed the channel." But that probably would have been closer to the truth.

If a defining feature of a successful television drama is that it requires of its audience as little exposure as possible to anything but the contemporary popular culture of which it is a part, *Carnivàle* fails the test, two thumbs down. To follow even the basic mechanics of what Strauss calls "the story," a viewer would have to bring to the screen a working knowledge of history that includes World War I, the Great Depression, the rise of radio broadcasting, and the failure of the Crusades to reclaim Jerusalem for Christendom. And that's not all—a passing familiarity with Western literature and art from, oh, the Bible to Todd Browning's 1932 film, *Freaks*, wouldn't hurt, either.

After the cancellation of *Carnivàle*, Daniel Knauf, the series' hyphenated *auteur*, returned to inputting episodes for prime-time network television, contributing to such series as *Supernatural* and *Standoff*. One can only hope Knauf will have the chance—and the will—to make the mistakes of *Carnivàle* again. Meanwhile, the complete set of episodes is available on DVD for viewers who find themselves above or beneath the vast sagging middle of generic programming and do not count "following the plot" among the great rewards of watching TV.

*Carnivàle* boldly pushes forward into the aesthetic territory of the twenty-first century to convey its early twentieth-century period piece. To experience it, the viewer must stop stumbling among the contradictory stories of universe, species, tribe, family, and ego that endlessly intrude upon each other through mass media, education, the dinner table, and the dark night of the soul, and leave the self as nothing more than a sum of confusions. In a monologue that opens the series, Samson (Paul J. Anderson), the line boss of the carnival, preps the audience for the show it is about to witness: "Before the beginning, after the great war between Heaven and Hell, God created the Earth and gave dominion over it to the crafty ape he called man. And to each generation was born a creature of light and a creature of darkness . . . [All that changed] the day that a false sun exploded over the Trinity, and man forever traded away wonder for reason." If we accept the fruits of technology as our "miracles," we are worshipping the power of humans at the expense of knowing the divine. We are begged to answer a question that forms outside the American loop: Are indoor plumbing, automobiles, and MP3 players just smokescreens behind which we allow ourselves to become dependent upon war? Are they distractions blinding us to the struggle between angel and beast that takes place in each of us at every moment of life?

Whatever the operative narrative of the universe, things are not going well for Ben Hawkins (Nick Stahl) when first we meet him. Out of the window of his New Canaan, Oklahoma, house, the topsoil of the family farm is blowing away in a dust storm. Geologists will find samples of it in Pennsylvania. Across the room, his mother lay dying. He goes to her, but she uses every ounce of strength to shoo him away. A half a dozen episodes later, it will start to become evident that Hawkins has the power to heal, and she just wants to give up the ghost. When she does just that, the dutiful son slings her body over his shoulder, grabs a shovel, and commences burial a few feet out the front door. He is interrupted by noise of a giant earth-moving machine with an appropriately unfeeling driver at the wheel, who has come to flatten the pathetic Hawkins family shack by order of its new owner, the First Persons Bank of New Canaan. An Okie with neither land nor a social utopian vision to guide him to California, Hawkins is recruited by a traveling carnival that happens to be passing through the dust storm. A carnival from hell? Despite appearances, no. They help Hawkins give his mother a proper burial, and one need not be an English major to know what a good thing that is. If fans of naturalistic storytelling think Hawkins a bit on the scrawny side to be chosen for work among the brawny roustabouts of the tent show, they are, as usual, correct. But Management, as Samson calls the guiding force of the traveling entertainment, sees a rarer talent in Hawkins—and Management, though disembodied, prevails. Hawkins steps up from his destitution in the carnival, gradually revealing himself as a Christ-like figure capable of healing the sick.

If all this is not bizarre enough, *Carnivàle*'s parallel plot, which gets almost as much screen time in the 22-hour drama, contains more than twice the narrative chaos. In it, we watch Brother Justin (Clancy Brown), a socially conscious Methodist minister at the podium of a respectable middle-class congregation, gradually reveal himself as an agent of Satan, or possibly the Evil One, himself, judging by what happens to his eyes when impure thoughts are incumbent upon him. Brown, whose best known role is the voice of Mr Krabs on *SpongeBob Squarepants*, gives an exceptional performance as the demonic mole who has invaded the body of the church to check out the use of radio broadcasting as a weapon against God in the war for human souls.

"The clock is ticking, brothers and sisters, counting down to Armageddon," Justin tells his loyal listeners. "The worm reveals himself in many guises across this once great land, from the intellectual elite cruelly indoctrinating our children with the savage blasphemy of Darwin, to the craven Hollywood pagans corrupting them in the darkness of the local bijou; from the false prophets cowering behind our nation's pulpits to the vile parasites in our banks and boardrooms and the godless politicians growing fat on the miseries of their constituencies."

In the early episodes, Brother Justin seems like a righteous Christian pastor attempting to move his middle-class parishioners from their middle-class complacency to compassion for the desperate and growing poverty engulfing them in mid-Depression America. Exasperated by their apathy, he leaves the parish to feed the poor and establish an orphanage downtown—a Christian act in defiance of the church. Things go haywire after this, and Justin is revealed as evil. A lifetime of American TV viewing sets up a reading of Justin as a "good" character who turns "evil." This can be read literally, for the benefit of Christians and believers in other monotheistic religions, or it can read as a familiar metaphor that is easily translated by secular humanist, atheist, and agnostic viewers: Justin is a healthy (sane) character who becomes sick (psychopathic). It requires an act of viewing beyond genre to ponder what's happened in *Carnivàle*'s own terms: the devil has won a victory on the battleground of Justin's soul—the same battleground that exists in each of us (us? viewers!).

*Carnivàle* dances through consciousness to its own tune. Familiar, naturalistic cutting, the kind used in most prime-time dramatic genres, bumps into epic subject matter, sometimes making for hilarious juxtapositions, as when Hawkins seeks interpretation of a medieval Christian symbol that may lead him to knowledge of his father from a family of backwoods rednecks from beyond the pale of *Deliverance*. In another episode, we are presented with the image of Hawkins healing the lame: an ex-baseball player, Clayton (Tim McKay). The use of iconological TV actors, including Adrienne Barbeau (*Maude*'s daughter) as the carnival's Roma-American fortune-teller and Ralph Waites (John-Boy's father on *The Waltons*) as a righteous clergyman and stroke victim, who Brother Justin takes in to live with him, for no other reason than to have a Christian around as silent witness to his evil.

Set in the blossoming mushroom of the age of mass culture, *Carnivàle* is a farce of the sacred and profane set in a society where that distinction has been trivialized into a matter of personal taste. The devil, disguised as the church, shows a good understanding of the emerging show business environment, jumping in early to take advantage of new media—in this case, radio. Meanwhile, the broken-down carnival of dreams, hungry, horny, preposterously devoid of quality control, rolls across the prairie to the promised land in sputtering old cars and wooden wagons, stopping in any town that will have it, at the mercy of corrupt sheriffs, hooligans, and the past chasing each member of its erratic labor force.

## Notes

1   Cawelti wrote about genre (or "formula," which he considered its closest English cognate) in *Adventure, Mystery and Romance* (1976), *The Six-Gun Mystique* (1970), and, to varying degrees, in most of his work. For Cawelti's theory of conventions and inventions in its most abstract form, see his application of it to bestsellers in the article "The Concept of Formula in the Study of Popular Literature" (1969).
2   For more on the decision, see Carugati (2006).

# Works cited

"*Carnivàle* Comes to a Close" (2005, May 11) Press release. www.hbo.com.

Carugati, A. (2006, October 10) "Interview with Carolyn Strauss". www
.worldscreen.com/print.php?filename=strauss1006.htm.

Cawelti, J. (1969) "The Concept of Forumla in the Study of Popular Literature", *Journal of Popular Culture* 3: 381–390.

Cawelti, J. (1970) *The Six-Gun Mystique*. Bowling Green: Bowling Green State University Press.

Cawelti, J. (1976) *Adventure, Mystery and Romance*. Chicago: University of Chicago Press.

Kuney, J. (1998, November 3) "Interview with Leonard Goldenson", unpublished. Center for the Study of Popular Television. Syracuse University Library.

Schatz, T. (1981) *Hollywood Genres: Formulas, Filmmaking, and the Studio System*. Philadelphia: Temple University Press.

# Chapter 6

# Challenging sitcom conventions

## From *The Larry Sanders Show* to *The Comeback*

### Lisa Williamson

As a pay-cable network, HBO successfully differentiated itself in the marketplace from its inception by actively avoiding the production of standard generic programming that appears on commercial network television. Instead of the half-hour sitcom, the hour-long drama, and the mini-series, HBO broadcast live sports events from around the country and overseas along with commercial-free movies. With the addition of stand-up comedy specials featuring comedians such as George Carlin and Steve Martin to its schedule, HBO focused on bringing events that viewers had previously enjoyed outside of the home and were accustomed to paying for, into the comfort of one's living room. However, with the advent of the video rental market and pay-per-view channels offering similar services, the programming tactics of the subscription-based service began to come under pressure. For HBO to attract new customers, retain loyal audiences, and increase market share in an increasingly competitive post-network era, it had to diversify its output. Thus, it began to develop original series programming.

In order to maintain its differentiated status in the marketplace, the pay-cable network attempted to produce series programming that was distinctive from its commercial network counterparts and that viewers were willing to pay for. In effect, it advertised itself as the producer of something "other" than conventional television, an ethos that was crystallised with the marketing slogan "It's Not TV. It's HBO." Yet, with regards to the sitcom, it appears that HBO is in fact primarily concerned with the nature of television. Rather than reproducing the sitcom's popular and somewhat rigid style, HBO shows challenge the conventions of the genre by appropriating the looks and styles of other television forms, such as the late-night talk show and reality TV. A large part of its comedic output is therefore based on pastiche and critique of the medium and its various forms.

In this essay I consider three such sitcoms, *The Larry Sanders Show* (1992–1998), *Curb Your Enthusiasm* (2000–), and *The Comeback* (2005). Through an analysis of the formal qualities of each program, I contend that these shows do not *look* like sitcoms. Instead, they knowingly showcase the documentary look through the continued use of what Caldwell refers to as "the docu-real" and Mills terms, "comedy verité" (Caldwell, 2002; Mills, 2004). This particular visual aesthetic not only works to complicate the notion of genre but also acts as a badge of prestige that helps differentiate each show from its network competitors. I also demonstrate the way in which these sitcoms purposely blur the boundaries between the real and the fictional in an attempt to highlight the artifice of television conventions and raise questions about the nature of performance. In each instance, HBO targets a media savvy viewer from which a certain level of knowingness is expected. Not only do the programs consciously draw attention to generic conventions and reference specific texts, but they also draw on the real-life backgrounds and public personas of their creators and stars.

Finally, I examine how each sitcom highlights the restrictions placed on broadcast networks by exhibiting strong language and controversial storylines that tackle adult themes. By emphasising the difference in standards and practices between commercial television and pay-cable, HBO attempts to place itself outside the political and economic realities of broadcast television and assure viewers that they are receiving something "other" than the standard fare offered to the mass audience. As such, the slogan "It's Not Network TV. It's HBO." would perhaps be more appropriate.

## Transforming the traditional sitcom

High-key lighting, multiple cameras, and a fixed studio setting have historically provided the sitcom with its definitive look. Such production techniques are generally preferred because they are economically effective, providing program-makers with a fixed, reusable set that can be utilised weekly for the duration of a 24-week season. This layout is also indicative of a theatrical mode of staging that was initially influenced by vaudeville. As noted by Medhurst and Tuck (1982: 45), the presence of a studio audience and the use of an audible laugh track can be viewed as an explicit attempt to conceive the sitcom as an "electronic substitute for collective experience." This approach has limitations, however, regarding form and visual style. The television viewer is only ever given access to a limited number of camera angles as the illusion of the fourth wall is rigorously upheld in order to accommodate the camera crew and the studio audience. The limited depth of the sets restricts the movement of both cameras and actors, requiring them to manoeuvre from side to side rather than *through* spaces (Butler, 2002: 95–96). And although the use of a fixed rig directly above the set produces lighting that is consistent from every angle, it often results in a flat effect that lacks dimension (Lury, 2005: 39). As a result, the sitcom has traditionally been understood as a low cultural text. Rigid in form and muted in style, it is considered a genre that signals its comic intent clearly and offers itself to the mass audience as mere light entertainment.

Such conventions are widely challenged by the HBO sitcoms *The Larry Sanders Show*, *Curb Your Enthusiasm* and *The Comeback*. Focusing on the daily lives of a late-night talk show host, a comedy writer, and a sitcom actress, respectively, these shows abandon the traditional characteristics of the sitcom and appropriate the look of the docusoap instead. Since the 1990s, reality programming has become a prominent category within broadcast television, with the docusoap emerging as a particular strand. As its name suggests, it is a hybrid genre that films "real-life people" over a period of time and combines the documentary style of observation with the dramatic structure of the soap opera (Bonner, 2003: 25). Although ostensibly factual in content, it prioritizes "entertainment over social commentary" and is therefore "more interested in characters' personalities than in their social roles or professions" (Bruzzi, 2001: 132).

Dispensing with the fixed studio setting, high-key lighting, and multi-camera setup associated with the sitcom, *The Larry Sanders Show*, *Curb Your Enthusiasm*, and *The Comeback* showcase this observational style through the use of handheld cameras, long continuous takes, and the occasional in-shot rack focusing. Whilst retaining the sitcom's comedic structure, each show affectionately imitates the visual conventions of the docusoap and thus operates as a pastiche of the latter form. It must be noted that my understanding of pastiche differs from Jameson's much-cited dismissal of it as "blank parody" (1991: 17). Instead, my analysis draws on Hoesterey's more positive assertion that although pastiche may involve the imitation and synthesis of "different styles and motifs", this does not necessarily mean that it is uncritical (2001: 46). HBO's conception of "real-life people" also differs somewhat from that of Bonner. For Bonner (2003: 53), the people who appear in docusoaps are special only in as much that they are being filmed for television. While this applies to the initial wave of docusoaps that appeared on our television screens, it does not account for subsequent "celebrity" versions, in which it is a well-known figure that forms the basis of the camera's attention. In this case the aim is not to simply combine the everyday with a driving narrative but to provide an insight into another world, a world that, regarding the HBO sitcom, revolves around the television industry.

By showcasing the visual style of the docusoap, this approach is representative of what is variously described as "docu-real fiction" or "comedy verité." According to Caldwell (2002: 259), the term "docu-real" refers to those episodes in entertainment programs that "self-consciously showcase documentary units as part of their narrative and plot/or documentary imaging as part of their mise-en-scène." Caldwell does not restrict his analysis to the sitcom but rather considers the docu-real as an emerging technique within episodic television in general. Mills (2004: 75), on the other hand, reserves the term "comedy verité" purely for instances in which "the visual characteristics of verité have been adopted for comedic purposes." These techniques are generally used as "stunts" through which certain episodes in a series are promoted as "events" or "must-see" television. Often occurring during sweeps weeks, such stunts are confined to one-off occasions with the aim to elicit widespread coverage before the show returns to its standard format. As a subscription service, however, sweeps week is not important to HBO. Instead, the pay-cable network must produce series programming in which every episode offers something distinctive from its broadcast network competitors. This means that *The Larry Sanders Show*, *Curb Your Enthusiasm*, and *The Comeback* utilize the "docu-real" as a type of "continuous programming stunt." By creating a distinct visual aesthetic that will attract sustained media attention, each show attempts to break through the clutter produced by the numerous broadcast and cable programs available in the post-network era and convince viewers that such sitcoms are worth paying for. In doing so, these shows alter the very nature of the sitcom form.

Mills (2004: 67) describes the sitcom as a "transparent" genre that works to highlight its artificial status rather than hide its codes of construction. The theatrical staging, foregrounding of performance, and audible laugh track encourage the audience to suspend their disbelief and judge it not on its verisimilitude but on its ability to entertain and ultimately produce laughter. By dispensing with such conventions, in favor of appropriating the characteristics of other television forms, the aforementioned sitcoms not only challenge the way in which humor is traditionally signaled, but also the way in which audiences make sense of both the sitcom form and the television experience in general. HBO shows have removed the traditional metacues that act as a signpost for comic intent and replaced them with signifiers of "the real," namely handheld cameras, location shooting, and understated performances. Although the intention is still to create humor, such techniques undermine the distinction between sitcom and documentary and blur the boundaries between the comic and the serious. The notion of the sitcom as a collective experience is also called into question, due to the removal of the studio audience and the audible laugh track. Unlike network sitcoms, which have historically been directed at the entire family, HBO's output signifies a distinct shift toward niche demographics that are formulated according to status and taste cultures.

Within his theory of "televisuality," Caldwell (1995) explains that by the 1980s, television viewers were beginning to possess certain cultural abilities that led to new stylistic appetites being cultivated: "Many viewers expected and watched programs that made additional aesthetic and conceptual demands not evident in earlier programming" (9). These segments of the audience are extremely valuable to HBO because as a pay-cable operator it has to convince audiences that its output is sufficiently different enough to require a monthly payment. In terms of the sitcom, this has led to a distinct shift away from comedy grounded in the vaudeville experience toward comedy that engages with other television forms. Dispensing with the notion of a collective experience, HBO sitcoms ask the audience to engage with the material on an individual basis and make sense of the comic intent by drawing on their knowledge and experience of television and its many forms and conventions. As such, *The Larry Sanders Show*, *Curb Your Enthusiasm*, and *The Comeback* are indicative of what Mills (2004: 78) describes as "comedy for audiences raised on television formats."

## The emergence of a reality aesthetic

*The Larry Sanders Show* is essentially a workplace sitcom that revolves around the production of a late-night talk show. However, it eschews many of the conventions of the genre and adopts characteristics from both the talk show and the documentary instead. The result is in parts a pastiche of the late-night form and a satire on the inner workings of the television industry. Each episode offers the viewer a look at the goings-on in front of camera as well as the rivalries, conflicts, and insecurities that take place behind the scenes. The divide between the talk show scenes and the backstage footage is marked visually through the use of videotape and 16mm film. The majority of each episode centers on the off-air antics of Sanders, his production team, and the weekly celebrity guests who appear on his fictional show. As a sitcom, it breaks with convention to film such segments using a single camera, but it is also a sitcom that operates as a pastiche of the talk show and, as such, must imitate the characteristics of that genre. The talk show is a relatively low-budget television form that shares many of its defining signifiers with the traditional sitcom. Thus, the on-air elements of the show are videotaped in front of an assembled studio audience using the aforementioned multiple cameras and high-key lighting. This results in a complex layering of styles that challenges the conceived notion of the sitcom as a visually muted and limited form.

In contrast to the talk show segments, the single camera technique that is utilised in the backstage footage dispenses with the studio audience and creates a fully realised set that both the camera and actors can move through without restriction. It follows the characters as they prepare for each episode in the production office and then moves with them as they walk through the corridors of the building and onto the studio set where the fictional talk show is filmed. It is here that the multi-camera setup and high-key lighting rig is on display, along with the autocue, television monitors, floor manager, and assembled studio audience. The viewer at home is then repeatedly exposed to two contrasting images as the action cuts between the talk show (shot on videotape using fixed cameras and flat lighting) and behind-the-scenes footage (captured on film using a range of camera angles and more sophisticated lighting techniques). In addition, the viewer is occasionally exposed to both images within the frame, particularly in instances when the single camera observes Artie the producer as he oversees the taping of the show on a television monitor.

The overall aim of this approach is to assign different levels of authenticity to contrasting visual styles. The use of videotape authentically recreates the look of the late-night form and Larry's self-effacing manner replicates that of the amiable talk-show host. Featuring saturated color, bright lighting, and a standard backdrop, the viewer initially experiences this section of the program as if it were an actual talk show. However, the action quickly cuts to a single camera shot of the wider studio, revealing the assembled audience and Larry's image replicated on numerous television monitors. This constant return to 16mm footage of studio areas that are usually kept from view is an attempt to remind viewers that what they are watching is in fact a pastiche. It also succeeds in positioning the audience in documentary terms. Even though the characters in the show never actually acknowledge the single camera or make reference to a documentary crew, the level of behind-the-scenes access provided and the unobtrusive but pervasive nature of the camerawork evoke the verité gaze of observational documentary. The fact that these segments also reveal another side to Sanders' personality—that of a somewhat egotistical neurotic—only adds to the implication that the off-air footage is a true depiction of the personalities and processes behind the late-night talk show. The show is therefore indicative of Caldwell's (2002: 259) latter description of the docu-real mode, that is to say, entertainment programs which self-consciously showcase "documentary looks and imaging as part of their mise-en-scène." By adopting the docu-real look as a "fictional house style" (268), *The Larry Sanders Show* not only defines its backstage footage in verité terms, but also attempts to draw attention to the constructed artifice of the talk show in comparison.

This has implications for the humor produced in the program. By exposing the audience to the making of the talk show, the comedy performed within such segments has less impact. The viewer knows, for example, that it is the show's writer Phil who provides Larry with his jokes because it is revealed in the backstage footage. In "Larry's Big Idea," Phil informs Artie that he has not had enough time to write any new, topical gags for that evening's show but is confident that those he has included are "good, solid jokes." Artie replies, "you know, there's a reason they sell day old bread at half price. I want twenty new jokes on Larry's desk in one hour." Revealing such production practices may result in the jokes having less of a punch when they are delivered on-stage but it aims to create humor in another way. Comedy in *The Larry Sanders Show* is based on the incongruity between what we see on-air within the fictional talk show and the behavior we witness backstage. The humor does not come from the traditional jokes, puns, or wordplay that are often employed in the talk show genre or from the contrived situations that are customary in sitcom.

A similar docu-real approach is adopted in *Curb Your Enthusiasm*, but in this case the show combines the docu-real form with HBO's own tradition of comedy specials rather than that of the late-night talk show. Initially produced and broadcast as a one-hour comedy entitled *Larry David: Curb Your Enthusiasm* (1999), the aim of the show was to document the eponymous David, co-creator of NBC's hugely successful sitcom *Seinfeld*, as he prepares to return to the stand-up circuit after an absence of more than 10 years. Rather than film a straightforward documentary, however, a fabricated element was introduced to the format. While a large part of the show did indeed center on David's stand-up routines in the comedy clubs of Los Angeles and New York, the off-stage footage was fictional with actors playing the role of his wife and manager. Further complications were added in the form of real-life celebrities appearing as themselves and the fact that all of the dialogue was improvised, with only selected cast members receiving a general outline for the fictional segments.

Based on the conceit that it is a literal documentary culminating in a live stand-up performance, *Larry David: Curb Your Enthusiasm* applies the rules of the fly-on-the-wall format to its modes of production. Shot on location and in sequence using handheld digital cameras, the cast members regularly acknowledge the camera and the occasional boom mic appears in shot to highlight the presence of a diegetic documentary crew. The verité action is also interspersed with a number of talking head interviews of various performers and production personnel discussing their actual experiences of working with David. Although it assumes the techniques of the comedy special, the show also challenges the conventions of the format by ultimately denying the audience a final stand-up performance when the comedian reneges on the deal at the eleventh hour. While this seemingly brings the on-screen relationship between David and HBO to an abrupt end, *Larry David: Curb Your Enthusiasm* effectively acted as a pilot for a subsequent sitcom series entitled simply *Curb Your Enthusiasm*. With David once again retired from the stand-up circuit, however, there is an inevitable narrative shift within the series that impacts on the style of the show. As the narrative no longer self-consciously revolves around the making of an HBO special, there is no need for the diegetic presence of the camera crew or for the inclusion of talking head interviews. Nevertheless, the verité style remains, albeit in a more relaxed form. Handheld cameras and real-life locations are still used to follow David as he goes about his everyday business and the action continues to be shot in-sequence to accommodate the improvisational techniques that are applied within the show. The characters move through spaces rather than from side to side in the theatrical manner typical of studio-based sitcoms and the camera often loses its focus slightly as it quickly pans between characters in an attempt to keep up with the dialogue. Ultimately, both the director and the camera are *reacting* to events, rather than anticipating them—the opposite of the rigid mode of filming applied to conventional network sitcoms.

This makes *Curb Your Enthusiasm* somewhat different from its predecessor, *The Larry Sanders Show*. Unlike the latter, which simply adopts the docu-real look as a distinct visual aesthetic, the former is actually filmed according to documentary practice. In an era in which there is "extensive borrowing of the 'documentary look' by other kinds of program," Corner (2000) asserts the importance of considering how a program was actually made. While I am not suggesting that *Curb Your Enthusiasm* functions as a documentary, I am suggesting that the verité mode of filmmaking is crucial in capturing the improvisational performances within the show. Improvisation is a key technique within stand-up comedy, in which comedians have to be able to interact with, and react to, a live audience. Television comedy, on the other hand, offers little opportunity for improvisation, as the demands of television production require a rehearsed performance that can be executed quickly and efficiently. By replacing the rigid production techniques of sitcom with that of documentary, *Curb Your Enthusiasm* is able to provide a more informal space in which the actors can perform and interact with each other in a spontaneous and unrestrained manner.

While *The Larry Sanders Show* appropriates the docu-real as its fictional house style and *Curb Your Enthusiasm* films according to documentary practice, *The Comeback* features an actual documentary unit as part of its essential plot and is thus, according to Caldwell (2002: 263–268), an example of a "classical docu-real fiction." Following the fortunes of Valerie Cherish, a faded former sitcom actress who agrees to star in a reality TV show in an attempt to revive her ailing career, *The Comeback* serves as both the title of the HBO sitcom and that of the fictional docusoap that forms its basis. In terms of its visual aesthetic and modes of filming, *The Comeback* adopts the characteristics and techniques of the docusoap. The majority of the action is recorded by a diegetic camera crew using handheld cameras while additional footage comes courtesy of a personal video camera that Valerie herself operates when recording her own video diary. There are also a number of fixed cameras strategically placed throughout Valerie's home to capture seemingly private moments as they unfold. Although the show adheres to the look and style of reality TV, each episode is prefaced with an opening title card that reads " '*The Comeback*'—Raw Footage—." This means that rather than being presented with the finished docusoap, what viewers are actually offered is access to the unedited material from the eponymous reality show.

Attempting to reveal the *reality* behind reality TV, *The Comeback* exposes the actual processes involved in its creation by highlighting the mistakes that occur during filming, the role of the production crew, and Valerie's struggle to assert her power over the situation. There are scenes in which the two handheld cameras used to film the fictional show appear in range of one another or are inadvertently reflected in a background mirror that is subsequently removed from the frame. With the camera still running, the action is sometimes put on hold in order for a microphone to be replaced or repositioned by a soundman or for Jane, the producer of the fictional show, to hand out release forms to people caught up in location shooting. Valerie not only addresses the camera throughout each episode but she is also seen debating the merits of different camera angles with the crew or asking Jane to take a time-out from filming, a request that is routinely ignored.

While these elements alone make for a complex image, a further complication exists in that Valerie's television "comeback" consists of her starring in an upcoming network sitcom entitled *Room and Bored*. This means that the reality cameras are often required to film her in the studio as each episode is rehearsed and then taped in front of an audience using multiple cameras and high-key lighting. In this sense, *The Comeback* is similar to *The Larry Sanders Show* in that both programs reveal the production practices of the sitcom and the talk show, respectively. However, while its predecessor assumed the characteristics of both the talk show and the docu-real in order to highlight the artifice involved in creating the former, *The Comeback* retains its classical docu-real approach throughout and resists offering the viewers a look at the action from a multi-camera perspective. By presenting raw footage of the eponymous reality show, the suggestion is that there will be an eventual disparity between the actual events as they play out in front of camera and the edited version prepared for broadcast. As the audience is expected to be knowledgeable regarding the construction and manipulation involved in the creation of reality TV, it is only Valerie who appears genuinely surprised at how she has been depicted when the final edit of the fictional show is revealed in the season finale.

## Inside humor and the nature of performance

Another of the essential aspects of the HBO sitcoms examined here is the way in which they each blur the boundaries between the real and the fictional. Not only do all three programs adopt a docu-real approach in terms of visual aesthetic, but they also draw on the real-life backgrounds of their creators and stars. Furthermore, they regularly feature well-known celebrities playing versions of their public personas. This means that viewers are expected to possess a certain level of media awareness if they are to recognize not only the visual signifiers of other television forms, but also the various levels of performance at work. This is made possible not just because viewers are familiar with the forms and conventions of television, but because television is no longer considered to be an anonymous medium (Caldwell, 1995: 10). Caldwell outlines how authorial intent is now used regularly within the industry to market programming as a prestige product to a knowing and discerning audience. Rather than showcase auteurs from the world of film, however, in an attempt to offer something "other" than television, HBO sitcoms are particularly concerned with those who have been successful or gained recognition within the network system. By offering a different platform from which to showcase their skills, HBO enables comedians to appropriate elements of their previous work in a self-conscious manner and play with notions of authenticity and performance. The result is a type of "insider" humor that operates as both a pastiche and critique of the network system and which is played out in a variety of ways.

For example, Garry Shandling, the creator and star of *The Larry Sanders Show*, is a comedian who initially came to the attention of television viewers via his frequent stand-up appearances on late-night talk shows and for his occasional role as a substitute host for Johnny Carson on *The Tonight Show*. Although playing a fictional character in *The Larry Sanders Show*, Shandling has real-life knowledge of such an environment and viewers are expected to be familiar with his performance as a talk-show host. As the overall aim of the program is to strip away the artifice of the talk-show form in an attempt to reveal the "true" personalities and production processes that lie beneath, this notion is lent credibility due to Shandling's insider knowledge of the form. There is a similar concept at work in *The Comeback*, which was created by former *Friends* star Lisa Kudrow, along with Michael Patrick King, the executive producer of *Sex and the City*. Featuring Kudrow as a former sitcom star named Valerie Cherish, *The Comeback* attempts to play with the phenomenal success achieved by the actress through her role as Phoebe in *Friends*. As noted by Lury (1995/1996), the distinction between the character and the actor is notoriously blurred in television and "this is part of the pleasure for the audience, to believe that the actor is (or is at least like) the character he or she plays" (118). By playing a faded sitcom star whose successful days are behind her, Kudrow seems to be self-consciously acknowledging the limited opportunities available in television for an actress who is closely associated with her previous role. Moreover, her sitcom experience in real life not only adds to the authenticity of her character, but also to the depiction of the television industry offered by the fictional reality show.

*Curb Your Enthusiasm* is different from the other two shows in this respect because instead of adopting a fictional persona that alludes to past perform-ances, Larry David plays an extension of himself, namely, the former stand-up comedian and co-creator of *Seinfeld* Larry David. Again, this is in keeping with the nature of stand-up performance that runs throughout the show. Limon (2000: 6) asserts that within the realm of stand-up comedy, the comedian is "not allowed to be either natural or artificial. (Are they themselves or acting? Are they in costume?)" This is similar to what occurs in documentary and reality TV. Due to the presence of the camera crew, the manipulation of the circumstances by technicians and producers, and the editing process, it is never entirely clear whether what the audience is witnessing is an authentic represen-tation or a performance. *Curb Your Enthusiasm* plays with this ambiguity exten-sively by adopting a reality aesthetic, applying improvisational techniques, and by featuring the "real-life" character of Larry David in the main role.

As each program is set within the television industry, the presence of celeb-rity guests is crucial in maintaining the reality conceit. Despite the fact that the shows rarely attempt to mock their celebrity guests, preferring instead to make the recurring characters the butt of any joke, playing with notions of their private persona is still a risky strategy for celebrities. This is because any change in the public's perception of them could be detrimental to their career. In an episode of *The Larry Sanders Show*, entitled "Everybody Loves Larry," *The X-Files* actor David Duchovny features within a narrative that raises questions about his sexuality. When Larry becomes convinced that Duchovny has a crush on him, the actor deftly toys with the talk-show host in an attempt to unnerve him before finally admitting that he is not gay but wishes he were because he finds Larry so attractive. Rather than damaging his image, Duchovny's appearance on the show was rewarded with an Emmy nomination and an American Comedy Award for the Funniest Male Guest Appearance in a Television Series. This level of acclaim can on some level be attributed to the fact that the show operates as an industry satire. By adeptly parodying the media industry, whose own members vote for and choose such award winners, the show targets the type of industry taste-makers who strongly influence trends and approval. This means that two types of "insider" viewers are targeted by such shows. On the one hand there are those who actually operate within the television system while on the other there are those outside the industry who nonetheless recognize and understand the conventions of the various forms and different levels of performance on dis-play. In each instance, a type of inside pleasure is expected to be derived in which viewers laugh knowingly and affectionately at the double standards and contradictions inherent in the portrayal of public and private personas.

## Constructing HBO comedy in opposition to the network sitcom

HBO sitcoms are an attractive prospect for celebrities because they are free of many of the restrictions and limitations placed on network programming. As a pay-cable network, HBO not only offers a space for self-parody, but it also allows serious subjects to be tackled and strong language to be used without fear of recrimination from potential advertisers. Even if the end result is less than flattering, actors are offered a certain amount of credibility by appearing on such shows as it demonstrates that they are willing to stand outside the confines of network programming and challenge conventions. This is in contrast to the polished appearances made on real-life talk shows, which generally function as a "prime site where celebrities are able to promote their most recent cultural products" (Bonner, 2003: 14). Despite these differences, it must be emphasized that HBO sitcoms also offer a promotional platform, albeit in a different form. Again, in an episode of *The Larry Sanders Show* entitled "The Talk Show," which aired in 1992, both Catherine O'Hara and Billy Crystal appear on the fictional show to discuss their real-life film releases *Home Alone 2* and *Mr Saturday Night*, respectively. This is significant for two reasons. First, it lends authenticity to the conceit that the viewers at home are witnessing the actual taping of a talk show in which the celebrities are appearing as themselves. Second, and perhaps more importantly, it acts as a space for product promotion that is not offered elsewhere in the HBO schedule. As a pay-cable network, HBO offers no advertising and neither does it produce the type of light entertainment programs that invite celebrities to discuss their latest cultural product. It does offer an opportunity for product endorsement however, and, due to its exclusive nature, this is considered to have a different type of value to network advertising.

*Curb Your Enthusiasm* explicitly highlights some of the other differences in standards and practices between network and pay-cable programming, particularly in relation to comedy programming. This is particularly apparent throughout Season Two when both Jason Alexander and Julia Louis-Dreyfuss appear on the show. As the actors who played George and Elaine in *Seinfeld*, respectively, they complain about how the industry has typecast them in these roles, a situation that inadvertently provides Larry with the inspiration for a new sitcom. In "The Shrimp Incident" Larry presents his concept to Julia and refers to the proposed sitcom character as Evelyn, a similar sounding substitute for Elaine. The conceit of the show involves a sitcom actress who is so identified with her former character that she cannot find any other parts. Deciding that the show should be called *Aren't you Evelyn?*, Julia suggests that they pitch it to HBO rather than the broadcast networks because, "I want to be able to say fuck

. . . you know, cocksucker." This particular episode features a highly self-conscious narrative that not only requires a prior knowledge of *Seinfeld*, but also expects viewers to be familiar with the distinctions between pay-cable and network programming. By highlighting the different types of language permitted, Julia's character suggests a sense of frustration that occurs within the creative process (and perhaps also on the part of the audience) when writers and actors are institutionally restricted by the type of language they can use. Later in the episode, Larry supports Julia's desire to be part of an HBO production by saying "you throw in a 'fuck,' you double your laughs." While freedom of language is undoubtedly an important issue within the discipline of comedy, this statement is not to be accepted as a universal comic truth as the relationship between HBO sitcoms and language is actually much more complex than this suggests.

The television sitcom is bound by a number of conventions and restrictions, and thus the inclusion of obscenities within what is considered a conservative form injects an element of comic surprise to a scene. In the case of HBO audiences, however, strong language is not always unexpected. Hence, the comic element of this scene has more to do with its self-reflexive nature. By highlighting the language restrictions placed on network television it assures the audience that they are receiving something "other" than the standard fare offered to the masses. This flatters viewers into thinking that only a select few share their tastes and that they are being offered more thought-provoking and sophisticated material as a result. The fact that *Curb Your Enthusiasm* is shot on location and in-sequence using improvisational techniques also suggests that David consciously creates obstacles that prevent the production of the relatively easy-to-produce sitcom form. Yet, the notion of HBO as something "other," and therefore "better," than standard network programming, is actually challenged by Larry within the show's narrative. After his deal with the pay-cable channel breaks down, Larry says to Cheryl, his on-screen wife, "It's not TV? It's TV. Why do they think people watch it? You watch it on TV don't you. You don't go to the movies to see it?" With this statement, Larry highlights the fact that HBO's position as something "other" than television is an effective marketing ploy used to differentiate it from the broadcast networks. At the same time, however, the use of strong language within the episode also works to demonstrate that pay-cable does offer opportunities that are not available to network programming.

*The Comeback* also deals with the television industry and in particular the recent institutional struggle between the sitcom and reality TV. As an enduring popular form that has been a staple of television scheduling since its inception, the sitcom has recently been challenged for dominance by reality-based programming. In "Valerie Demands Dignity," the fall of the sitcom genre in popularity is highlighted when the ratings share for the first episode of *Room and Bored* are revealed to be disappointingly low. While this could be attributed to the fictional show itself being unpopular with audiences, the fact that Valerie is starring in a reality show presents a different perspective. There is the understanding within the narrative of *The Comeback* that Valerie would prefer to be successful as a sitcom star, but she is also aware that success may result from her reality show instead. Thus, she keeps her options open by starring in both.

The fact that this particular episode raises the notion of dignity in its title is also indicative of the way in which *The Comeback* operates as a critique of reality programming. Valerie is consistently subjected to moments of embarrassment and humiliation throughout the series. This is partly due to the way in which she consistently fails to recognize her lack of power over her image and also because the creators and cast of the fictional sitcom regard her as something of a failure due to her decision to appear in a reality show. Much of the attraction of reality TV is based on the spectacle of real people laying themselves bare for the cameras and *The Comeback* questions the ethics surrounding the production of reality programming and the pleasure it offers. Discussing the appearance of ordinary people in such programming, Lury (1995/1996: 126) suggests the audience is often aware that the subject is being "coerced into making a fool of themselves and that their presence or image on screen has been manipulated by technicians, producers and bullying presenters." Valerie makes explicit reference to this in the final episode of the series, "Valerie Does Another Classic Leno," when she condemns reality TV as "humiliation TV that destroys people's characters so that other people have something to TiVo."

This is an interesting process to occur within the sitcom. In general, the production of humor requires viewers to assume a position of superiority in which they laugh at the "misfortunes and incapacities of others" in order to assert their knowledge that it will not happen to them (King, 2002: 10). By incorporating the production techniques and performance style of reality television into the sitcom, however, a sense of "uneasy ambivalence" is created that makes the production of humor problematic. Even though the audience may empathize with the performer's lack of control, there is also the suggestion that they are somewhat complicit in the humiliation process, thus making for an uncomfortable, rather than pleasurable, viewing experience. As a result, I would suggest that not only do the programs discussed here challenge the conventions of the sitcom genre in order to differentiate HBO from its network competitors, but they also present the viewer with more challenging material in the process. By abandoning the safe, familiar, and moral world of network sitcoms, in which comic intent is clearly signaled, HBO has retreated into a risky and uncomfortable place that is not so easy to negotiate and for which audiences are ultimately expected to pay.

## Works cited

Bonner, F. (2003) *Ordinary Television: Analyzing Popular TV*. London: Sage.
Bruzzi, S. (2001) "Docusoaps (Accidental Footage)", pp 132–134 in G. Creeber (ed.) *The Television Genre Book*. London: BFI.
Butler, J.G. (2002) *Television: Critical Methods and Applications*. Mahwah: Lawrence Erlbaum Associates.
Caldwell, J. (1995) *Televisuality: Style, Crisis, and Authority in American Television*. New Brunswick: Rutgers University Press.
Caldwell, J. (2002) "Prime-Time Fiction Theorizes the Docu-Real", pp 259–292 in J. Friedman (ed.) *Reality Squared: Televisual Discourse on the Real*. New Brunswick: Rutgers University Press.
Corner, J. (2000) "Documentary in a Post-Documentary Culture? A Note on Forms and Their Function", Changing Media—Changing Europe, Programme Team One (Citizenship and Consumerism), Working Paper No. 1. European Science Foundation, http://www.lboro.ac.uk/research/changing.media/publications.htm.
Hoesterey, I. (2001) *Pastiche: Cultural Memory in Art, Film, Literature*. Bloomington: Indiana University Press.
Jameson, F. (1991) *Postmodernism, or, The Cultural Logic of Late Capitalism*. London: Verso.
King, G. (2002) *Film Comedy*. London: Wallflower.
Limon, J. (2000) *Stand-Up Comedy in Theory, or, Abjection in America*. Durham: Duke University Press.
Lury, K. (1995/1996) "Television Performance: Being, Acting and 'Corpsing' ", *New Formations* 27: 114–127.
Lury, K. (2005) *Interpreting Television*. London: Hodder.
Medhurst, A. & Tuck, L. (1982) "The Gender Game", pp 43–55 in J. Cook (ed.) *Television Sitcom*. London: BFI.
Mills, B. (2004) "Comedy Verité: Contemporary Sitcom Form", *Screen* 45 (1): 63–78.

# Chapter 7

# "Cocksucker, Motherfucker, Tits"

*Marc Leverette*

- **L** for strong course language
- **V** for extreme graphic violence
- **S** for explicit sexual situations

Tonight's essay by Marc Leverette contains segments that include strong and frank language.

*"And this leads us to the filth . . ."*

—George Carlin

## That's how HBO rolls, bitch

And there it was.

I was sitting on my couch sometime in July or August of 2006, after having dinner with Brian Ott, and we were viewing a mini-marathon of the short-lived series *Lucky Louie* (which had already been cancelled by then for all we knew). And, of course, since we are both scholars working in media studies, the soundtrack of the show was drowned out by our own meta-commentary tracks, on-the-spot criticisms, and, of course, the occasional: "Can you believe some of the shit they're saying in a sitcom?"[1]

And there it was. Sometime around the second episode, "Kim's O" as I recall, star Louis C.K. leaps up from the post-coital rap session he and the Mrs are having (after he helps her "find" her first orgasm) and we get a full view of Louis' "C dash dash K." And we said, "well isn't that ballsy—pardon the pun—a bit of male full frontal in what is clearly the most self-reflexive sitcom on television. Clearly this must be some kind of commentary on the form itself from within HBO's privileged position outside of FCC regulation." I said we were media scholars (your TV watching conversations don't sound like this?).

Anyhow, we kept watching. We watched through the constant profanity, which seemed to get more explicit the more we got used to the characters. We watched through what was the most doomed marriage, perhaps filled with the most symbolic violence and verbal abuse, on TV since Ralphie-boy kept threatening to send Alice on a nonstop trip to the moon. And we watched as Kim's brother Jerry wandered into the kitchen, completely naked, only to wake Louie up by almost rubbing his penis on his face. This was the second appearance of male full-frontal nudity in almost as many episodes in a show that, interestingly enough, publicly announced that it would have no female nudity whatsoever—unique for an HBO series.[2] The show, which Walter Metz (2005) hailed as being one of the most brilliantly intertextual moments in recent television history—one that relied entirely on viewer knowledge of not only the form, but more specifically the genre—was at once an anti-sitcom and a hyper-sitcom, challenging and reifying the generic conventions of the form. And, it might be worth mentioning, the show was absolutely brilliant and completely God-awful at the same time. With its highlighted laugh-track and overly cramped sets—too shallow for even the most ardent of sitcom viewers—and its standard sitcom stories involving the working-class doofus of a husband and his ineptitude for even the most basic of familial responsibilities (Butsch, 2003), *Lucky Louie* seemed to be everything HBO doesn't want to be. It seemed, in a word, like TV. However, *Lucky Louie* was complicated—even for a working-class doofus. Much of its critical commentary came from the fact that it was *so much like* the rest of TV—formulaic plots, poorly developed characters, its aesthetics, etc. However, its main points of interest, at least for Brian and myself that night, were not what it had in common with network sameness, but what it didn't. In the first few episodes we see Louie get caught masturbating, repeatedly offend a black neighbor, ask for and be denied anal sex, hang out with a drug dealer, call his young daughter a "fucking asshole," and give and take some major verbal punches with his under-appreciating yet overly-forgiving wife. Or, as Brian put it, "is this HBO giving network TV the finger or what?"

And this is what interests me here, not how HBO is like TV, but, to be one of the only contributors to this volume who seems to buy into HBO's slogan, how's it's not like other TV.[3]

Television as a medium has traditionally been defined by its limitations—technological, political, and cultural. In this essay I seek to explore the expansion of television's norms and constraints through an extended discussion regarding the possibilities of HBO being something other than TV, specifically through an exploration of profanity, violence, and sexuality and how each of these acts as a cultural marker within HBO's brand identity. From its early broadcasting of feature films not suitable for networks, its pioneering place in the dissemination of stand-up comedy, its large swathe of control over the broadcasting of boxing, its adult-oriented "late-nite" programming, and its early attempts at original programming through its most successful shows in the post-network era, HBO, as a "premium brand," seems to have the televisual market cornered on the dirty underbelly of the tube of plenty, continually using explicit content as a way to position itself outside televisual normativity.

Dick Hebdige (1979), in his now canonical piece on subculture, reads a notion of style through the dirty, sweaty themes of Jean Genet: style as revolt, style as refusal, crime as art. Much of what is discussed here as HBO's "style" has, in the various histories of our culture, been considered criminal or obscene at varying times. If we follow Genet and Hebdige's trail of subversive breadcrumbs, we are left with a channel that sells a subculture. While often discussed in terms of "quality" (see McCabe and Akass in this collection) or being a "premium brand" (see Santo here as well), HBO's marketing and clientele clearly smack of a kind of elitism and exclusion, the hallmarks of any subcultural movement/moment. But what does the consumer of HBO get out of being in this club?

In his 2007 book, *The Small Screen*, Brian Ott (2007) updates Burkean theory by arguing that "television equips us to live in the information age." His extended examples are the categories of nostalgic TV and hyperconscious TV (with *Dr Quinn, Medicine Woman* and *The Simpsons* as exemplars). I will consider in this chapter how HBO essentially provides a forum for transgression as equipment for living. And while subscribing to HBO may not be the same kind of cultural marker as the safety pins and Edwardian garb of Hebdige's punks and teddy boys or the Vaseline that so tipped off the Spanish police to Genet's predilections, it might not be too distant or difficult an articulation to make.

For John Jervis (1999: 4), the transgressive is "reflexive, questioning both its role and that of the culture that has defined it in its otherness." However, as Jervis continues, it is not simply a kind of reversal or opposition, rather, transgression "involves hybridization, the mixing of categories and the questioning of boundaries that separate categories." Michel Foucault (1977: 34) argues that the act of transgression is no doubt enthralling to witness because "the limit opens violently on to the limitless, find[ing] itself suddenly carried away by the content it had rejected and fulfilled by this alien plentitude which invades it to the core of its being." The limit of which Foucault speaks is, of course, subjectivity. And those moments of transgression are, of course, when we strive to overstep the boundaries of our individual subjectivity. Thus, the *jouissance* we find in watching and hearing profanity, violence, and sex on HBO is a kind of "mode of 'expenditure' or *dépense* that, pushed to the limit of all reason, utility, morality, sense of meaning, takes experience beyond experience itself, opening what was once oneself on to an apprehension of an impossible totality" (Botting and Wilson, 1998: 1). The viewer of HBO's titillating programming crosses the boundary of what is taboo, at once corporeal and ephemeral. Yet we find intense pleasure in these transgressive moments—as its millions of subscribers would attest. Perhaps we buy into HBO in order to "hoodwink ourselves . . . We want to get across without taking the final step" (Bataille, 1986: 141).

We are always and already locked in dialectic with style. Originality can thus only ever be an aura. HBO, in this way, can only be transgressive in relation to other modes of televisual discourse. And since HBO is all about the "buzz," we might well begin to examine HBO by looking at the first of what Mark Hughes (2005) has called "the six buttons of buzz": the taboo. Since profanity, violence, and sexuality are still taboo areas of discourse on the tube, I wish to explore them here through HBO's various presentations of stand-up comedy and its use of profanity, violence specifically found in the racialized, sexualized presence of boxing, and sex as it is presented in the post-Fordist dramas of labor as evidenced by the channel's infatuation with sex workers. As such, I argue here that HBO's transgressive behavior is a kind of philosophy toward television and its content: the philosophy of "cocksucker, motherfucker, tits."

## Cocksucker

> Those are the ones that will infect your soul, curve your spine, and keep the country from winning the war.
>
> George Carlin

I've been told I use "fuck" like it's a comma. I love to swear. I can't help it. In some utopian linguistic hierarchy, I imagine, some words are just better than others. Clearly, I'm not the only one. As Larry David argues in "The Shrimp Incident" episode from season two of *Curb Your Enthusiasm*, "you throw in a 'fuck,' you double your laughs"—this is the same episode where Julia-Louis Dreyfus insists they pitch their show idea to HBO so she, in fact, could say fuck (and she then proceeds to actually call him a cocksucker).

But beyond HBO's original programming, which clearly affords its characters plenty of opportunities to say things they otherwise couldn't, it is HBO's pioneering use of stand-up comedy as a branding tool that has perhaps most fully explored the channel's "cocksucker" aesthetic. And while stand-up comedy has been glaringly absent from much critical discourse (Limon, 2000), I still write with the presumption that most people know what it is when they see it.[4] As such I wish to focus on the HBO "work" of one comedian in particular here, one who pushes the boundaries of language and, as such, makes that boundary the subject of his material: George Carlin.

While much of the recent comedy on HBO would make the FCC's policies on obscenity implode, I'm thinking here of the charged and profane discourse that is the standard fare of the post-hip-hop shows such as Russell Simmons's *Def Comedy Jam* and Sean "Diddy" Combs's *Bad Boys of Comedy* (both named after their labels, respectively), it was the groundbreaking use of language on HBO by Carlin that both popularized comedy specials, as well as having a normalizing effect regarding profanity.

Carlin is, without question, one of our most daring social critics, acutely aware of the dangers of censorship and the constant problematization political correctness is in need of. As nearly all of the material Carlin writes has the potential to make its way into one of his numerous HBO specials, the met-acommentary he provides about language and its (ab)uses on television are a perfect place for us to examine HBO and the "cocksucker" dynamic it produces with stand-up comedy (Carlin, 2005). As Ruth Wajnryb (2005: 12) observes:

> Talking about swearing can stimulate a great deal of hilarity, a fact well known to comedians, who use it to their advantage. There must be a basic handbook for wannabe stand-ups: When in doubt or in need of a quick laugh, dip into toilet humor or pull out a dick joke or throw in a few FUCKS. People laugh, almost by reflex. It's the result of a flouting of a taboo. The comic is allowed to say it, and we're allowed to laugh. It's a ritual. Take, for instance, George Carlin's recital of his infamous list of seven major words you can't say on television. Audiences delighted in hearing Carlin say "shit, piss, fuck, cunt, cocksucker, motherfucker, and tits."

And it's Carlin and those seven little words I want to focus on for a moment. On his 1972 album *Class Clown*, Carlin first released the monologue called "Seven Words You Can Never Say on Television." And he clearly knew the power of this statement and what he was getting into. Simply consider the sentence immediately following the words' first utterance:

> There are some people that aren't into all the words. There are some people who would have you not use certain words. Yeah, there are

400,000 words in the English language, and there are seven of them that you can't say on television. What a ratio that is. 399,993 to seven. They must really be bad. They'd have to be outrageous, to be separated from a group that large. All of you over here, you seven. Bad words. That's what they told us they were, remember? "That's a bad word." "Awwww." There are no bad words. Bad thoughts. Bad Intentions. And words, you know the seven don't you? Shit, piss, fuck, cunt, cocksucker, motherfucker, and tits, huh? Those are the heavy seven. Those are the ones that will infect your soul, curve your spine and keep the country from winning the war.

Later that year he was arrested for performing a bit called "Seven Deadly Words" at "Summerfest" in Milwaukee, Wisconsin. On the follow-up record a year later, *Occupation: Foole*, a similar routine was included, this time called "Filthy Words." "Filthy Words" was broadcast by the Pacifica radio station WBAI in New York City. This broadcast ultimately led to the Supreme Court case, "FCC v. Pacifica Foundation," in 1978 that, in many ways, defined the limits of acceptable language on radio and television in the United States even through to the present.[5]

Carlin's first HBO special was part of their initial stand-up series *On Location*, usually run in conjunction with their variety/burlesque show *Standing Room Only*. Carlin's *On Location, George Carlin at USC*, was filmed in the summer of 1977. His performance lasted 85 minutes. What is interesting about this particular show is that word had spread so quickly about Carlin doing a television special that the FCC had a legal hearing regarding what should and shouldn't be Carlin's content. As such, for most of the performance, Carlin does an unusually high amount of inoffensive material. However, the federal court ultimately ruled in Carlin and HBO's favor. And this is why viewers are greeted at the opening of the special by *Newsweek* columnist Shana Alexander, who proceeds to explain that this kind of material is rarely seen on television or heard on the radio. As the taping draws toward its end, with about 25 minutes left, the screen freezes and a title card reads: **"THE FINAL SEGMENT OF MR. CARLIN'S PERFORMANCE CONTAINS ESPECIALLY CONTRO-VERSIAL LANGUAGE, PLEASE CONSIDER WHETHER YOU WISH TO CONTINUE VIEWING."** And for the remainder of the special Carlin performed "Seven Dirty Words" for the first time on television. And while this landmark in televised stand-up comedy truly paved the way for today's comedians to be as filthy as they want, it was Carlin's follow-up HBO special which is perhaps the more brilliant of the two, specifically regarding langauge and HBO's airing of it.

*George Carlin: Again!* (sometimes rebroadcast as *On Location: George Carlin at Phoenix*) is Carlin's second HBO special, performed in the round and first broadcast on July 23, 1978. In an October 31, 2004 appearance on *Inside the Actor's Studio*, Carlin says this HBO special was his major comeback. The special features much trademark Carlin material: "goofy shit," why there is no blue food (which was originally performed on the first episode of *Saturday Night Live*), a lengthy routine about time ("who has the time?"), specifically the odd ways in which we describe time ("Sooner than you think. Sounds spooky doesn't it?"), a version of his well-known "New News" routine complete with an appearance from Al Sleet, "the hippie-dippie weather man," as well as a newer version of "Death and Dying," along with other scattered material from the albums *An Evening with Wally Londo Featuring Bill Slaszo* (1975) and *On the Road* (1977). But the real gem in this special, and the piece that really matters here, is the finale, which features what is arguably the most well-known version of the "Seven Words You Can Never Say on Television" routine. This section of *Again!* is even featured as the centerpiece of the DVD release *George's Best Stuff*.

In *Again!* Carlin is in pure deconstructive mode, beginning the bit by arguing that one of the most interesting things about dirty words is that we have more ways to describe dirty words than we actually have dirty words:

> Someone was quite interested in these words. They kept referring to them: they called them bad, dirty, filthy, foul, vile, vulgar, coarse, in poor taste, unseemly, street talk, gutter talk, locker room language, barracks talk, bawdy, naughty, saucy, raunchy, rude, crude, lude, lascivious, indecent, profane, obscene, blue, off-color, risqué, suggestive, cursing, cussing, swearing . . . and all I could think of was: shit, piss, fuck, cunt, cocksucker, motherfucker, and tits!

At that point the crowd loses their mind and comedy (and television) history is made. But for Carlin, this list, which got him in so much trouble just a few years earlier, is seemingly incomplete. His first alteration is the addition of fart, turd, and twat, all the while assuring the audience that "some of your favorites might make the list this year." A few more words are added: asshole, ballbag, hard-on, pisshead, blueballs, nookie, snatchbox, pussy, pecker, peckerhead, peckertracks, jism, joint, dork, poontang, cornhole, and dingleberry ("innocent sounding word; sounds Christmas-y to me.").

Carlin also feels the list needs to be tightened a bit. "Motherfucker came off the list immediately." He claims he had a call (that day in fact) from an "English language purist" who explains to him that motherfucker is simply a duplication of the word fuck . . . technically, "because fuck is the root form, motherfucker being derivitive . . . And I said, 'Hey, motherfucker, how did you get my phone number anyway?' " Carlin's additional response to the purist is quite interesting again, because it's a further linguistic antagonizing of the limits of "what can't be said": "Look man, it may be derivative, but you still can't say it. You can't say motherfucker on TV, can you? He said, 'No, but you can't say fuckee, fucking, fuckola, fuckarooni, or fuckareeno either.' I said, 'Well, yeah, that would crowd up my list something awful. So I just struck that motherfucker away."

After his conversation with the "purist" convinces Carlin to drop motherfucker, the list, for Carlin, lacks its original rhythmic quality. "Shit, piss, cunt, cocksucker, tits . . . Does it sound like something's missing?" For Carlin, it sounds like "an old friend is gone . . . Remember the old rhythm . . . cocksucker, motherfucker, tits," he performs in a sing-song way, "cocksucker, motherfucker, tits." Additionally, cocksucker has taken over as the dominant word in a series that simply falls off and goes nowhere for Carlin, which is to say that cocksucker was balanced out somewhat by motherfucker as the only multisyllabic words on the list. Standing alone, cocksucker thus takes over: "shit, piss, cunt, COCKSUCKER, tits." But this outing of cocksucker by implication brings up its legitimacy as a dirty word as well. For Carlin, "sucker" is "suggestive as hell," but not dirty, and "cock" isn't dirty all the time ("it's only partly filthy")—and for Carlin, the real danger of puritanical linguistic relativism can be seen here as he asks how did cocksucker come to mean "a bad man," when it's really "a good woman. How did they do that?" So cocksucker is gone.

We are thus left with tits. For Carlin, this word simply does not belong on a list like this with real "heavyweight filth." "Cute thing, cute idea, great fun, great name." But in evoking tits as problematic Carlin is also pointing to the arbitrariness of attempts to govern obscenity. "But the word tits is on the list because you can't say it on television . . . You can say boobs. Boobs is spelled the same forwards and backwards too . . . you can't say tits but you can say boobs . . . You can say teats, provided you're on at five in the morning and a cow is your guest. But you can't say juggs and you can't say knockers . . ." So tits are problematic as well.

Carlin then goes on to consider the words he just added to the list: fart, turd, and twat (very interesting considering the commonality of the first two on American television today). The most interesting thing about "fart" for Carlin, besides the fact that it's "shit without the mess," is its complex relationship to fuck and television.

> You can't say fart on television, and you can't say fuck either on television. However, you can refer to fucking. You can talk about fucking . . . Fucking is alright. Fucking is part of the plot. Lotta plots are based on fucking. Will they fuck? Should they fuck? Have they fucked? Will they fuck again? Will they get sick from fucking? Are they fucking too much? Will they fuck each others' friends? Will they have a baby from fucking? Will they be

sorry they fucked? Will they be glad they fucked? . . . They talk about fucking all they want, they just don't call it what it is. They call it other things . . . making love . . . going to bed with someone . . . having an affair, sleeping together. But they don't call it fucking. On the other hand, fart. Not only is fart a word you can't use on television, but they never even refer to them. That's how bad farts are compared to fucking.

While much has changed regarding fart and its presence in American television (an almost central presence some critics might say), fuck has changed little in the three decades since this monologue. He gets back on track and returns to the new words. "Turd's another word you can't say on television . . . but . . . when you get right down to it, who wants to say it? I don't even care if I ever hear that one again." Twat, for Carlin, is on the list because, like cunt, it doesn't mean anything else, unlike prick which is "one of those part-time dirty words." "It only has that one meaning. Twat's twat and that's that." Prick, unlike twat, points to the ambiguity and ridiculousness that Carlin is calling into question: "You can say prick on television. 'I pricked my finger.' Just don't say 'I fingered my prick.' " Ball, for Carlin, suffers the same undecidable malady as prick.

Carlin ends *Again!* with an appeal to rationality with regard to language. He says that he wishes he thought of "Make love, not war," so he could simply retire now and go to the beach. The problem with the phrase for Carlin, though, isn't simply in its overuse, it's that it lacks power. Carlin tells us that the real power, if these words are so dangerous, would be found in a phrase like "Make fuck, not kill" (he follows: "I'm not looking to retire anytime soon.").[6] As such, Carlin is polticizing and rendering problematic the understandings of acceptable language and violence (or perhaps it's just that "Shamu, the fucker whale" just sounds funnier).

Since these specials, thousands of comedians have been broadcast by HBO saying piss or shit or any other fucking thing they damn-well please. One can now occasionally even hear "tits" on network television, and piss (usually as in "pissed off") is so prevalent that those original Supreme Court justices who sided with the FCC must be well . . . pretty pissed off. Shit occasionally makes its way onto network TV, but is becoming a staple of cable—pun intended—with shows like FX's *The Shield* or AMC's *Mad Men* giving HBO and Showtime a good game of "anything you can do I can do better." However, since HBO is outside of FCC obscenity guidelines it has never had to be concerned with those guidelines. The guidelines do not apply to any subscription-based media, such as pay-cable television, satellite radio, or pay-per-view services. And while there are numerous groups in the United States today calling on Congress to step in and take control over FCC obscenity guidelines, at the moment at least, network Standards and Practices departments will continue to self-censor to avoid FCC intervention. Cable outlets continue to push the envelope a little at a time (*South Park*'s "It Hits the Fan" aired the word "shit" 162 times while alluding to Carlin's list and adding two extra words—"asshole" and "mee krob," the Thai dish that Cartman would rather "scarf down a whole wet bucket full of shit before [he eats] another plate of mee krob," later noting that "God must hate it as much as I do!"). Additionally, Comedy Central over recent years has taken to showing R-rated films uncut, as well as uncut performances from comedians such as Richard Pryor or Carlin himself, after 1:00am. Yet, even while the profane is increasingly becoming the mundane, there is still something tantalizing, taboo, and, indeed, transgressive in turning on the television set and hearing "shit, piss, fuck, cunt, cocksucker, mother-fucker, and tits." As Kate Burridge (2002: 220) observes, "As with most things forbidden, dirty words have a special fascination. What is taboo is revolting, untouchable, filthy, unmentionable, dangerous, disturbing, thrilling—but above all powerful."

But this is not to say that we can't forget, mustn't forget, that the times are indeed a-changin'. We have to remember, for example, that since Lenny Bruce was arrested in 1964 and spent four months in jail, no comedian has served real time in the United States for their words (Epstein, 2001). But Carlin bridges the old world of comedy and the new, the world where "Saint Lenny . . . died for our sins" (Bogosian, 1992: vii) and the world where profanity has become so commonplace that it is perhaps more shocking—and indeed transgressive—to hear programs without "bleeps" scattered throughout—even on "real TV."

## Motherfucker

> *Sport is at once both trivial and serious, inconsequential yet of symbolic significance.*
> John Sugden and Alan Tomlinson (1994: 3)

One major aspect that often gets overlooked in discussions of HBO and pay television is its relationship with professional boxing—and sport in general.

The first thing ever broadcast by HBO, to viewers in the community of Wilkes-Barre, Pennsylvania, was a hockey game between the New York Rangers and the Vancouver Canucks. Thirty-five years later, while HBO no longer broadcasts live major league hockey (or football, basketball, or baseball for that matter), boxing still manifests as a major earner for HBO. As such, with its early roots in televised sport, and its contemporary stake in professional boxing, HBO has also had a major impact in defining other television, as has been widely known, even from its earliest days (Lockman and Sarvey, 2005). For example, the success of HBO during cable's earliest years—along with that of Ted Turner's Superstation—"showed it was possible for nonnetwork, alternative programming to work, much to the distress of the networks" (Freeman, 2000: 55–56). The developments in satellite technology, coupled with audience willingness to watch other sites of programming, made possible the coming of channels such as ESPN and the rewriting of the history of televised sport. From that first hockey game shown in November of 1972, HBO has had a real presence in the often overtly sexualized, racialized, and violent world of professional sport. HBO's use of boxing as part of its brand identity will be discussed in this section as we look at how "the sweet science" reinforces HBO's "motherfucker" attitude.[7]

*HBO World Championship Boxing* premiered in 1974 and has continually shown major fights for the past three decades. Its first broadcast was the George Foreman defeat of Joe Frazier from Kingston, Jamaica in January 1974 when Foreman took the prize of World Heavyweight champ in two rounds. Other major events the show covered were the Ali–Foreman "Rumble in the Jungle" from Zaire, the third Ali–Frazier installment known as the "Thrilla in Manila" (the first satellite broadcast), the Holmes–Cooney heavyweight championship, "The Battle of the Champions" (Pryor versus Arguello in what was called the 80s fight of the decade), the Haggler–Hearns "War," "Thunder Meets Lightning" when Chávez beat Taylor with two seconds left in the twelfth round, and, of course, the biggest upset in the history of the sweet science: "Buster" Douglas knocking out Mike Tyson for the heavyweight title in Tokyo in February 1990. (Tyson was a 42:1 favorite.) The series also had two spin-offs, *Boxing After Dark*, which premiered in 1996 showing major fights, but often not with a title on the line, and *KO Nation*, which profiled up-and-comers in a hip-hop format. The latter featured dancers and hip-hop performances, along with radio personality Ed Lover as the ring announcer. The Saturday afternoon show failed to find "a young male audience" and was cancelled after only eight episodes (Lee, 2001). Additionally, in 2000, Time Warner released for PlayStation a game titled *HBO Boxing*, carrying the HBO brand. Finally, just to situate HBO's presence in the world of boxing, it is worth noting that many high-profile bouts and title fights take place in London—often at midnight or later so HBO can show the fight live to its (North) American prime-time audience.

But much of the critical discourse about boxing has little to do with its mediation or political economy, rather it is a discourse of society and race. There has been much written about the representation and (often metaphorical) implications of the "black athlete" (Bruce, 2004: 862; see also, Andrews, 1996; Lafrance & Rail, 2001; Sabo & Jansen, 1994; Sabo et al., 1996; Sloop, 1997; Wilson, 1997; Wynn, 2003). Additionally, someone like Mike Tyson—and black boxers in general—is, for Neil Wynn (2003), a kind of "American icon." Boxing, as John Sugden (1997: 33–34) illustrates in his study of the sport in Ireland, Cuba, and the United States, has historically been used to promote, maintain, and naturalize ideological myths of race, ethnicity, and nation in Western culture. The irony, of course, is that these institutional and systemic discriminations are what draw minority men (particularly black and Hispanic men) into the sport out of economic necessity, with many boxers coming from inner cities and ghettoes with their success due to a complex set of sociocultural circumstances (Heiskanen, 2006; Sugden, 1997; Wacquant, 1995, 2000, 2004).

And what HBO subscribers get with their monthly fee when they turn on *World Championship Boxing* is a kind of story, a story about race and about masculinity, a kind of "iconic embodiment of masculinity" that reifies "representations of the masculine body and their psychic underpinnings" (Jefferson, 1998: 78–79). The story of boxing, then, as Raymond Boyle and Richard Haynes (2000: 137) argue, is one of "an exclusive, essentialist masculine domain . . . dominated by metaphors of power, strength, ferocity of the competitive spirit, and courage." These discourses are retrieved, circulated and reinforced in media coverage of boxing. However, these stories are not simply what get broadcast: boxing is still, simply put, and what most viewers are concerned with most of the time, two people beating the living hell out of one another. Participants are injured, bloodied, brain-damaged, and even killed— and they are acutely aware of these possibilities (Sugden, 1997; Wacquant 1995). But "violence in sports" simply "sells" (Bryant, Zillman, and Raney 1998: 253). It's entertainment. It's violence. It's sport. It's boxing. It's not TV. It's HBO.

And this real and symbolic violence is not simply about men.[8] As Boyle and Haynes observe (2000: 141), "women's role in boxing has stereotypically been consigned to scantily clad models strolling around the ring holding up number cards that precede the next round." In November of 2006, how HBO perpetuates this hegemonic masculinity became decidedly clear when it chose to *not* cover the Wladimir Klitschko–Calvin Brock bout at Madison Square Garden, instead opting to rebroadcast the Floyd Mayweather–Carlos Baldomir welterweight bout from a week prior. The problem was, the undercard match had the "wrong chromosomes": Laila Ali (then 22–0 and daughter of Muhammad), was facing Shelley Burton. HBO, which has never shown women's boxing, is, according to Ali, "missing the big picture." She said rather frankly on ESPN2 during the press before the fight, "I am kind of like the headline. I'm selling the tickets." And while this may have been the case, HBO Sports President Ross Greenburg noted that the event wasn't worthy of live coverage, stating, "It's a very young sport and the athletes need to develop." In the end, HBO simply aired highlights of the Ali bout, with much of its airtime being devoted to her father who was present at the fight (Heistand: 2006, 3c). According to Boyle and Haynes (2000:141), "The marginalization of women's boxing is perhaps the clearest manifestation of patriarchal hierarchies in sport." Boyle and Haynes (2000: 141) go on to note:

> The gendered values of sport are acutely realized when the physical capital ascribed to men and women's bodies differs so greatly. Female muscularity is viewed as distasteful and inhumane. Masculine strength and bravura are celebrated and viewed as heroic.

What we can see in boxing as a whole then is also what we find in James McBride's (1985) examination of the psychodynamics of patriarchal culture, wherein men, identifying with the victim of violence, can generate rage and anguish that becomes projected on to a female other (Sabo and Jansen, 1998). McBride is largely drawing on the work of Georges Bataille (1986) and Luce Irigaray (1985), arguing that the "masculinitist psychic economy" of American culture, war, and sport are all interpellated expressions of a patriarchal desire for power and control. For McBride, however, the suppression of these needs results in a kind of emotional ambivalence and frustration, which, in turn, gets manifested and channeled through collective, personal, and spectacular violence. HBO, it would appear, is always already leading and reifying the heterosexist "twinning" of sport and sex (Houck, 2006: 552; Miller, 2001; Guttman 1996).

It makes sense that HBO, with its emphasis on "quality TV" and representations of true daily life, would have the boxing connection. For, as Aaron Baker (1998: 161) points out, "boxing presents a dramatic metaphor for the rugged individualism that has traditionally been a central element of Hollywood's mythology." And as part of that mythology, and how it still gets perpetuated today through its televisuality, it will be likely to continue to draw "youth from subaltern groups who have very little opportunity for self-determination" (Baker, 1998: 161). But it is also the narrative of animality, coupled with that of race and socio-inequality, which sets the stage for professional boxing. As the attorney Gerry Spence (quoted in Sloop, 1997: 102) once remarked with regard to Tyson's case: "Anger is what drives a champion . . . He cannot rid himself of that any more than he can rid himself of the color of his skin . . ." Yet why do we watch? For me, this is an unanswerable question, but a question worth asking nonetheless. If we reconsider again HBO's positioning of itself as a "quality," even luxury, brand, why then does it partake in the dissemination and perpetuation of violence—both physical and symbolic? What does the HBO viewer get out of seeing often minority men—from the subaltern position of having grown up in a world where HBO was probably not in their homes for obvious reasons—pummel each other?

The most commonly offered rationale to explain televisual, mediated, or really any kind of violence with regard to sport usually stems from the notion of catharsis—a kind of "purgation of pent-up feelings of hostility" (Bryant, Zillman, and Raney 1998: 258–259). Yet for many, violence is as good a reason as any to watch televised sport, and that violence—and often a highly sexualized form of it—is a hugely important factor in attracting and maintaining audience members. "The persisting popularity of combative sports, and of wrestling and boxing in particular, would seem to give sufficient support to the contention that at least a good portion of sports spectators enjoy bruising activities that often lead to the temporary incapacitation, by knockout or injury, of some competitors" (Zillman and Paulus, 1993: 606).

The sport is clearly a messy, sweaty affair, with racial metaphors playing out in the squared circle. HBO viewers get something from watching boxing, and even though we can't smell it through our televisions, we know there's an odor there. So the question remains: Who wants to see two "motherfuckers" beat the shit out of each other?

## Tits

*If you don't want to fuck me, baby, well baby, fuck off.*
Wayne County and the Electric Chairs

In celebrating *The Sopranos* as a "triumph of non-network TV," Paul Levinson (2002: 29) said something quite brilliant: "Speaking as a male viewer, I can't say that curse words are as pleasurable to hear as nudity is to see [at the] Bada Bing!" This is to say that within HBO's content branding philosophy Levinson has a predilection for "tits" over "cocksucker"—but since he is an unabashed *Sopranos* fan, he clearly has a taste for both.

In this section I will briefly discuss, after Levinson, some of the characteristics and virtues of sex and nudity and then problematize some of the ways in which these are "exploited" by HBO.

For Levinson (2002: 28), even as much as he seemingly enjoys it, nudity "is not all it's cracked up to be." The problem, for Levinson, is that nudity must exist to serve the story—otherwise it's simply a distraction. This makes sense when one considers the role of love scenes in narrative terms, or the fact that a good deal of *The Sopranos* does take place at "the Bing." HBO, however, gets around this "story problem" in a rather unique way. Unlike Cinemax, whose "after-dark" programming consists of banal soft-core pornography, HBO utilizes the "docu-drama" format for some rather complicated purposes. In these pseudo-reality shows, we find sex and nudity a-plenty, all under the guise of "informational TV." So whatever the purposes of viewing—from a genuine interest in people who pretend to be horses when they have sex to wanting to know about the daily lives of hookers in America's fiftieth state to the simple desire to get off without the attached stigma that comes with consuming pornography—HBO offers viewers a wide array of sexual peccadilloes for the "elite" HBO consumer. Two things are evident here, however, with just a simple perusal of how HBO sells these shows: (1) They don't market them as quality TV—at least not in the same way that they might sell a show like *Six Feet Under*; and (2) they are not pornographers—rather they provide an informational service that fulfills the interests of an astute, intelligent clientele. We can make of that what we will.

One of the first programs to establish HBO in the arena of adult programming was *Taxicab Confessions*. Filmed in taxi-filled cities such as New York or Las Vegas, it has a cast of regular producers who pose as drivers. Once a passenger hails and gets in the cab, they are recorded on hidden cameras. At the end of the ride, passengers sign waivers explaining they will be on *Taxicab Confessions*. What often takes place, though, aren't really "confessions" of the purist sort, rather it is often the driver/HBO investigator coaxing stories from people who are often too drunk to remember their name. What this often produces is verbally (and often visually) quite graphic and sexually explicit discussions—or even sex taking place in the back seat. This is, as HBO puts it, America undercover and out in the open. But to further legitimize what we could call the "porning" of quality TV, the first episode won an Emmy for "Outstanding Informational Special."

The success, both critically and commercially, of *Taxicab Confessions* gave way in the 1990s to *Real Sex*, a "news-magazine" that explores "sex '90s style" in its full explicitness.[9] The show explores a variety of aspects of sexuality, usually three or four packages to an episode (with episodes now in the thirties), focusing on fads in consumer sex culture such swinging parties, subcultures, and so on. Much of the series, however, is devoted to the sex industries, from the production of "love dolls" to going behind the scenes at porn shoots. Other episodes focus on sex education, from a cunnilingus seminar to men learning how to masturbate to their full potential. And while segments are separated by on-the-street interviews with presumably non-actors, much of the series is focused on those who work in the business of sex. For example, *Real Sex* "specials," or "Xtras," have focused on the porn industry in Southern California (*Pornucopia: Going Down in the Valley*) or features about porn stars (*Katie Morgan: A Porn Star Revealed*—which featured a 90-minute interview with a completely nude Morgan and various high-brow questions about where men can come on her and what she will or will not do during a scene).

Which brings us to *Real Sex*'s two spin-off series, *G-String Divas* and *Cathouse*, each of which focus on the daily lives of sex workers. *G-String Divas* focuses its lens on strippers on and off the pole, while *Cathouse* is an extended profile of the Moonlite Bunny Ranch, Nevada's most well-known legal bordello. In *Cathouse* we find a strict business-like atmosphere as Dennis Hof and Madame Suzette orchestrate "parties" between "clients" and the "girls." *Cathouse*'s hidden cameras focus not simply on sex, but also upon the negotiations between the prostitutes and their johns—who include everyone from widowers, brother "teams," virgins, to husbands and wives.

What we are seeing in the connections across *Cathouse*, *G-String Divas*, *Real Sex*, and *Taxicab Confessions*, as well as the series of "Hooker" documentaries (*Pimps Up, Hos Down*, *Atlantic City Hookers: It Ain't E-Z Bein' a Ho*, *Hookers on the Point*, and *Downtown Girls: The Hookers of Honolulu*), is a kind of documenting of the post-Fordist "cultural body work" that occurs on a different scale in post-industrial societies that are marked by an increasing amount of individualiza-tion and part-time, temporary, or insecure work (Beck, 2000; Schilling, 2005: 88; Sennett, 1998). Here we can even see the division of social bodies between the sociological theories of Georg Simmel (1971: 133) and Georges Bataille (1993: 168), perhaps two of our greatest "body" theorists, in that HBO's use of "tits"

> enables individuals to experience their bodily being as a positive resource rather than a constraint, and [as] a domain of sovereignty in which people feel themselves to be acting freely, away from the burdens and inequalities that confront them in the rest of their lives. (Schilling, 2005: 150)

For Bataille (1991: 22, 27), the body is possessed of an excess of energy and how this excess is used is telling about the societies individuals inhabit. Simmel (1971), however, views the body as basically possessed with a drive to socialize, a "drive linked to the intrinsic satisfaction gained from merging into a 'union with others' " (Schilling, 2005: 150). These bodily manifestations get played out rather unmetaphorically in the sexually explicit congresses shown through-out these bodywork programs. This embodiment of the subject, particularly by briefly considering two thinkers of the industrial age, becomes a story of social bonding. If we consider HBO's post-Fordist "tits" as a kind of body labor, then, we can consider what it means to "union with others" in an age of "semiotic excess" (Collins, 1995), wherein our postmodern superficialities are being "exploited" as people seek bodywork that enables them to be sociable on the most intimate of levels. This gets complicated, however, by HBO's exploitation of this labor and begs the question: Are shows like *Cathouse* or *G-String Divas* now a televisual sweatshop taking advantage of post-Fordist body labor? Is HBO the biggest pimp in the Time-Warner empire's army? The changing nature of obscenity certainly doesn't help answer this question. Even though we see "the work of being watched," to steal Mark Andrejevic's (2004) phrase, in the post-Fordist set of "tits" every time HBO premieres a new *Undercover* or *Real Sex* documentary, we still do not see mainstream Hollywood films following suit. NC-17 films, for example, are rarely, if ever, shown on the channel (and if they are it is usually in the wee small hours), nor are they on Cinemax, The Movie Channel, Showtime, Starz, or Encore for that matter.[10]

And yet even though these taboo series, these televisual transgressions, seemingly respond to something lacking in the rest of viewers' choices, the "sex-media as equipment for living argument," at least to me, doesn't really hold up when considered as really simply another trope about life in post-modernity and the liquidity of sexual, personal relations under the logic of neoliberal post-Fordism.[11] The dynamic between "television" and "tits" depends in part on our cultural, (bio)political, personal, and policed perspectives on sexuality, pornography, and obscenity—as well as the erotic, the titillating, and the arousing—as a kind of displaced discourse, particularly in America, that goes unmentioned and, perhaps more potently, unmention*able*. The numbing that occurs with "tits" on TV, which is really a kind of deadening of erotism, clearly impels an almost antithetical position to HBO's "transgressions," whereby the reader/viewer's engagement is ultimately impelled by the writer/producer's output, which is to say that HBO's "tits" as found in their faux-reality porndocs really fail, more than anything else on the channel, to establish what Roland Barthes (1975: 4) called a "dialectics of desire."

## HBO's money shot: Network and cable take it on the chin (and not just on Sunday nights anymore)

Now that I have looked at how "cocksucker, motherfucker, tits" gets played out in complex cultural ways through stand-up comedy, boxing, and reality-sex programming, it's worth finally noting that nearly all of the original programming that makes HBO "HBO," aside from its children's shows on HBO Family, embodies the "cocksucker, motherfucker, tits" philosophy. Consider, for example, the following exchange between Larry David and his manager, Jeff Greene, in the second season episode of *Curb Your Enthusiasm*, "The Shrimp Incident":

JEFF GREENE: All of the women at HBO, they don't want to work with you.
LARRY DAVID: Oh, come on. That's ridiculous.
JEFF: They think you're misogynist.
LARRY: Why, 'cause I called the guy a cunt? So what!
JEFF: 'Cause you called the guy a cunt.
LARRY: Big deal, I call men pricks all the time, men want to work for me.
JEFF: Well, cunt's worse.

LARRY: Cunt's not worse. Pricks and cunts, they're equal. Pricks, cunts, come
   on. They balance out.

JEFF: No, cunt is worse. Cunt's much heavier.

LARRY: Why? Why is cunt heavier?

JEFF: I never questioned, it just is.

LARRY: That's sexist to me! Come on.

What this highly offensive, and comically genius, back-and-forth illustrates is
not simply the bickering at the heart of so much of *Curb*'s hilarity, rather this is
a telling comment about the packaging of and understanding about "cocksucker, motherfucker, tits" that so embodies HBO's cultural production. A
profane conversation about a violent, sexualized word, Larry and Jeff are
manifesting what makes HBO "HBO." And since *Curb* is not stand-up comedy
(at least not since its original documentary inception), and it's not boxing, and
it's certainly not reality-sex programming, this conversation is illustrative of
the fact that nearly all of HBO's original programming (the good stuff that
most people cop to watching) use this model. Every HBO original program has
exploited "cocksucker, motherfucker, tits" to make the most of its place outside
of "TV." And what we don't have is a splintering of HBO based on these
transgressive televisualizations (outside of the most obvious HBO Family). We
don't have HBO Profanity, HBO Violence, or HBO Sex and Nudity. Rather
we have the normal HBO offerings that just so happen to contain all three. We
haven't got TV. It's HBO. As such, it is not coincidental that HBO has a series
called *Undercover*, since the channel itself offers content that involves rhetorical
tropes and discursive patterns that transgress the everyday. But those transgressions, however taboo, on mainstream television are at the center of what
makes HBO "not TV." For example, Jane Arthurs (2003: 81) finds in *Sex and the
City* a kind of novelty that lies "in the migration of women-centred and explicit
sexual discourse into television drama." But the combination of profanity,
violence, and sex doesn't always mean an edgier kind of hit. For example, one
critic described the Showtime drama *The Street*—which the critics saw as an
unnecessary rip-off, paling in comparison to HBO's *The Wire* and FX's *The
Shield*—in the following way: "Take away the jittery camera work—and the
*breasts, profanity* and *violence* that mark it as a pay-cable product—and you could
be watching *Hunter*" (Bianco: 2002, 7e, emphasis mine). Furthermore, each
category I've discussed here—stand-up (profanity), boxing (violence), and sex
(sex)—is now or has been its own reality show. From the obvious reality
programs based on sex, we've also got *Dane Cook's Tourgasm*, which reminds
us that comedians are just as dirty offstage and the four-part prelude *De La
Hoya-Mayweather 24/7*, which followed Oscar De La Hoya and Floyd Mayweather in preparation for their bout "De La Hoya vs. Mayweather: The World

Awaits." The show aired in installments on the Sundays leading up to the match with the fight broadcast by HBO Pay-Per-View (HBO PPV) on May 5, 2007.

In John Caldwell's *Televisuality* (1995), he argues that television defines itself through the ways in which networks and programs distinguish themselves from what Newcomb (2007: 573) calls a "welter of available content spread across multiple television offerings." Caldwell (1995: 5) notes:

> Televisuality was a stylizing performance—an exhibitionism that utilized many different looks . . . For example, the miniseries proved to be a quintessential televisual form, while the video-originated sitcom—at least with a few notable exceptions—resisted radical stylistic change. Conceived of as a presentational attitude, a display of knowing exhibitionism, any one of many specific visual looks and stylizations could be marshaled for the spectacle. The process of stylization rather than style—an activity rather than a static look—was the factor that defined televisual exhibitionism.

And while we are now seeing a sea change in aesthetics with the "resistive" sitcom at the center (consider post-sitcom sitcoms such as *Arrested Development, My Name is Earl* or either version of *The Office*—all of which, it's worth noting, followed *Sex and the City*, *Curb Your Enthusiasm*, and *The Mind of the Married Man*), HBO stands as a spectacular, both in Caldwell's sense and in Guy Debord's (1977), triumph of post-televisuality. By turning its everyday content into the spectacular and aestheticizing the taboo, HBO is an example *par excellence* of what Caldwell (1995: 106–107) himself termed "boutique television":

> Boutique programming constructs for itself an air of selectivity, refinement, uniqueness, and privilege. The televisual excess operative in boutique programming then, has less to do with an overload of visual form than with two other products: excessive intentionality and sensitivity. Programming's cult of sensitivity may involve the kind of spectacular cinematic spectacle more typical of loss-leader event programming, but it may also involve more restrained forms of drama, writing, and cinematography—subtle orchestrations of televisual form that create the defining illusion of a personal touch.

Such is clearly the case for HBO on numerous levels (Newcomb, 2007: 573). Unlike the case with network shows that ostensibly have no "author," HBO is always already in auteur-celebration mode with "David Chase's *The Sopranos*," "Alan Ball's *Six Feet Under*," or "David Milch's *Deadwood*." But this logic is also at work in how HBO defines itself as "not TV," something consumers seemingly buy into—a slogan and product that is outside of normal televisual discourse, selectively cultivated by HBO, selectively *chosen* by HBO's audience. Here again we can see a return to Ott-cum-Burke's "equipment for living argument" and pose the question: what are viewers getting from HBO that they can't get from "TV?" The simple answer: "cocksucker, motherfucker, tits."

A recent example of HBO's "cocksucker, motherfucker, tits" philosophy that is seemingly the next logical step for "not television," is the *HBO Voyeur Project*, a kind of Warholian multimedia experience—that's really just an elaborate marketing campaign—launched in the summer of 2007. By framing the series (though that's not really the appropriate word) around the assumption that HBO viewers are willing to go along on a voyeuristic tour, the content is made less for television and more for filling a gap in what I've called "transgression as equipment for living." While there are five locations upon which we the voyeur can choose to peep, for the most part, the main frame, which consists of a wall-less apartment building, wherein we can see the daily going-ons of its tenants, features eight fictional residents at the corner of Broome and Ludlow Streets in New York City on the nights of June 28–July 1, and again from July 5–July 8, each from 9:00–11:00pm.[12] The footage seemingly plays out in an endless loop on the HBO website, where a viewer/voyeur is confronted with the slogan: "See what people do when they think no one is watching." However, unlike Warhol who truly did film the empty vacuous-ness of daily life with his pieces such as *Sleep*, *Eat*, *Empire*, and even *Blow-Job* to some extent, the *Voyeur Project* seems hinged on reifying HBO's mantra of "cocksucker, motherfucker, tits," as the building at Broome and Ludlow, of course, offers the standard fare of murder, violence, sex, marriage, romance, and adultery, etc. Consider simply the names of each story for each apartment: 1A, "The Tempted," 1B "The Departure," 2A, "The Discovery," 2B, "The Proposal," 3A, "The Killer Within," 3B, "The Grown-Up Table," 4A, "The Delivery," and 4B, "The Temptress."

As this content clearly fits into HBO's "cocksucker, motherfucker, tits" attitude toward programming outside the boundaries, *HBO Voyeur*, perhaps more than anything else HBO has ever done, speaks to its "It's Not TV" manifesto. HBO subscribers can watch on HBO Online; they can also peer via HBO On Demand, wherein they can see additional content including trailers for the elaborate website, as well as paired apartment storylines from Broome and Ludlow (at about eight minutes or so), plus an extra—perhaps metatextual?—story called "The Watcher." As content related to storylines and characters is sprawled across a variety of web pages and blogs, both fictional and real, as well as having clips and images circulate online, again both through genuine fan participation and elaborate multimedia programming, we have "not TV" for the "not TV" consumer. Since there is ostensibly no "show" in the traditional sense, rather what we lay our gaze upon are a series of interconnected, yet independent clips, we are seeing television post-YouTube. When we find HBO's programming not simply as a two-hour block on Sunday night, but as part of a postmodern televisual flow that knows no borders or boundaries, we haven't got TV. We've got Flickr and YouTube; we've got Facebook and MySpace; we've got mobile content for the iPhone set; we've got self-surveillance to the point where Big Brother is looking for a new job (Andrejevic, 2007). Who needs TV when you've got all that? It makes sense then, given HBO's place on the leading edge for almost three decades, that its latest foray in transgressive content comes to us as less "TV" than ever (Van Tassel, 2001).

*Voyeur* was developed not by a traditional production company, but by Batten, Barton, Durstine & Osborn, the advertising agency branch of the Omnicorp Group. The main "wall" was directed by film and television director Jake Scott, with the exclusive four interactive stories being directed by Chris Nelson. The project was estimated to have cost between seven and ten million dollars, and took about a year to create. Without having a season, or even real episodes for that matter, *Voyeur* is a complex tapestry of extratextual narrative space including the main HBO website, HBO On Demand and HBO Mobile exclusive content for subscribers, MySpace pages for the characters from the stories, as well as supporting websites and additional content for those willing to follow the breadcrumbs or "artifacts" hidden in the other media outlets. For example, clues and discussions about voyeur "artifacts" found at the promotional blog http://www.thestorygetsdeeper.com further complicate and enhance the experience for those interested in becoming an interactive media consumer by way of the "voyeur" brand.

In the end, Scott and Nelson aren't responsible for a traditional TV show as we normally conceive of the medium. We are seeing a push, by HBO, to again be on the leading edge, one that I believe further pushes their claim of not being TV away from simple hyperbole into a much more realistic positing.

In HBO's use of "cocksucker, motherfucker, tits" we find a precise equivalent in their presentation of profanity, violence, and sex to what in hardcore pornography is referred to as the "money shot," the culminating visual evidence of male ejaculation (see Williams, 1989). We find this paroxysm in the moment of "did I just see that?" or "did they just say?"—as Brian and I found that July night as we watched *Lucky Louie*. From a brutal knockout early in a fight[13] to Tolliver making Joanie shoot a young scheming girl "on the con" in the head on *Deadwood* to a woman going down on a "love doll" during an episode of *Real Sex*, from Chris Rock nearly advocating the murder of Nicole Brown Simpson or trying to explain why he "loves black people" but "hates niggers" in *Bring the Pain* to an over-lunch conversation about golden showers on *Sex and City* to Ari's wife's clear offense taken at his nonchalant use of the term "cuntmuscle" in *Entourage*, we find HBO's "money shots" coming at us with potency and frequency. If HBO is simply "TV" as so many critics espouse, why did we never hear Marie call Frank a "cuntmuscle" on *Everybody Loves Raymond*?

HBO, as a premium brand, offers its consumers a place where it's okay to be transgressive with regard to mainstream television.[14] As such, the discretionary income that HBO's customers offer up every month as a kind of tithe to television's dark side creates a particular kind of subculture of distinctly elite, yet transgressive cultural citizens/postmodern subjects (Miller, 1993, 1998, 2007). Yet because of its place as both a premium brand and a transgressive outlet, HBO attains a kind of cultural authority between popular culture and "mature" content. Kant (1983) once said that the connection between the Enlightenment and maturity defined authority as a kind of transgression of self-imposed immaturity. Perhaps this explains why people pay so much money to consume media they don't want people to know they watch, HBO being a unique example here: as a premium brand one can take pride in being a consumer of HBO, but a very specific HBO—i.e. its original programming in the form of its Sunday night shows. Perhaps HBO has created a uniquely complex "cosmopolitan consumer" (Cannon & Yabrak, 2005), who seeks out the taboo and pays for the privilege. Consider the fact that critics regularly duke it out over which of HBO's original programs is the "best TV show of all time."[15] I, however, have never heard someone claim they subscribe to HBO just so they can watch *Cathouse* or *G-String Divas*; certainly none of the other authors in this volume cop to it (nor do they discuss people who might), but that just might be my experience.

Transgressions aside, we can't forget that HBO is still part of Time Warner and exists first and foremost to make money. As the rock critic Dave Marsh (1985: 15) once put it rather succinctly, "all culture is made in an industrial complex." Even though viewers may have various uses for HBO, it is HBO that is using those viewer needs to offer something people can't really get else-where (save for the trickle down effect as Showtime, FX, and AMC start to pick up where HBO leaves off). Scholars such as Amanda Lotz (2004) or Newcomb (2007) have recently suggested that we are in the post-network era, but HBO's utilization of "cocksucker, motherfucker, tits" would make it seem that we are somewhere even beyond that, somewhere in a post-television era, where our once easily relied-upon understandings of the medium are consist-ently called into question by technology, content, and reception.[16] Addition-ally, considering Caldwell's (1995: 2–5) documentation of how production, promotion, and programming processes have shifted toward "excessive style" and "visual exhibitionism," it is clear to see how HBO's utilization of televisual transgressions (and the ultimate [perhaps unwitting] mainstreaming of those transgressions, thus making them nontransgressive in the process) is a kind of branding push toward gaining a specific (read elite) audience amidst a world of churn and fragmentation. However, while HBO has from the beginning claimed to eschew formula in its programming, it is now rather obvious that eschewing formula is just as formulaic—(non)transgressive McTelevision for the post-television international audience (Waisbord, 2004; Moran, 1998).

Without question, HBO and its brand of profanity, violence, and sex is "popular" in the sense that Stuart Hall (1981: 231) used it to describe any kind of cultural text consumed by large audiences. But HBO and its philosophy of "cocksucker, motherfucker, tits" is also popular in the second sense Hall (1981: 235) used the term, existing "in a continuing tension (relationships, influence and antagonism) to the dominant culture." And while it is most evidently popular, there is also something clearly spectacular about "cocksucker, motherfucker, tits." As Debord (1977: section 3) notes in *the* definitive statement on the topic, spectacle functions as "the existing order's uninterrupted discourse about itself, its laudatory monologue." As we have seen, "cocksucker, motherfucker, tits" is always and already about othering and the process of exoticizing that other; yet without an other there is no I. We cannot watch from without without questioning from within. Considering the appeals of "cocksucker, motherfucker, tits" from within the perspective of HBO's "upscale" clientele, it becomes apparent that it is a discourse of our own transgressions, our own perversions, and our own desires.

There is much I haven't discussed here, such as race or gender in stand-up comedy, the socioeconomic ironies of HBO broadcasting and controlling boxing, or the exploitation and perpetuation of patriarchy and heteronormativity in their reality programming. I have also attempted to not make moral judgments of HBO or its viewers. The most interesting thing about the profanity, violence, and sex that comes through HBO's "cocksucker, motherfucker, tits" brand philosophy is that they simply are. Are they not enough to make HBO "not TV?" If not, then what is "TV?" What are our expectations of the medium? What do we want from it? What do we get from it? Does HBO offer something different? I believe that it does. It may not be the things we brag about watching—or even things HBO brags about offering, but they are there. We can hear it, feel it, and see it almost every hour of every day on the HBO family of channels. Whether this is good or bad is not something upon which I wish to comment. I honestly don't care. I think it's fascinating enough that this conversation is taking place. In *Contingency, Irony, and Solidarity* (1989: xiv), Richard Rorty makes the following remarks about our contemporary moral compasses:

> This process to see other human beings as "one of us" rather than as a "them" is a matter of detailed description of what unfamiliar people are

like and of redescription of what we ourselves are like. This is not the task of theory but for genres such as ethnography, the journalist's report, the comic book, [and] the docudrama . . . The novel, the movie, and the TV program have, gradually but steadily, replaced the sermon and the treatise as the principle vehicles for moral change and progress.

With that having been said, I don't know how comfortable I am in giving Rorty the last word. Instead, I'll hand that privilege over to someone who truly deserves it, George Carlin (from *George Carlin: Again!*): "Thank you all and good night! I love you . . . and fuck you!"[17]

## Notes

1   I will, throughout this essay, varyingly refer to HBO as HBO, it, them, they, etc. Deborah Jamarillo (2002: 73–74, n.1) makes a complicated effort to consistently ascribe agency to the channel. I am less concerned with that here, as I am more interested in HBO's content on a largely phenomenological level.
2   Louis C.K., on the message board of his website, wrote that the reason for this was that "you can't laugh and jerk off at the same time."
3   Horace Newcomb (2007: 561) has presented one of the most sustained arguments that HBO is, in fact, just TV. I wish to counter his argument here by examining that its "content" and "style" is something that is indeed something that can be "distinguished from 'TV'." To offer an entirely tautological explanation of how HBO is different "because it's different," consider the fact that when TBS airs *Sex and the City*, Bravo shows *Six Feet Under*, or A&E rebroadcasts *The Sopranos*, each of the shows is "edited for time and *content*."
4   David Marc (1987: 348–349) and Philip Auslander (1992: 125–167) each provide an interesting comparison of stand-up comedy with more conceptual forms of performance art.
5   The specific decision of the case involved the Supreme Court upholding the FCC action with a 5:4 vote that the routine was "indecent but not obscene." For the entire text of the decision, see: http://www.eff.org/legal/cases/FCC_v_Pacifica/fcc_v_pacifica.decision.
6   Here Carlin is somewhat recapitulating phrasing from *Class Clown*'s original "Seven Words" bit: "I would like to substitute the word fuck for the word kill in all those movie clichés we grew up with. 'Okay Sheriff, we're gonna fuck ya now. But we're gonna fuck ya slow.' "
7   While HBO is probably most known for its coverage of boxing, it's worth mentioning that from 1975 to 1999 it covered Wimbledon annually—the coverage has since moved to sister network TNT, then on to ESPN2. During the mid-1970s, HBO also broadcast NBA and ABA games (perhaps most famously the last ABA Finals in 1976 between the New York Nets and Denver Nuggets). In 1977 the channel began airing *Inside the NFL*, which is the longest running program in the history of HBO. HBO and NFL films currently jointly produce *Hard Knocks*, a reality series that has, since 2001, followed a team through training camp as they prepare for the upcoming season. As of this writing, the Kansas City Chiefs are currently being profiled. Additionally, a World Wide Wrestling Federation championship between George "The Animal" Steele and Pedro Morales aired from Madison Square Garden in 1973. A blip on the radar of popular culture history, this recently appeared as part of the WWE 24/7 On Demand package. Finally, and

perhaps most important for the current discussion, HBO operates HBO PPV (formerly known as TVKO) which is the industry leader in broadcasting boxing matches through pay-per-view.

8 As Rose and Friedman (1998) point out, even though televised sport is uniquely a masculine experience of spectatorship, there is also an interpellation that occurs wherein the male spectator is distracted, both reflecting the ideological contradictions of masculine identity, while at once destabilizing the feminization of consumer culture.

9 HBO does have its limits. The hallmarks of the pornographic, erect penises, penetration, and visible ejaculation, etc., are all glaringly absent from HBO's version of "real" sex.

10 While this is really not the place for a discussion about how NC-17 films get much maligned within Hollywood (see, for example, Kirby Dick's wonderful documentary about the racism and heternormativity involved in *This Film is Not Yet Rated* [2006]), NC-17 rated films are not shown at multiplexes and not available at Blockbuster, Wal-Mart, or K-Mart. But, as Jon Lewis (2001: 26) illustrates, "such an industry policy has nothing to do with sex or morality or larger legal questions regarding censorship or obscenity. In Hollywood, or so the saying goes, 'when they say it's not about the money . . . it's about the money.' "

11 Additionally, the fact that the porn industry in the United States alone is a giant, organized, now nearly mainstream, industry with revenues of upwards of $11 billion annually, saying that sexually explicit media is taboo or transgressive may simply be untrue at this point.

12 Aside from the Broome and Ludlow building, at West 41$^{st}$ Street we find "The Artist," "The Housewife" on East 85$^{th}$, "The Meditator" on Prince, and "The Mortician" on West 72$^{nd}$.

13 David Rowe (1999: 126) argues that sports photography offers a key analogy to the money shot, essentially building from an earlier argument made by Toby Miller (1990).

14 Since HBO is almost entirely made up of transgressive content, for it to truly be transgressive regarding its own subscribers it would have to start to genuinely look more and more like regular TV.

15 The day I wrote this sentence in fact, Rebecca Traister and Laura Miller (2007), two critics for *Salon*, debated whether or not it was *The Sopranos* or *The Wire* that holds that honor. In any event, HBO wins. I wish to thank Guy McHendry for sharing the article with me.

16 Lotz (2004: 23) argued that the "post-network era refers primarily to changed institutional structure and industrial practice; however, these adjustments cannot be isolated from the industry's creative output: television texts." Yet, even though cable passed network TV in total numbers of viewers back in 2002, with television no longer being TV as we know it, the phrase post-network is becoming increasingly impotent. With the rise of YouTube, the iPhone, iTunes downloading of shows, DVDs, and On Demand services, television is increasingly less like television, existing in no singular time, place, or technology.

17 An extra special thank you (and fuck you) must go to Lehne Leverette, Guy McHendry, Josh Riggs, and Toby Miller for conversation and comments and to Brian Ott for his inestimable patience.

## Works cited

Andrejevic, M. (2004) *Reality TV: The Work of Being Watched*. Lanham: Rowman and Littlefield.

Andrejevic, M. (2007) *iSpy: Surveillance and Power in the Interactive Era*. Lexington: University of Kentucky Press.

Andrews, D.L. (1996) "The Fact(s) of Michael Jordan's Blackness: Excavating a Floating Racial Signifier", *Sociology of Sport Journal* 13: 125–158.

Arthurs, J. (2003) "*Sex and the City* and Consumer Culture: Remediating Postfeminist Drama", *Feminist Media Studies* 3 (1): 81–96.

Auslander, P. (1992) *Presence and Resistance: Postmodernism and Cultural Politics in Contemporary American Performance*. Ann Arbor: University of Michigan Press.

Baker, A. (1998) "A Left/Right Combination: Populism and Depression-Era Boxing Films", pp 161–174 in A. Baker & T. Boyd (eds) *Out of Bounds: Sports, Media, and the Politics of Identity*. Bloomington: Indiana University Press.

Barthes, R. (1975) *The Pleasure of the Text*, R. Miller (trans). New York: Hill and Wang.

Bataille, G. (1986) *Erotism: Death & Sensuality*, M. Dalwood (trans). San Francisco: City Lights.

Bataille, G. (1991) *The Accursed Share: An Essay on General Economy, Volume 1: Consumption*, R. Hurley (trans). New York: Zone.

Bataille, G. (1993) *The Accursed Share: An Essay on General Economy, Volume 2: The History of Eroticism and Volume 3: Sovereignty*, R. Hurley (trans). New York: Zone.

Beck, U. (2000) *The Brave New World of Work*. Cambridge: Polity.

Bianco, R. (June 21, 2002) "The 'Street' is Just a Waste of Time", *USA Today*. 7e.

Bogosian, E. (1992) "Introduction", pp vii–x in L. Bruce, *How to Talk Dirty and Influence People*. Chicago: Playboy.

Botting, F. & Wilson, S. (1998) "Introduction", pp 1–23 in F. Botting & S. Wilson (eds) *Bataille: A Critical Reader*. Oxford: Blackwell.

Boyle, R. & Haynes, R. (2000) *Power Play: Sport, the Media and Popular Culture*. Harlow: Longman.

Bruce, T. (2004) "Marking the Boundaries of the 'Normal' in Televised Sports: The Play-by-Play of Race", *Media, Culture, and Society* 26 (6): 861–879.

Bryant, J., Zillman, D., & Raney, A.A. (1998) "Violence and the Enjoyment of Media Sports", pp 252–256 in L. Wenner (ed.) *MediaSport*. London and New York: Routledge.

Burridge, K. (2002). *Blooming English: Observations on the Roots, Cultivation, and Hybrids of the English Language*. Sydney: ABC Books.

Butsch, R. (2003) "Ralph, Fred, Archie, and Homer: Why Television Keeps Re-creating the White Male Working-Class Buffoon", pp 575–585 in G. Dines & J.M. Humez (eds) *Gender, Race, and Class in the Media: A Text-Reader*. Thousand Oaks: Sage.

Caldwell, J. (1995) *Televisuality: Style, Crisis, and Authority in American Television*. New Brunswick: Rutgers University Press.

Cannon, H. & Yaprak, A. (2002) "Will the Real-World Citizen Please Stand Up! The Many Faces of Cosmopolitan Consumer Behavior", *Journal of International Marketing* 10 (4): 30–52.

Carlin, G. (2005) "Napalm, Silly Putty, and Human Nature", pp 188–202 in D.J Brown, *Conversations on the Edge of Apocalypse: Contemplating the Future with Noam Chomsky, George Carlin, Deepak Chopra, Rupert Sheldrake and Others*. New York: Palgrave MacMillan.

Collins, J. (1995). *Architectures of Excess: Cultural Life in the Information Age*. New York and London: Routledge.

Debord, G. (1977) *The Society of the Spectacle*, F. Perlman & J. Supak (trans). Detroit: Black and Red.

Epstein, L.J. (2001) *The Haunted Smile: The Story of Jewish Comedians in America*. New York: PublicAffairs.

Foucault, M. (1977) "A Preface to Transgression", pp 29–52 in D. Bouchard (ed.) *Language, Counter-Memory, Practice: Selected Essays and Interviews*, D. Bouchard & S. Simon (trans). Ithaca: Cornell University Press.

Freeman, M. (2000) *ESPN: The Uncensored History*. Dallas: Taylor Publishing.

Guttman, A. (1996) *The Erotic in Sports*. New York: Columbia University Press.

Hall, S. (1981) "Notes on Deconstructing the 'Popular' ", pp 227–240 in R. Samuels (ed.) *People's History and Socialist Theory*. London: Routledge and Kegan Paul.

Hebdige, D. (1979) *Subculture: The Meaning of Style*. London: Methuen.

Heiskanen, B. (2006) "On the Ground and Off: The Theoretical Practice of Professional Boxing", *European Journal of Cultural Studies* 9 (4): 481–496.

Heistand, M. (2006, November 10) "HBO Isn't in this Corner", *USA Today*. 3c.

Houck, D.W. (2006) "Sporting Bodies", pp 543–558 in A.A. Raney & J. Bryant (eds) *Handbook of Sports and Media*. Mahwah, NJ: Lawrence Erlbaum.

Hughes, M. (2005) *Buzzmarketing: Get People to Talk About Your Stuff*. New York: Portfolio.

Irigaray, L. (1985). *Speculum of the Other Woman*, G.C. Gill (trans). Ithaca: Cornell University Press.

Jamarillo, D.L. (2002) "The Family Racket: AOL Time Warner, HBO, *The Sopranos*, and the Construction of a Quality Brand", *Journal of Communication Inquiry* 26 (1): 59–75.

Jefferson, T. (1998) "Muscle, 'Hard Men' and 'Iron' Mike Tyson: Reflections on Desire, Anxiety and the Embodiment of Masculinity", *Body & Society* 4 (1): 77–98.

Jervis, J. (1999) *Transgressing the Modern: Explorations in the Western Experience of Otherness*. Oxford: Blackwell.

Kant, I. (1983) "Beanwortung der Frage, Was ist Aufklärung?", in *Kants gesammelte Schriften*, Berlin and New York: Walter De Gruyter. Vol. VIII. 35.

Lafrance, M. & Rail, G. (2001) "Excursions into Otherness: Understanding Dennis Rodman and the Limits of Subversive Agency", pp 36–50 in D.L. Andrews & S.J. Jackson (eds) *Sport Stars: The Cultural Politics of Sporting Celebrity*. New York: Routledge.

Lee, W. (July 9, 2001) "*KO Nation* Down for the Count", *Cable World*.

Levinson, P. (2002) "Naked Bodies, Three Showings a Week, and No Commercials: *The Sopranos* as a Nuts-and-Bolts Triumph of Non-Network TV", pp 26–31 in D. Lavery (ed.) *This Thing of Ours: Investigating The Sopranos*. New York: Columbia University Press.

Lewis, J. (2001) "Those Who Disagree Can Kiss Jack Valenti's Ass", pp 23–32 in J. Lewis (ed.) *The End of Cinema as We Know It: American Film in the Nineties*. New York: New York University Press.

Limon, J. (2000) *Stand-up Comedy in Theory, or Abjection in America*. Durham: Duke University Press.

Lockman, B. & Sarvey, D. (2005) *Pioneers of Cable Television*. Jefferson, NC: McFarland.

Lotz, A. (2004) "Textual (Im)Possibilities in the U.S. Post-Network Era: Negotiating Production and Promotion Processes on Lifetime's *Any Day Now*", *Critical Studies in Media Communication* 21 (1): 22–43.

Marc, D. (1987). "Beginning to Begin Again", in H. Newcomb (ed.) *Television: The Critical View, 4th edition*. New York: Oxford University Press.

Marsh, D. (1985). "It's Like That: Rock & Roll on the Home Front", in D. Marsh (ed.) *The First Rock & Roll Confidential Report*. New York: Pantheon.

McBride, J. (1985). *War, Battering, and Other Sports: The Gulf Between American Men and Women*. Atlantic Highlands, NJ: Humanities Press.

Metz, W. (2006, August 18) "Sitcom Aesthetics, Intertextuality, and Lucky Louie", *Flow*. http://flowtv.org/?p=23. Retrieved July 1, 2007.

Miller, T. (1990) "Sport, Media and Masculinity", in D. Rowe and G. Lawrence (eds) *Sport and Leisure: Trends in Australian Popular Culture*. Sydney: Harcourt Brace Jovanovich.

Miller, T. (1993) *The Well-Tempered Self: Citizenship, Culture, and the Postmodern Subject*. Baltimore: Johns Hopkins University Press.

Miller, T. (1998) *Technologies of Truth: Cultural Citizenship and the Popular Media*. Minneapolis: University of Minnesota Press.

Miller, T. (2001) *Sportsex*. Philadelphia: Temple University Press.

Miller, T. (2007) *Cultural Citizenship: Cosmopolitanism, Consumerism, and Television in the Neoliberal Age*. Philadelphia: Temple University Press.

Moran, A. (1998) *Copycat TV: Globalization, Program Formats, and Cultural Identity*. Luton: University of Luton Press.

Newcomb, H. (2007) " 'This is Not Al Dente': *The Sopranos* and the New Meaning of Television", pp 561–578 in H. Newcomb (ed.) *Television: The Critical View, 7th edition*. New York: Oxford University Press.

Ott, B.L. (2007) *The Small Screen: How Television Equips Us to Live in the Information Age*. Oxford: Blackwell.

Rorty, R. (1989) *Contingency, Irony, and Solidarity*. Cambridge: Cambridge University Press.

Rose, A. & Friedman, J. (1997) "Television Sports as Mas(s)culine Cults of Distraction" pp 1–15 in A. Baker & T. Boyd (eds) *Out of Bounds: Sports, Media, and the Politics of Identity*. Bloomington: Indiana University Press.

Rowe, D. (1999) *Sport, Culture and the Media*. Buckingham: Open University Press.

Sabo, D. & Jansen, S.C. (1994) "Seen But Not Heard: Images of Black Men in Sports Media", pp 150–160 in M.A. Messner & D. Sabo (eds) *Sex, Violence and Power in Sports: Rethinking Masculinity*. Freedom, CA: The Crossing Press.

Sabo, D. & Jansen, S.C. (1998). "Prometheus Unbound: Constructions of Masculinity in the Sports Media", pp 202–217 in L. Wenner (ed.) *MediaSport*. London and New York: Routledge.

Sabo, D., Jansen, S.C., Tate, D., Duncan, M.C., & Leggett, S. (1996) "Televising International Sport: Race, Ethnicity and National Bias", *Journal of Sport and Social Issues* 20: 7–21.

Schilling, C. (2005) *The Body in Culture, Technology and Society*. Thousand Oaks: Sage.

Sennett, R. (1998) *The Corrosion of Character*. New York: Norton.

Simmel, G. (1971) "Sociability", pp 127–140 in D.N. Levine (ed.) *Georg Simmel on Individuality and Social Forms*. Chicago: University of Chicago Press.

Sloop, J.M. (1997) "Mike Tyson and the Perils of Discursive Constraints: Boxing, Race, and the Assumption of Guilt", pp 102–112 in A. Baker & T. Boyd (eds) *Out of Bounds: Sports, Media, and the Politics of Identity*. Bloomington: Indiana University Press.

Sugden, J. (1997) *Boxing and Society*. Leicester: Leicester University Press.

Sugden, J. & Tomlinson, A. (1994) "Soccer Culture, National Identity, and the World Cup", in J. Sugden & A. Tomlinson (eds) *Hosts and Champions: Soccer Cultures, National Identities, and the USA World Cup*. Aldershot: Arena.

Traister, R. & Miller, L. (2007, September 15) "The Best TV Show of All Time", *Salon*, http://www.salon.com/ent/tv/feature/2007/09/15/best_show/. Retrieved September 15, 2007.

Van Tassel, J. (2001) *Digital TV Over Broadband: Harvesting Bandwidth*. Boston: Focal Press.

Wacquant, L. (1995) "Pugs at Work: Bodily Capital and Bodily Labour Among Professional Boxers", *Body & Society* 1 (1): 65–93.

Wacquant, L. (2000) *Corps et âme. Carnets ethnographiques d'un apprenti boxeur*. Marseilles and Montréal: Agone, Comeau & Nadeau.

Wacquant, L. (2004) *Body and Soul: Notebooks of an Apprentice Boxer*. New York: Oxford University Press.

Waisbord, S. (2004) "McTV: Global Trade in Television Formats", *Television and New Media* 5 (4): 359–383.

Wajnryb, R. (2005) *Expletive Deleted: A Good Look at Bad Language*. New York: Free Press.

Williams, L. (1989) *Hard Core: Power, Pleasure and the "Frenzy of the Visible."* Berkeley: University of California Press.

Wilson, B. (1997) " 'Good Blacks' and 'Bad Blacks': Media Constructions of African-American Athletes in Canadian Basketball", *International Review for the Sociology of Sport* 32: 177–189.

Wynn, N. (2003) "Deconstructing Tyson: The Black Boxer as American Icon", *International Journal of the History of Sport* 20 (3): 99–114.

Zillman, D. & Paulus, P.B. (1993) "Spectators: Reactions to Sporting Events and Effects on Athletic Performance", pp 600–619 in M. Murphey & L.K. Tennant (eds) *Handbook of Research on Sports and Psychology*. New York: MacMillan.

# Chapter 8

# Baltimore on *The Wire*

## The tragic moralism of David Simon

*Blake D. Ethridge*

Blue and red lights illuminate trails of blood on a street in Baltimore, sirens sound, a detective collects evidence, a uniformed officer fills out paperwork, a body lies in the street, and the first episode of David Simon's *The Wire* begins, as if it were just another iteration of the television police procedural or cop drama. If it was, it is likely that an hour later the audience would be entertained and satisfied. The police would have identified the evil criminals and brought them to some sort of justice, and, in so doing, they would have reassured viewers that theirs is a moral, just and legitimate society. Simon, however, takes audiences in a different direction. Simon's project is to make a moral appeal to his viewers showing the lives of many in Baltimore as tragically bound by the institutions in their lives. In so doing, he challenges both city leaders and their booster representation of the city as well as the foundational myths of American society. Simon's challenge, though, lacks a clear articulation of an affirmative social and political project.

The opening scene then cuts to the other side of the street. A span of asphalt separates the murder scene from Detective James "Jimmy" McNulty, who is talking with an unnamed friend of the murder victim, Omar Isaiah Betts, commonly known as Snot Boogie. McNulty learns that each and every Friday Snot Boogie would play in the alley craps game with the guys from the neighborhood, and, when there was a lot of money on the ground, he would steal it and run. Snot was usually caught and beaten for his crimes, but he must have sometimes escaped with the cash if he kept doing it. He had now done it for the last time. McNulty is tempted by the obvious question, "I gotta ask you, if every time Snot Boogie would grab the money and run away, why did you even let him in the game?" The answer coming back at him is simple, "You got to, this is America, man." The theme song and introductory credits begin to roll.

Surely, this is a place in America. It is a street, a sidewalk and a stoop near Fulton and Lexington streets in West Baltimore. This physical location is important. Locating *The Wire* in Baltimore gives the show particularity and character or, as locals might say, charm. Baltimore is a poor, second-tier city that has seen rough times since World War II. Deindustrialization, suburbanization, segregation and globalization have not been kind to the city. At least 40,000 buildings are now vacant, many abandoned as the population shrank to less than two-thirds of its peak. Also, crime and drugs have besieged the city, and the homicide rate is a constant problem. It is also a city with a long, fascinating history and a quirky, vital culture. Yet, stepping back a bit, Simon is as much interested in accurately and caringly depicting the character and difficulties of his city as he is in projecting a criticism of the ideas and myths of America. Baltimore is a part of America, but it is also separated from much of the country.

There is tragic irony in the declaration of Snot's friend. He depicts America as a place of inclusion. You cannot leave anyone out, even if you know that they might cause problems or even steal from you. Snot's friend earnestly means what he said, but McNulty, Simon and the audience are supposed to understand a deeper significance of his declaration. Snot and his friend are part of the urban underclass shunned by and segregated from the rest of the country. Simon, in an audio commentary track, explains that he thinks Snot's friend's response is a "wonderful metaphor for what is going on in the American city, that those who are excluded from the legitimate economy make their own world. And we're trying to depict the world that they've created upon being excluded from the rest of America." What makes this interaction even more poignant is that it actually happened.

Simon recounts Terry McLarney, a Baltimore Homicide Detective, telling the parable of Snot Boogie in his first book on Baltimore, *Homicide: A Year on the Killing Streets* (Simon, 2006: 562–563), which later became the television series *Homicide: Life on the Streets*. In fact, *The Wire* is Simon's fourth engagement with representing Baltimore and Baltimoreans. *Homicide*, his second engagement, was written about Baltimore homicide detectives and their work after Simon left his first engagement with Baltimore, covering the police beat for a major daily newspaper. *The Corner: A Year in the Life of an Inner-City Neighborhood*, his third project, portrayed the life of a family involved with drugs in Baltimore and the effects of the war on drugs (Simon & Burns, 1997). *The Corner* was written with Ed Burns, a former cop and teacher in Baltimore and now writer, producer and collaborator for *The Wire*. Simon and Burns's book *The Corner* was also adapted into a mini-series for HBO.

Simon's earlier projects have been widely celebrated, but *The Wire* is a maturation of his work. Simon has expanded from the limited environments and time periods of the first two projects to encompass the entire city, allowing him to take on more issues, themes and conflicts. Although the first season of *The Wire* dealt primarily with the drug trade and the police who battle it in

West Baltimore, each season has expanded to involve another part of the city, state, nation, and world, as well as issues of deindustrialization, jobs, gentrification, security, politics, corruption, schools, and economics. This accumulation is really what makes up a city, a plural set of neighborhoods, subcultures, institutions, individuals, and problems. They are all included.

Ostensibly, the title, *The Wire*, suggests that the show is about a wiretap case and electronic surveillance, which comes to be associated with quality police work targeted at serious criminals as opposed to the kids who actually sell drugs on the street corners. It is about that, but, Simon explains, it is also about division or exclusion:

> The title really refers to almost an imaginary but inviolate boundary between the two Americas, between the functional, post-industrial economy that is minting new millionaires every day and creating a viable environment for a portion of the country, and the other America that is being consigned to a permanent underclass, and this show is really about the vagaries and excesses of unencumbered capitalism and what that has wrought at the millennium and where the country is and where it is going, and it is suggestive that we are going to a much more divided and brutish place, and I think we are, and that really reflects the politics of the people making the show. It really is a show about the other America in a lot of ways, and so *The Wire* really does refer to almost a boundary or a fence or the idea of people walking on a high wire and falling to either side. It really is sort of a symbolic argument or symbolic of the argument we are trying to make. (Andelman, 2007)

*The Wire* has an argument, and Simon and the creative staff have a politics. The political position is composed of a frustration with the division between a wealthy America and the other America as well as with a two-part myth of America that enable this division to exist with little conflict. The myth is of the American dream and a related, humbler myth of bootstraps and hard work. The first myth is that anyone who makes a better product or innovates in some way will be able to make it rich. America is the land of opportunity and excess. The second myth, though, is the more important for Simon. It is that even if you are not the most innovative person, but you are willing to work hard, there is a place for you. According to this myth, if you are "willing to get up every day and work your ass off and be a citizen and come home and be committed to your family and every other institution you are asked to serve, then there is a portion for you" (Simon, 2004: 5–6). America is a place of inclusion. For Simon (2004: 6), though, it is important to be direct and clear about the status of this myth in America: "It is, in a word, a lie."

It is a lie because many Americans, many Baltimoreans, are no longer socially and economically marginalized. They are "excess Americans" who have been left behind. They make up the contemporary other America, and they populate the streets and homes and corners of Baltimore. They are:

> Ex-steelworkers and ex-longshoremen; street dealers and street addicts, and an army of young men hired to chase the dealers and addicts; whores and johns and men to run the whores and coerce the johns—and all of them unnecessary and apart from a new Millennium economy that long ago declared them irrelevant. (Simon, 2004: 7–8)

Thus, *The Wire* is as much a show about these people as it is about, "at the risk of boring viewers with the very notion, macroeconomics. And frankly, it is an angry show" (Simon, 2004: 8). What is to be done about globalization, poverty and the economic problems of the city is not directly articulated. What is important for Simon is the representation of the problem and the provocation of the audience. Unlike the entertaining and affirming morality play and cop drama, Simon wants his anger and the anger of the show to influence the audience. And he wants to do this in a particular way.

Simon does not want to tell people how to feel and insists that people should and will respond in their own manner. But, he does want to provoke them, to incite them to think hard about a story that he believes to matter and "ought to matter to other people" (Simon, 2007). The politics, then, of Simon and the creative staff is one frustrated and angry with an America that is leaving much of Baltimore behind and leaving its residents with little or no opportunity to build a stable life. His argument comes from how he tells his story and his chosen genre, a modernized and American version of Greek Tragedy.

Simon does not believe in whimsical or vengeful Olympian gods hanging over the city of Baltimore and playing with the insignificant lives of Baltimoreans, and he does not expect anyone else to. He does, though, see the late-modern institutions of the city and nation as similar to indifferent gods:

> *The Wire* is really constructed as Greek tragedy. . . . If you supplant the idea of those old Greek gods with post-modern institutions, with the police department, with the drug organization, with government, with the union, with the Catholic Church, with Enron, you start layering over the institutions that determine how individuals are going to be served by our severe society. Now you have some really indifferent gods. (Andelman, 2007)

The lives of many Baltimoreans are tragically bound for ruin by the fates created by these institutions. Simon, again in an audio commentary, notes that institutions strongly regulate the lives of people, and "regardless of what you are committed to whether you are a cop, a longshoreman, a drug dealer, a politician, a judge, a lawyer, you are ultimately compromised and must contend with whatever institution you have committed to." Like Antigone who is tragically caught between two powers, the will of the gods and the will of the state, Baltimoreans are similarly caught between institutions and suffer terrible consequences. Also, Simon equates traditionally opposed institutions such as the police departments and drug organizations in terms of how they nurture, then consume and destroy individuals. For example, the first season carefully tracks Detective Jimmy McNulty and mid-level drug dealer D'Angelo Barksdale through their conflicts with institutions to which they have sworn their allegiance.

In fact, D'Angelo Barksdale's story is a prime example of tragedy in *The Wire*. D'Angelo, or Dee, is a mid-level dealer for his family's drug organization. The season begins, after the parable of Snot Boogie and the credits, with the organization, and particularly second-in-command Stringer Bell, spending a considerable amount of money and effort to bribe and intimidate witnesses so that Dee can beat a murder charge and return to the family and the corner. D'Angelo is thankful and recommits to being a dealer and making his uncle, Avon Barksdale, proud. In the final episode, Dee finds himself again incarcerated and facing a major drug charge. He also believes he has been betrayed by his uncle. Because of this and the fact that he is never fully committed to the life of a drug dealer, he considers a proffer agreement that would put him in witness protection with a chance to start over in exchange for testifying against his uncle and other members of the drug organization.

Rhonda Pearlman, an assistant state Attorney, is handling the proffer agreement along with Detectives McNulty and Bunk Moreland. They keep placing gruesome homicide photos in front of D'Angelo and asking him what he knows about each murder. His court appointed attorney begins to flinch and is clearly wondering if she is defending some sort of a monster. Judgment hangs in the air, and Dee takes advantage of a pause to explain:

D'ANGELO BARKSDALE: Ya'll don't understand man. Ya'll don't get it. You grow up in this shit. My grandfather was Butch Stamford. Know who Butch Stamford was in this town? All my people, man, my father, my uncles, my cousins, it's just what we do. You just live, with this shit, until you can't breathe no more. I swear to God, I was courtside for eight months, and I was freer in jail than I was at home.

RHONDA PEARLMAN: What are you looking for?

D'ANGELO BARKSDALE: I want it to go away.

RHONDA PEARLMAN: I can't . . .

D'ANGELO BARKSDALE: I want what Wallace wanted. I want to start over. That is what I want. I don't care where, anywhere. I don't give a fuck. I just want to go somewhere, where I can breathe like regular folk. You give me that, and I'll give you them.

Wallace was a 16-year-old who worked for D'Angelo, but decided he wanted out of the game and wanted to go back to school. Alas, he ended up murdered and his homicide photo was one of those on the table in front of D'Angelo. D'Angelo is desperate and knows that he, like Wallace, will be destroyed by the game unless he makes a definite and final break by turning on and betraying everyone in his life, his family and friends.

Later in the episode, D'Angelo's mother, Brianna Barksdale, the sister of his uncle and a major player in the drug organization, comes to visit her son. She clearly understands that he has made some sort of deal. Brianna Barksdale is there to convince her son not to turn on her and the family:

BRIANNA BARKSDALE: So, they got you all the way out here, huh? . . . I started out thinking you was in Jersey. You ain't in Jersey. I figured they still got you down in Central Booking. But, all the way out here . . . Do send a message, though.

D'ANGELO BARKSDALE: Yeah, a message needs sending. How y'all even find me?

BRIANNA BARKSDALE: Ain't no one going to keep a mother from her son, right?

D'ANGELO BARKSDALE: You know, he's always talking family. "Family is the heart," he say. Well, I'm family . . . ain't I? What about me for once? It ain't right.

BRIANNA BARKSDALE: What's right? Hmmm? You like for him to step up, take all the weight, and let you walk? Because he will. You know he will. But if he got to go away . . . that mean you got to step up and fill his shoes. You ready for that?

D'ANGELO BARKSDALE: Ma, you know I ain't. I ain't ready, and I'm never gonna be ready for this game.

BRIANNA BARKSDALE: Dee, come on.

D'ANGELO BARKSDALE: Look. They giving me a chance to walk away . . . to start again someplace else.

BRIANNA BARKSDALE: And what you giving them? . . . Look. He messed up, Dee. He knows it. Now if you want to get even with him, you can. But if you hurt him, you hurt this whole family. All of us. Me and Trina and the cousins. And Donette, too. And your baby. Your own baby boy. This right here is part of the game, Dee. And without the game . . . this whole family would be down in the fucking Terrace living off scraps. Shit, we probably wouldn't even be a family. Start over? How the fuck you going to start over without your peoples? Without your own child, even? If you ain't got family in this world . . . what the hell you got?

D'Angelo is tragically caught between two institutions. His mother is right. He might gain some sort of freedom by working with the police and district attorney, but he would end up alone with nothing, not even his own son. D'Angelo will be destroyed, either by his family and their business or by the state that will destroy everything he cares about, and probably even take away his name, in giving him freedom. D'Angelo decides to remain with his family and go to jail for them. Later, in season two, he is killed on a contract issued by a suspicious Stringer Bell, the one who freed him at the beginning of the show.

Frank Sabotka is another tragic character. In his role as a local union leader, and in a desperate attempt to save the lives and jobs of his fellow stevedores, he gets involved with smuggling drugs, prostitutes, and other unknown materials. He does this in order to acquire the money necessary to retain a lobbyist and thus a voice in the realm of politics in the state capital. His hope is that his purchased voice will lead to public projects that will make the harbor of Baltimore a more attractive port for ships. Primarily he needs an expensive project, the dredging of the C & D Canal, to be approved. This would result in more work and jobs for his union and other dockworkers, and would help to stabilize his community and way of life. His belief is that without such plans, Baltimore will change more and more into a city for people other than himself, his family, and his community. He fears gentrification and the slow death of his community due to unemployment or underemployment. Yet, Sabotka is a moral man and becomes overwhelmed by the complexity of these arrangements, which are brought to a head by the asphyxiation of several prostitutes, due to a crushed vent, in a container he helped to smuggle. His tie to this criminal element also leads to the self-destruction of his son. When Sabotka tries to get out of this situation and agrees to testify for the police, the smugglers discover his agreement and kill him.

Frank Sabotka has little choice. If he did nothing, his way of life, work and community along with the future of his son and nephew would slowly die. His only way of gaining the economic and political power to fight this decline was by getting involved with criminal activity. This activity leads to the ruin of his local, his son, and himself. No matter what he did, Frank Sabotka was fated for destruction.

Howard "Bunny" Colvin, the major in command of the Western District of the Baltimore Police Department, is never tragically bound to the degree of

D'Angelo Barksdale or Frank Sabotka, but he does endure several inescapable binds in his attempts to serve and improve the city. In the third season, he is stuck between bosses who want him to reduce violent crime in his district and the belief that the only way to do this would be to reduce the violence of the drug trade. So, Colvin attempts to reduce crime by quietly calling off the enduring and, what he believes to be ineffectual, war on drugs in the Western District. In so doing, he reduces violent crime as he was commanded, but he enrages his superiors, the mayor, press and even federal government officials. As punishment he is demoted to lieutenant before his immediate retirement, and his superiors make sure he loses his comfortable retirement job working security for Johns Hopkins University.

No longer a major and in need of work, Colvin takes a job as director of security for a downtown hotel. He quickly finds himself in another difficult situation. A john has beaten a prostitute in a hotel suite. He wants to arrest the john, but the hotel manager stops him because this particular john is a representative of a national consortium of convention planners. To arrest him would be to sour him and potentially his consortium on Baltimore as a convention site. He takes the cuffs off of the john and leaves the suite. Simon and writer Richard Price are not so subtly critiquing Baltimore's relationship with tourism and conventions. Ultimately, Colvin finds himself working with disruptive and violent kids in a Baltimore middle school. Along with a professor from the University of Maryland and others, they create a pilot program for these kids that focuses on social skills and tries to find a way in which they can learn in the school environment. They are having success, but the program is cancelled because of politics and administrators who do not understand what the program might accomplish.

Colvin is a tragic reformer. He tries to work within the system of the police department and the schools, but his potential improvements are repeatedly destroyed because, although they might solve a problem, they become problematic for the particular institutions. Toleration or legalization of drugs might free police to attend to other crimes and the community, but it runs the risk of appearing to actually condone drugs. This is politically dangerous for those in charge. The police commissioner and deputy of operations have to cover up Colvin's experiment, and the mayor is left to repeatedly apologize to the federal officials who threaten to withdraw federal funds if the city ever attempts another such project. Similarly, school administrators fear that a special program that spends substantial time on socialization of troubled students looks too much like tracking, which equates to having different standards for different students. Having different standards for different students then equates with leaving some students behind. Exasperated, Colvin declares to Mayor Tommy Carcetti's Chief of Staff, "As it is, we're leaving them all behind.

We just don't admit it." His plea, though, falls on deaf ears, and the program is cancelled. The criticism here is that effective and pragmatic reform is stifled because it might represent institutions unfavorably to people who make political judgments on abstract ideals as opposed to truly understanding the problems at hand.

The scene of Carcetti's office canceling Colvin's school program at the end of season four demonstrates how Carcetti is also a tragic reformer. It shows how in the space of a year he has become what he criticizes. As a young, passionate City Councilman in season three, Carcetti is tired of the city's decline, stagnation and despair. He makes a spontaneous speech in a committee meeting that is reviewing Colvin's decision not to fight the war on drugs in West Baltimore. At this moment, Carcetti launches his public run to become mayor of the city, to take control and really make a change:

> We can forgive Major Colvin who out of his frustration and despair found himself condoning something, which can't possibly be condoned. We can do that much. But, gentlemen, what we can't forgive, what I can't forgive, ever, is how we . . . you, me, this administration, all of us, how we turned away from those streets in West Baltimore, the poor, the sick, the swollen underclass of our city trapped in the wreckage of neighborhoods which were once so prized, communities, which we've failed to defend, which we have surrendered to the horrors of the drug trade, and if this disaster demands anything of us as a city, it demands that we say "enough." Enough to the despair that even makes policemen think about surrender. Enough to the fact that these neighborhoods are not saved, or beyond the saving. Enough to this administration's indecisiveness and lethargy, to the garbage that goes uncollected, the lots and row houses which stay vacant, the addicts who go untreated, the working men and women who every day are denied a chance at economic freedom. Enough to the crime, which every day chokes more and more of the life from our city. And the thing of it is, if we don't take responsibility and step up, not just for the mistakes and the miscues, but whether or not we are going to win this battle for our streets, if that doesn't happen, we're going to lose these neighborhoods and ultimately this city, forever, if we don't have the courage and the conviction to fight this war the way it should be fought, the way it needs to be fought, using every weapon we can possibly muster, if that doesn't happen, well, then we are staring at defeat. And that defeat cannot and should not and will not be forgiven.

The tragedy of Carcetti is that even when he wins and becomes the mayor he has little power over institutions. He becomes besieged by crises and financial problems, as well as by his own ambition for higher office, which condition him to be a functionary of the institutions he criticizes in his impassioned speech. Aside from the final part, which might mean escalating the war on drugs, Carcetti's speech about having had enough with indecision and stagnation and failure rearticulates the politics of Simon and the creative staff of *The Wire*. The tragedy is that even if Simon or one of the creative staff were mayor it is likely that they would be similarly bound. This is why the medium of television and HBO become the critical space of affect and argument. Simon rejects the morality play of other cop dramas, but he asserts a moral and political argument of his own in *The Wire*. If the audience accepts his portrayal of Baltimore and America as accurate and just as real for D'Angelo Barksdale and Frank Sabotka as it is for a significant portion of the population in Baltimore, then viewers have to realize that the American myth is, in fact, a lie. They are then left with four options. One, they can do nothing, eschewing the dilemma of tragic urban poverty with indifference. Two, they can do nothing and accept a utilitarian logic that declares that these institutions overall create the greatest happiness for the greatest number in America. Simon and the creative staff would not agree with either. The third option would be to reject the institutions that have led to and perpetuate these tragedies. Simon does not articulate what might replace these institutions or how they could be radically altered.

A fourth response would be to stigmatize Simon and *The Wire* as a threat to the city of Baltimore, and particularly to its economic health and prosperity. Martin O'Malley, then mayor of Baltimore and now Maryland's governor, declared that "along with *The Corner*, [*The Wire*] has branded us in the national and metropolitan eye in a way that is very counterproductive to growth, hope, violent-crime reduction, and recovery" (Alvarez, 2004: 229). Landor Associates, a marketing firm contracted by the city in November of 2005, has identified the "harmful characterizations" of *The Wire* as one of the greatest threats to Baltimore's "upward momentum" (Landor, 2005). After the airing of the first season, 13 of the 15 members of the Baltimore City Council introduced a resolution condemning Simon's work. The resolution, titled "Let's Not Just Imagine a Better Image for Baltimore," quotes five major newspaper commentaries of *The Wire* describing each as "vying to outdo the other in gritty depictions of a crime ridden hell-hole and in clever expressions of chagrin at Baltimore's fate as the patsy for blood and guts storytellers" (Baltimore City Council, 2002: lines 18–20). The resolution also cites one travel publication's rosy description of Baltimore and concludes that, "It is imperative to the economic, social, and spiritual well-being of our hometown that the city 'gleaming with new-found optimism' is the picture that remains in the hearts and minds of residents of, and visitors to, Baltimore City" (Baltimore City Council, 2002: lines 22–24). Officially, Simon and *The Wire* are a threat to the city.

One is tempted to see this conflict as the age-old story of the city boosters versus the muckraking journalist. In many ways it is. Yet, there is more to this story. In the early twenty-first century this conflict is more intense, as there is more at stake. In order to understand this intensification, one must recognize the admixture of several changes cities have faced in the postwar era. First, the economic bases of second-tier cities like Baltimore have shifted more and more from industry, manufacturing and shipping to tourism, leisure and culture. Second, cities are now, more than ever, controlled by the external forces of the federal government, mobile capital, and mobile residents rather than by their internal politics. Third, the changing geography of cities due to suburbanization, highways, transportation technology, and demographic shifts have intensified the fragmentation of urban space and ghettoization of poverty and social challenges. Fourth, drugs have exacerbated the problems of urban America. Fifth, arguments and sentiments against economic redistribution and government social services have gained increasing salience in government and politics, and this has resulted in movements to reduce or eliminate social welfare programs and restrain government from creating new programs to address social problems.

City leaders function in this context. Their dominant approach has been a neoliberal economic development model with a utilitarian logic. This basically means that particular interests, needs or wants of residents must be ignored in favor of the needs of the export industry of the city. It is this export industry that will bring additional wealth to the city. It is then thought that the rising tide in the harbor of Baltimore will lift all boats. Although shipping and manufacturing are still essential to the city, the export "industry" on the rise and of increasing significance is that of culture, leisure and tourism. This economy functions differently than the import of materials, refinement of those materials or manufacturing of new goods, and the export of finished products with an increased value. Instead, what is sent out is an image made up of slogans, brochures, and representations of the city as a desirable place for a conference, visit or vacation. The business or personal tourist is then drawn to the city to consume the leisure services and leave their money in the city. The two keys to this economy are the marketing or branding of the city as a destination and the invention and reinvention of the city as a destination. Once the basic infrastructure of urban industry was a good transportation network, adequate labor, and basic services like water and electricity, policing and schools. Now, the basic infrastructure of the economy is its branding as a tourist destination, the branding that brings jobs and revenue to the city.

This is the logic that allows Mayor O'Malley to declare *The Corner* and *The Wire* not only counterproductive to growth and recovery but also to hope and violent crime reduction. The idea is that the representation of troubled institutions and crime and drugs and other social problems scares people. Potential tourists as well as potential and current residents do not want to be wrapped up in or victims of these problems. Officials and boosters then try to shift the public focus. By representing the city as reborn, as a renaissance city, with new life, culture and opportunities for leisure, more tourists will then be attracted to the city, more residents will stay, more will come and employers will be more likely to locate in the city. This helps address recovery and violent crime reduction by increasing revenues for the city. This revenue can then be used to fund policing, education, social work and other programs that improve the condition of the city. Thus, it is in the interest of reducing violence, crime, drugs and poverty that these phenomena should not be publicized.

Viewers of *The Wire*, along with Baltimoreans and Baltimore's leaders are then left in a bind. They might go along with O'Malley and other boosters in obscuring social problems to try to grow the economy of the city. Alternatively, they might side with Simon and hope that enough people are sympathetic to the moral appeal of his tragic argument. Such viewers would then become so wary of, and angry at, American myths and institutions that they would enact or demand some sort of change. *The Wire* might also stimulate viewers to recognize that individuals compose these institutions and put pressure on individuals who perpetuate institutional problems. The problem with this moral appeal made in an entertainment television medium is that it lacks an articulation of an affirmative political project. Viewers are then just as likely to be inoculated from working to change the circumstances of the tragic characters of *The Wire*. They might also be so convinced by the bounded character of life in much of Baltimore that they decide that there is nothing to be done. This form of political and cultural agitation can lead to the support of established institutions just as much as traditional police procedurals. This is because the brief exposure with problems might agitate viewers, get them angry about something that matters, as Simon might say, but then give them no direction in using their agitation for action.

The above criticism, though, places too much responsibility on Simon, and the creative staff of *The Wire*, to both agitate for change as well as to also direct that agitation. What is needed then is not to embrace the economic booster representation of the city that would work only to confirm Simon's thesis that the people of Baltimore are excluded and unnecessary or even detrimental to the recovery of the city. It is also not to rely entirely on *The Wire* to agitate for change and direct it. Simon's work may build sentiments that would support ending the war on drugs, but it has to be joined by thoughtful arguments, articulated by others, about what that would look like and how the epidemic of drugs would be dealt with. Simon's work must be joined by additional engagements with the problems of Baltimore and affirmative articulations of political and social projects capable of transforming the tragic conditions of the city.

## Works cited

Alvarez, R. (ed.) (2004) *The Wire: Truth be Told*. New York: Pocket Books.

Andelman, B. (2007) "Fridays with Mr. Media: The David Simon/*The Wire* Interview", *The Mr. Media Interviews*. St. Petersburg, FL.

Baltimore, C.C. (2002) "Let's Not Just Imagine a Better Image for Baltimore", City Council Bill 02–0917.

Landor, A. (2005, November 7) "Presentation to the City Council of Baltimore".

Simon, D. (2004) "Introduction", in R. Alvarez (ed.) *The Wire: Truth be Told*. New York: Pocket Books.

Simon, D. (2006) *Homicide: A Year on the Killing Streets*. New York: Henry Holt and Company.

Simon, D. (2007) "On the Wire: A Night with David Simon", Urban Spaces, Urban Voices: The 2007 Humanities Symposium. Loyola College in Maryland. Baltimore.

Simon, D. & Burns, E. (1997) *The Corner: A Year in the Life of an Inner-City Neighborhood*. New York: Broadway Books.

# Part III

# Audiences and identity

# Introduction: The not TV audience

*Cara Louise Buckley*

The audience in Shakespeare's time was a stridently segregated group. The strategic separation of Elizabethan audiences was based upon class, with the upper-class patrons of The Rose theater adorning the balconies, seated in their ornate dress. A sharp contrast were the poorer audience members standing on the bare floor in front of the stage—both their positioning and dress denoting their place. And while it may seem that the lower-class patrons were unusually honored with the best seats in the house, this actually increased the societal perception of lowliness—theater, and particularly the work of Shakespeare, was seen as an entertainment venue for the peasants, a low-minded frivolity meant to evoke the basest of emotions. Therefore, those who engaged fully from the ground level—laughing, crying, shouting, stamping their feet— betrayed their inferiority when juxtaposed with the removed (both emotionally and physically) and composed upper-level patrons. There remains today a sense of a binding, even branding, relationship between audiences and their choice of pop cultural "poison." And while our perceptions of the work of Shakespeare in terms of its place within culture may have changed since that time period, the complexity of the relationship between audiences and their popular culture has only increased since the advent of the televisual audience.

Theoretical examinations of television audiences have been continuously mutating and evolving, moving scholarly conceptions of viewers from that of a mass both easily swayed and barely participatory, to more current understandings of a people engaged in "an area of cultural struggle" (Ang, 1996: 20). This notion of struggle not only raises the intensity of participation on the part of the viewer, but also increases the significance of critical examinations of audiences. In particular, the HBO audiences possess a unique placement both within the popular and (perhaps only perceptually) somewhere outside of it in the nebulous realm known as "quality television." Therefore, their cultural struggle can tender unique perspectives, positionings, and offerings, which are examined by the essays in this section. The relationship between

HBO television and its audiences is a complicated one and addressing issues such as loyalty/betrayal, voice, and identity often play as important a role in its maintenance/success as they do in interpersonal relationships.

The first essay of this section, Conor McGrath's "*K Street*: 'Raping HBO' or 'What HBO is All About'," examines this complex relationship between HBO television and its audiences, utilizing a form of voice that has permanently altered the communication between the two: the web forum. In responding to what was to become the member of a rare classification on HBO, the failed show, audiences took to the forum provided by the network to voice their frustration, pleasure, and even concerns regarding *K Street* and what effects it could have on HBO's legacy. In exploring the nature of audience members' interaction with each other as well as the show's creators/producers, McGrath illuminates the sense of ownership audiences can come to have over not just a show, but also a network/brand.

Beyond merely the privilege of ownership felt by audiences toward their televisual counterparts, this relationship often extends into the personal and emotional realm, as Rhiannon Bury explores with, "Praise You Like I Should: Cyberfans and *Six Feet Under*." Again turning to the web forum as the primary form of voice for television audiences in the postmodern culture, Bury utilizes the influential work of F.R. Leavis on the distinctions of taste and culture in opposition to the self-positioning that occurs on the *Six Feet Under* forum. The self-positioning addressed speaks to the effect the televisual experience has upon identity formation—particularly in regard to the HBO viewer as the "quality" TV viewer—and the sharply protective attitudes of the audience toward the identities offered by not just particular shows but the HBO network overall.

Whereas Bury examines the outward expression of identity on the part of HBO viewers, Cara Buckley and Brian Ott seek the possible offerings of identity and identity management *within* programming in their essay, "Fashion(able/ing) Selves: Consumption, Identity, and *Sex & the City*." In particular, they take up the paradoxical and often frustrating consum(ing/er) self that pervades postmodern culture and explore the popular, even beloved, character of Carrie Bradshaw in *Sex & the City* who both models postmodern identity— specifically through the realm of queerness—and furnishes actual cultural resources for enacting postmodern identity through her consumption of fashion. Buckley and Ott look at the dependence between audiences and programming, arguing that in watching Carrie perform a queer sense of self through her fashionable attire and choices, viewers observe and acquire symbolic equipment for fashioning selves of their own.

Audiences, members of a televisual culture, are also members of a larger culture, one that, while largely reproduced in the programming with which they align themselves, can also be at odds with that very programming. Joanna Di Mattia takes on this contrast and the role that new kinds of visibility can have on the identity of audiences in her essay, " 'No Country for the Infirm': Angels in an Unchanged America." Moving from the postmodern/queer identity explored in the previous chapter, Di Mattia engages the queer body and asks what place exists for images of the queer body and representations of sexual pleasure and practice in visibility debates. It explores *Angels in America*'s unique place in the public domain as a text that negotiates these paradoxes and posits the sexual corpus as a positive site of queer difference and political power as well as the uniqueness required of a network for this type of programming to air.

These essays take on the audiences that HBO has worked long and hard to not only gain but also shape. For a network built on the notion of standing apart, an audience that perceives itself as conforming would never do. Unlike the dominant culture of Elizabethan England, HBO does not want its "quality" patrons sitting idly by as consumers of their programming, working instead to court those most raucous and vociferous in their viewership and, most importantly, loyalty.

## Works cited

Ang, I. (1996) *Living Room Wars: Rethinking Media Audiences for a Postmodern World*. New York: Routledge.

# Chapter 9

# K Street

## "Raping HBO" or "What HBO is All About?"

### Conor McGrath

In its fall 2003 season, HBO ran a 10-part series, *K Street*, on the world of Washington lobbying and political consultancy. It attracted relatively small audience figures, and plans for a further series were shelved.[1] The program's supporters claimed that *K Street* was: "as close to the truth of politics as anyone gets" (Taubin, 2003: n.p.); "the most stylistically innovative series to air on American TV since HBO's 'The Larry Sanders Show' or maybe ABC's 'Twin Peaks' . . . It represents an evolutionary advance in TV drama" (Seitz, 2003: n.p.); and "a shrewd, experimental, mind-bending TV drama" (Rosenthal, 2003: 39). For its critics, though, *K Street* represented an interesting experiment, but: "does not make for especially good TV" (Genauer, 2003a: 21); "the fact-and-faux style can be problematic as well as innovative" (Abramson, 2003: 8); and "while *K Street* may not constitute anything that Peter Jennings would call 'news', it does share one key quality with it: sometimes—especially when real politicians are in it—it's boring" (Hagan, 2003: 1).

This chapter examines the nature of *K Street*'s innovation, primarily through an analysis of comments made by viewers on the program's forums on the official *K Street* section of the HBO website. Each week, viewers were invited to post their thoughts about the last episode, and other forums related to the show's cast, questions for the producers, its production technique, and so on. While these forums are no longer accessible on the HBO website, I printed them out at the time and draw extensively upon them in this chapter to chart the reaction of viewers to this program.[2] It has been suggested that, "In the discussion around fandom, the authentic voices of fans themselves are rarely heard" (Harris, 1998: 5). This chapter seeks to redress that imbalance a little, rather than to theorize about the sociological significance of fans as other academics have done extensively.

Most academic accounts of "fandom" relate to more or less independent groups of fans operating entirely amongst themselves, and most of the classic academic work relates to offline fan communities (Tulloch, 2000). This chapter looks at something slightly different—an online community of fans (and some critics) brought together specifically by the show's producers. The online forums were an element of HBO's official *K Street* site, though it should be noted that there was no evidence that HBO were in any way censoring or moderating the postings made. Baym (2000: 3) suggests that both fan groups generally and online groups particularly, "have been better discussed and theorized than documented." This chapter seeks to document how *K Street* viewers interacted with the program and with each other. In particular, it assesses what the postings reveal about the nature of the relationship between viewers and HBO.

Comments made on the *K Street* forums were hugely varied, as the title of this chapter suggests. One viewer wrote that, "this show alone is raping hbo of the special place that it had on television" (F/GC, posting 277). Another suggested that, "This show is a fascinating mess—interesting, layered, but a frigging mess" (F/GC, posting 301). Others, however, were wildly enthusiastic about the program: "Try to remember that is what HBO is all about, making your entertainment different from the networks. . . . bring this show back for a second season . . . The public gave you (HBO) that chance and look what happened" (F/FW10, posting 4). Similarly: "It is very refreshing to find HBO once again taking risks and stretching the medium further than anyone ever imagined" (F/FPP, posting 16). Interestingly, though, both supporters and critics of the series appear to share a clear identification with the HBO style and brand, and in consequence have very particular expectations of what a HBO series should deliver for them.

## *K Street* on screen and online

Without question, *K Street* was technically innovative. Its executive producers —including actor George Clooney and Oscar-winning Steven Soderburgh (whose previous movies included *Sex, Lies and Videotape*, *Traffic*, and *Erin Brockovich*)—conceived a program which fused politics and entertainment in ways not previously tried. Work on each episode began on Monday mornings, with the episode being transmitted that Sunday evening. Issues were taken from current political events, and a rough storyline would be developed. Fragments of dialogue would be written at the Monday meetings, but each episode was largely unscripted and improvised (Borger, 2003; Frey, 2003; McConnell, 2003; Taubin, 2004). The intention was not to produce a documentary showing how laws are made and how congressional committee hearings are organized (essentially, the stuff of C-SPAN), but rather to go behind the formal processes and reveal something about the nature of politics. As James Carville put it, "I envision a show about power: building power, applying power. There will be a lot of conniving going on" (quoted in McConnell, 2003: 18).

Behind the scenes *K Street* was staffed by people who mixed entertainment and political experience. The show's co-producer, Stuart Stevens, worked as a Republican media consultant and had been a writer for network TV programs, including *Northern Exposure*. A consulting producer, Jon Macks, had worked as a speechwriter for elected officials, before becoming a writer for Jay Leno's *Tonight Show*. Another consulting producer, Michael Deaver, spent over 20 years as one of Ronald Reagan's closest advisers, after which he became one of the most prominent lobbyists in Washington. Mark Sennet, an executive producer, who had worked at Merv Griffin Entertainment and Columbia Pictures Television, previously collaborated with Deaver on *The Reagans: A Love Story*.

The program was set around a political consultancy called Bergstrom Lowell, staffed by a mixture of actors and real-life political figures (including the husband-and-wife team of James Carville [Bill Clinton's campaign manager in the 1992 election] and Mary Matalin [George H.W. Bush's deputy campaign manager in 1992 and more recently an assistant to President George W. Bush and counselor to Vice President Cheney]). For readers not already familiar with *K Street*, a brief summary of the series may be useful (although the episodes unfolded in a much less linear way than this précis suggests). While Carville and Matalin are the partners at Bergstrom Lowell, the firm is financed by a mysterious New Yorker named Bergstrom. The firm's original—fictional—assistants are Maggie Morris (a lesbian who is somewhat obsessed with a lover) and Tommy Flanagan (who, while married, uses pornography and prostitutes, and is haunted by a shadowy "Woman in Red"). In the first episode Francisco Dupré is also hired by the firm (he had been recommended by Bergstrom).[3]

Among the issues that the firm addresses at some point are the Democratic presidential primary debates, the downloading of music from the Internet, energy policy, and the California gubernatorial recall election. The firm is asked to represent a new client, The Council for Mid-East Progress. It eventually emerges that this Saudi Arabian-funded group is under investigation by the FBI into whether it has channeled money to terrorists. The FBI and Department of Justice begin to focus their attention on the firm, setting the characters against each other and paralyzing its work.[4] It appeared that the enigmatic Bergstrom may have intentionally caused the firm to take on the client knowing that it was under investigation; but the show never made it clear why he would do this. Finally, the firm collapses, and Carville and Matalin close it and sell the office furniture.

While the show was originally promoted by HBO as being about lobbying, in fact relatively little lobbying is evident in the series. One viewer, noting

Michael Deaver's involvement with the program, wrote that: "I think it's interesting that Deaver is the only one of the cast who has actually worked as a lobbyist. The others have done public relations, campaigning but I don't think they've actually lobbied the Hill, have they?" (F/CMD, posting 1). Deaver himself said that, "I think they [the firm's members] do a lot of things. They do some advocacy on the Hill. They do media work and crisis management and image work. They will sort of be the ultimate generic D.C. consulting firm" (quoted in Frey, 2003: C03).

Actual politicians played cameo roles as themselves—among them Howard Dean, Senator Chuck Hagel, and Hillary Clinton—as did other Washington insiders like lobbyist Jack Quinn, former White House Press Secretary Joe Lockhart, and commentators Joe Klein and William Kristol. For these people, a guest appearance on *K Street* meant not just some social cachet among their peers but a rare chance to highlight a pet issue on a prime-time entertainment show (Lee, 2003). The blurring of fictional characters and actual political insiders was made even more profound by the fact that the people playing themselves were not always identified clearly (sometimes, not named at all in the program's dialogue), although they were usually listed on the *K Street* episode guides on its website (Seitz, 2003). Some viewers asked for these figures to be identified by an on-screen caption when they first appeared:

> It would help a lot if the producers would use fonts to ID the "real" people in the show, as opposed to the actors. I am not talking about Carville and Matalin, of course, but people like John Breaux from Week 6. His dad is a senator from Louisiana, but I did not know who Jr was until I read it here. (F/FW7, posting 6)

From the beginning, this blurring of fact and fiction was interesting, even if occasionally unsettling (Allen-Mills, 2003). For instance, during a debate among candidates for the Democratic presidential nomination on September 9, 2003, Howard Dean asserted that if he was seen as weak on racial issues simply because Vermont had a mostly white population, then the logical conclusion would be that, "Trent Lott would be Martin Luther King." The line went down well at the debate, and got good media coverage (Kurtz, 2003). Less amusingly, though, when the first episode of *K Street* aired on September 14, viewers saw that Dean had been given this line by James Carville in a scene where Carville is prepping Dean before the debate took place—not only was *K Street* portraying politics, it was participating in politics (Hagan, 2003; Rosenthal, 2003; Stanley, 2003).

Visually too, the show was often confusing—shot with handheld cameras, often from a distance with a zoom lens and often in a real location (like the street or a restaurant) that was too noisy to allow viewers to properly hear the dialogue; using no makeup or special lighting; and with no second takes (Taubin, 2004). James Carville has said that acting in *K Street* involved, "No lines, no memory, no nothing. No makeup, no lighting. It's completely different than anything that's ever been done before. We don't reshoot anything" (quoted in Darman, 2003: n.p.). As one reviewer put it, "Think *Curb Your Enthusiasm: The Washington Years*" (Shister, 2003: E08). The effect was intended to give the show an insider edge, to make the viewer feel that he or she was eavesdropping on events rather than watching a scripted and slickly produced program; essentially to use *cinema verité* techniques to make a TV show (Seitz, 2003). Not all viewers found these techniques attractive or effective: " 'Blair Witch' on Capitol Hill. Sheesh . . . I've seen first time student documentaries that looked better" (F/PTF, posting 2).

Moreover, *K Street* was an unusual TV series in the sense that it tended more to have individual episodes with some flashback and some reference to events seen in past episodes, rather than presenting a single continuing narrative across the series. This did make it difficult to follow and somewhat disjointed—one viewer wrote: "I have no idea what is happening, and I love the show. . . . I just watched the season finale, and I can say that I don't know no more than a fool" (F/CJC, posting 51). The extent to which even those who were participating in the online forums (presumably those viewers most interested and involved in the show) could be confused by the plotlines is evident in a number of postings about the ninth episode. One viewer asked:

> Can someone please confirm for me if the woman that Tom Flannegan slept with in last night's episode who ended up in the bathroom whacked out on some type of prescription drugs is the same woman that Tom's father proposed to before asking his son for $10,000. (F/FW9, posting 11)

The responses indicated that others were equally confused: "It looked like it was his father's bride to be" (F/FW9, posting 12); "I thought that she was his father's wife. When dad asked Tommy for the money, he mentioned something like, '. . . I'm paying your mother's mortgage, I've got a new wife . . blah blah blah'." (F/FW9, posting 13); "Yes, it was his fathers wife . . . Or were they really married?" (F/FW9, posting 14).

It's hard to imagine another TV series not making relationships like these between the characters more explicit, but one of the defining features of *K Street* as a television program was its refusal to give viewers any detailed background to the characters whose relationships with each other had to be surmised as plots unfolded. Another viewer wrote after the initial episode: "This show leaves you the distinct impression that you missed a main plot line—even though you know that a) it is the first show and b) that you started watching it from the very beginning" (F/GC, posting 127). As one journalist has asserted: "K Street presented the viewer with a jigsaw puzzle structure where each piece had to be examined from all angles in order to find its relationship to the others" (Taubin, 2004: n.p.).

On the *K Street* section of its website, HBO included a number of features, such as summaries of each episode, information about the cast and crew and those making guest appearances, polls which allowed viewers to express their opinion about a particular question, and so on.[5] This website was highly informative—as one viewer put it: "I find a lot of the extra material mentioned on this website very helpful. Too helpful, in fact—it makes me wonder why the show is not easier to follow on its own" (F/GC, posting 301). Another wrote that,

> I still feel like I am missing a lot of information while watching the show. Wanting to know more, I looked up the HBO K Street web site. It does wonders for clarification of uncertain points in the show itself. . . . Please tell us Producers of K Street is this intentional new form of viewing, where the internet is a vital, perhaps even essential? Was the Internet interaction or more specifically, the web site, looked at as an integral partner in the development and/or enjoyment of this show? (F/GKSP, posting 177)

While the *K Street* website seems to me to have been a useful supplement to the show, it was by no means essential to it, to anything like the same extent as the site for a British series, *Attachments*, which ran in 2000: in that case, the website functioned as an extension of the program with clips of unscreened footage, additional dialogue and emails between the fictional characters, and emails/ postings from the characters to viewers (Brooker, 2003). Similarly, a 2007 BBC drama series set around the lives of young lobbyists and political researchers, *Party Animals*, used a section called "Village Vermin" on its website where characters and fans could interact and chat.

This chapter focuses on the online forums that were created by HBO as a way of enabling viewers to post comments and questions. These forums were categorized as: feedback on each episode; each cast member; production techniques; general comments about the series; and questions for the producers. The online forums were not wholly successful, in the sense that while viewers were able to interact with each other, there was no discussion between fans and the program's producers. Occasionally, people would appear frustrated by the fact that no response to comments was ever posted by those making *K Street*. On the forum dedicated to George Clooney, one viewer wrote:

I hope that you and Steven are reading some of these postings. People are talking to both of you and if you had any sense you would post some-thing. . . . Feed them a bone, anything just so they know you really do care and appreciate the time and effort they have put into this project on both of your behalves. (F/CGC, posting 34)

Another viewer noted, "the Producers' absent participation on THEIR desig-nated corner of this Board" (F/QKSP, posting 198).

## Fandom: TV programs, viewers, and interactivity

We are all consumers of the media and popular culture. Fans, though, tend to focus on a particular person or thing to a greater extent than most. One scholar suggests that fans "attend to media texts, icons, stars, or sports teams in greater than usual detail . . . Fans use intertextual cues, such as previous story lines and their understandings of the world, to help construct the meaning of their favorite text" (MacDonald, 1998: 135). Fans are identified entirely based upon their shared interest in a particular celebrity, TV show, singer, sports team, and so on. They produce and share fanzines, talk to each other on the phone, attend conventions, and so on. Clearly, these avenues remain open to fans, but the development of the Internet has given fans virtually unlimited opportunities to interact with each other, with literally tens of thousands of websites devoted to particular movies, TV shows and performers. The Internet has changed fandom in another sense—not only is it easier for fans to com-municate with each other, but they can do so in real time. Hills (2002: 178) notes that, "fans now go online to discuss new episodes immediately after the episode's transmission time—or even during ad-breaks—perhaps in order to demonstrate the 'timeliness' and responsiveness of their devotion."

Fans have often complicated relationships with producers. It has been sug-gested that television fandom has its origins in efforts (usually unsuccessful) by fans banding together in order to influence networks and producers not to cancel TV shows—or, as Bird (2002) and MacDonald (1998) suggest, to pres-sure producers to make follow-up movies even after a TV series has been cancelled, as was the case with *Dr. Quinn Medicine Woman*. According to one scholar, "Many have traced the emergence of an organized media fan culture to late 1960s efforts to pressure NBC into returning *Star Trek* to the air" (Jenkins, 1992: 28). Another notes letter-writing campaigns by fans which played some part in ensuring the survival of *Cagney & Lacey*, *Hill Street Blues* and *St. Elsewhere*, and argues that these fans were fundamentally "challenging the very structure of the industry and the 'prevailing taste' the networks claim is revealed by the ratings. [They] argued instead that their programs *should* be continued because of a 'quality' that admittedly only a minority seemed to prefer" (Brower, 1992: 168). More recently, HBO agreed to produce two final two-hour specials of *Deadwood* following a month-long online campaign by fans who called for a "Cancel HBO Day" when it was announced that the show would be dropped after its third season (Bird 2006); similarly, CBS ordered seven new episodes of *Jericho* and promised to continue the show beyond that if ratings improved, in response to the fan-based Nuts For Jericho campaign (one of the show's characters had said "nuts" to a demand to surrender in the first-season finale, prompting fans to send 50,000 pounds of peanuts to CBS executives) (Associated Press, 2007).

From the point of view of the culture industry, fans constitute "an additional market that . . . provides valuable free feedback on market trends and preferences" (Fiske, 1992: 47). And clearly, online forums such as were set up for *K Street* viewers are a relatively cheap means by which HBO could access this sort of feedback or market intelligence. The fragmentation of the television audience and breakdown of the major networks' near-monopoly of that audience—a process which HBO has played its part in—have in addition led the makers of TV series to think in terms of niche rather than mass audiences: as one writer puts it, "From 1990 onwards, a number of television series have been produced and marketed precisely in order to attract particular microcultures and to foster within them not just regular viewers but also a high proportion of fans" (Gwenllian Jones, 2003: 166). It is certainly at least arguable that *K Street* was conceived of as being likely to attract a particular "microculture"—the political junkie.

## Politainment: The fusing of political fact and fiction

While there have always been occasional works of fiction (novels, movies, TV shows, songs, and so on) that have dealt with political issues or institutions, the last decade has seen a much more concerted trend in this direction. Clearly, the most successful and long-lasting marriage between fiction and politics has been *The West Wing*, but other television programs have been set in Congress (such as *Mister Sterling* and *Charlie Lawrence*) and we saw a female President in *Commander In Chief*. Movies based around politics have included *The American President*, *Dave*, *Absolute Power*, and many others. Politicians now court guest appearances on talk shows in order to demonstrate their winning personalities, and much of the content of cable news networks and talk radio shows is explicitly political. As Abraham Genauer (2003b: 37) has written, the entertainment industry has consciously created a new form of programming which, "seeks to portray government and politics in a believable way that can entertain everyone, not just those with an advanced degree in public policy"—this he terms "politainment."

Some people noted that this blend of fact and fiction had been used to good effect on previous programs—one viewer wrote that, "I loved Larry Sanders and Arli$$, other HBO shows that used actual celebrities as themselves, both giving a similar reality-based look at their respective industries" (F/GC, posting 51). Certainly, one of the loose inspirations for K Street was Tanner '88 (co-produced for HBO by cartoonist Garry Trudeau and Robert Altman) in which a fictional presidential candidate's campaign was backlit by the actual election taking place then—but technological advances allowed K Street to go even further in allowing their characters to interact with real politicians in real time.[6]

However, the concept was by no means universally acclaimed. One journalist suggested that: "Instead of blurring lines between fiction and reality, 'K Street' sharpens them, making us so aware of the manipulations and setups and improvised moments that we can't remotely get involved in the drama" (Havrilesky, 2003: n.p.). Conversely, another reason why some criticized the program was that by its blurring of reality and fiction, it threatened to deepen popular distrust and cynicism about politics and politicians by appearing to make politicians seem even more scripted and more removed from reality.

## K Street forums and political debate

Technology now permits fans (often in their millions) to actually participate and intervene in TV programmes such as Big Brother and Pop Idol. And many see a connection between the development of interactive shows such as these and the democratic process. In her analysis of the similarities between fan communities and political constituencies, van Zoonen (2004: 49) concludes that, "the representation of politics on television, generically entertaining, may be seen as inviting the affective intelligence that is vital to keep political involvement and activity going." Some viewers clearly saw K Street as having the potential to stimulate and invigorate wider political involvement:

> This is a dangerous show. There is a nice blend between fiction and reality challenging the viewer to be aware. To be aware of current events, and be aware of their representatives' opinions on those issues. With any luck, this show will shake the cloak of apathy off of this country and inspire the people to participate in their government. (F/GC, posting 195)

One regular criticism made of K Street, with some foundation, was that several episodes were based around real and current public policy issues, but that these policies were not adequately introduced or explained. As one viewer expressed it: "Unless you come armed ahead of time with a grasp of the issues, this will only serve to further confuse or worse, give someone erroneous perceptions of the truth" (F/GC, posting 249). The second episode of K Street dealt with the issue of music file sharing: the firm prepares a pitch to the Recording Industry Association of America (RIAA) on how record companies could fight against consumers copying CDs and downloading songs from the Internet. Quite a number of viewers found this episode unsatisfactory in its treatment of the issue. One viewer, for instance wrote that it, "fell disappointingly short of fairly representing both sides of the issues . . . we were clearly delivered the pro RIAA perspective, but the anti-RIAA perspective was weak and uninspired. There was very little if any mention of . . . the more obvious counter-points" (F/GC, postings 227). Others said that, "the whole show seemed like a primer on the RIAA position" (F/GC, posting 243), and "I'm terrified that the 'consultants' in the show are depicted having such pedantic opinions, and are successful in selling them. Did you see any character with an original thought on the RIAA/filesharing issue?" (F/GC, posting 206). Before K Street had even aired, there were suggestions that guest appearances by real politicians could be construed as a way in which HBO's parent company, AOL Time Warner, could ingratiate itself with policymakers as media consolidation was being debated (McConnell, 2003). This was picked up on by a viewer thus:

> You guys just lost me with this one. You don't even have the balls to take on your own vested interest. HBO is a division of Warner Brothers, one of the Big 5 record companies . . . basically 20% of the RIAA's financial backing. So we should think you guys are "controversial" and "edgy" for basically licking the hand that feeds you? This stupid show turned into a goddamn lobbying effort of its own in less than 2 weeks. (F/FW2, posting 22)

Not only did viewers respond to the particular issues presented in K Street episodes, they additionally made suggestions as to other issues that could feature in future shows—such as, "the proliferation of DU (deleted uranium) weapons and the government's/pentagon's active denial of their environmental and personal impact" (F/GC, posting 259); the Washington DC statehood movement (F/GC, posting 183); the use of electronic touchscreen voting machines (F/CGC, posting 11); and the political involvement by the pharmaceutical industry (F/GC, posting 366).

## *K Street* and HBO: Viewer perceptions

There were a number of viewers who strongly felt that *K Street* was not up to usual HBO standards. Comments posted regarding the tenth and final episode included: "Hopefully HBO will not waste anymore of anyone's time with another stupid series like this" (F/FW10, posting 50); and

> Sunday night at our house: The kids are bathed and put to bed early. The wife and I settle into our couch and pop the cork on a bottle of wine. The familiar HBO (static then tone) alerts us that our favorite night, and only night to watch together is about to start. Then comes K Street. Sorry— I've started surfing other networks. HBO you broke my heart. (F/FW10, posting 52)

Another viewer—one of the most prolific posters of messages as well as one of those most critical of *K Street*—suggested that HBO was doing the country a disservice:

> mixing "the fake" with real politics in an age when the American people are spun, manipulated, and generally messed with enough already, is just WRONG. It's as if somehow, HBO forgot the power of the medium. . . . There is simply too much at stake right now in the REAL WORLD to be this careless with distinguishing between reality and fiction. (F/GC, posting 139)

Others were hugely enthusiastic about the show, to the point where they positively welcomed the fact that it was confusing:

> I ALSO don't think the show needs to be made simpler. That would mean making it a little like TV, and you know, "it's not TV" people, "it's HBO"! There's plenty of that predictable, I could write the next episode my damn self, television out there for anyone who wants it. Isn't it liberating to not really know what the f—is going on sometimes? I think it's narratively and cinematically edgy because it assumes that we can follow something that ISN'T so linear and spoon fed, because we ARE intelligent, and engage and watch the news and read the paper, and we have a context to draw from. (F/FW3, posting 13)

Another wrote: "Enjoy how the story keeps you slightly off balance—the fact that you don't know for sure what is going on, keeps me interested" (F/GC, posting 337).

Some viewers used the online forums to call on HBO to commission a second series: "Bring K-Street back so it can tie up loose ends . . . to provide those storylines and clear up unfinished business. HBO give them that second chance. Sometimes that's all it takes. After all you got a second chance" (F/FW10, posting 40); and "Bravo HBO! Keep up the great work. This kind of cutting edge programming is exactly why we pay for our subscriptions" (F/GC, posting 343). Another wrote:

> This show has been a fantastic experience, and I couldn't be happier with HBO for taking a chance on it. I think HBO produces shows that will keep their subscribers supplied with the edgiest shows on TV and they have done that. I consider "K Street" an unmitigated success. (F/CJC, posting 50)

In truth, though, the show's ratings were relatively low, and in the end it was probably not a difficult decision to axe *K Street* after one series; the first episode was reported as being watched by less than half of the HBO audience drawn by *Sex and the City* (Rich, 2003). One viewer wrote: "thank you HBO for bringing us the smartest show on television. I was distressed to hear ratings are not so great and there is talk of canceling??? Say it isn't so!!!!" (F/CJC, posting 47). However, the audience figures for *K Street* were generally between two and three million each week, similar to the ratings for *The Larry Sanders Show* but well below the six to ten million viewers of *The Sopranos* or *Six Feet Under* (Seitz, 2003).[7]

Some viewers noted that the *K Street* online forums were generating substantially fewer postings than those for other programs: "Wow, I just realized only 12 messages had been posted about week four's episode. The producers have to know they're in trouble if they can't get more feedback than this!!" (F/FW4, posting 13); "As you can all tell by just the sheer lack of participation in this forum, nobody really gives a shit about this show. . . . A whole season, and not even averaging 100 posts per show. That really sucks" (F/GC, posting 349); and "I was surprised to find that there are not too many postings on this site, and almost all seem self-congratulating and uninspiring, at least when compared to the vast quantity, sophistication and variety of postings at HBO's Carnivale site" (F/FW10, posting 18). There were only 1,109 postings in total to the *K Street* forums during a three-month period in 2003; compare this with 32,253 postings to a Usenet soap opera newsgroup (which admittedly covered 11 programs) in a 10-month period in 1992 when Internet usage was substantially lower than in 2003 (Baym, 2000). And, while there was some evidence of a sense of community displayed between the *K Street* fans (in that people would respond to each other's messages and banter or joke with each other), this was limited. One *K Street* fan suggested that people should share their email addresses so that they could communicate directly with each other—"We all need to change emails so we can discuss the show after they take this board down" (F/FW10, posting 13)—but the suggestion was ignored by the rest of the viewers. This is not, though, inconsistent with the theory that the, "nature of the ties which bind an online fan community is different from that of the ties which bind other genres of cyber communities. Fans are less 'bound' to each other and more tied to the object of their fanaticism" (Bird, 2002: 36). Thus, it may be that *K Street* viewers were interested in communicating with each other only while the series was airing.

## Conclusion

I have argued elsewhere that, "Lobbyists will find it difficult to enhance their public standing or reputation—and the electorate will continue to hold gross biases about [them]—until novelists and screenplay writers begin to present more realistic and rounded lobbyists in their literary works" (McGrath, 2003: n.p.). Ironically (given what we now know about his business practices) a similar view was expressed by the lobbyist, Jack Abramoff, who told a journalist that if the show's makers, "are able to accurately show the thousands of professionals who abide by a strict code of ethics and treat Congress and the administration with respect, then [*K Street*] would positively influence America's perception of lobbyists" (quoted in Genauer, 2003a: 21). Actually, although much of the early press comment on the show was based (presumably) on HBO publicity to the effect that it would be illuminating the world of DC lobbying, there was not much lobbying evident in the series, leading many journalists to criticize it for not offering an accurate portrayal of lobbyists (Genauer, 2003a; Jones, 2003).

That *K Street* blended fact and fiction in an innovative way is undeniable, but it is clear that the program makers faced a constant challenge to deal with real issues through an entertainment medium. James Carville told one journalist that:

> I think that to like this show you would have to have some interest in public policy. And it's a kind of—for lack of a better word—for television, it's kind of artsy, it's kind of a subtle form. You know, it's not a sitcom or something. They don't try to hit you over the head with something. (quoted in Darman, 2003: n.p.)

Ultimately the show struggled to both present complex public policy debates and engage viewers' interest in the personal lives of the characters—as one person asked: "Is K Street a new fangled soap or a backdoor to useful information? I'm hoping for the Trojan Horse" (F/GC, posting 269). Some viewers wanted a more "hard core" approach to the issues—for instance:

> Please explain how storylines regarding a mildly staking lesbian and kinky sex in Vegas add to anyone's understanding of the business of lobbying. Marginal views into the characters' personal lives add some depth and sympathy, but the show is too short and stylized to not focus on the primary subject matter. (F/QKSP, posting 204)

Others felt that the program had to fit the issues around a more entertaining and engrossing mode of character development: "The back stories of the fictional characters had better liven up this show pretty soon or we are looking at that rare failure (Mind of the Married Man ring any bells?) of an HBO series" (F/GC, posting 258). Certainly, it was not until the sixth episode that many viewers thought the show was getting the balance right between fact and fiction:

> This was the best one yet. Tommy's propensity to stray from his marriage was elaborated upon. The young associates bicurious tendencies were explored. And enough politics and back room action to feed my need for political curiousity. . . . Enough content to keep me interested, enough questions left unresolved to keep me watching. (F/FW6, posting 1)

Another viewer agreed: "The show has finally reached a point of cohesion: balancing fiction and non-fiction, mystery, insight—essentially what it aspired to be in its initial trailer. Keep 'em coming!" (F/FW6, posting 3).

Writing following an advance screening party of the first episode, Howard Kurtz (2003, n.p.) asked whether viewers would really be very interested in a show that featured the workings of a Washington firm: "It wouldn't be 'Sex and the City', unless some lobbyists start taking off their clothes, but could it be 'Curb Your Enthusiasm'?" Kurtz suspected that it had the potential to become a popular show, given the success of The West Wing. In reality, though, it seems that K Street was unable to convert interest in the show among political junkies into a broader and more general viewing public. One viewer (who described themselves as a lobbyist) stated that, "If this ain't flying inside the Beltway, I can only imagine how it is being received outside of it" (F/GC, posting 167).

Even though K Street was not conspicuously successful in commercial terms—and even, arguably, in an artistic sense—it can still tell us something useful about HBO. To begin with, *K Street* unquestionably represented at least an attempt to meet HBO's vision of itself: it was innovative and creative, it was not a traditional network program, and it certainly made demands of the audience in ways which more mainstream shows do not. One thing which was clear from the online forums was that viewers have a strong sense of what sort of programming they expect from HBO; some felt that *K Street* delivered that, others felt that it did not match up to other HBO series. But there was certainly a general identification with HBO itself, and a decided sense that HBO had a particular style and image. Critics of the show were forceful: "K Street has NO RIGHT to be on the air, let alone on HBO. Sunday nights used to be strictly HBO night. K Street has put an end to that" (F/GC, posting 271); and "Given HBO's past performance on their Original Series, I am surprised that this show is even on their lineup" (F/GC, posting 285). Others disagreed robustly. As one viewer wrote:

> HBO is consistently featuring progressive original programming that pushes the boundaries of what's acceptable (and controversial) within our culture. It's exciting. In fact, I believe it's presently the only television worth watching. Overall, kudos to HBO and the entire team at K Street for giving me one of the most delightful half-hours of my week. (F/GC, posting 94)

Another praised the show by differentiating it from the offerings of other media outlets—"Kudosm . . . for continuing to provide programming that goes beyond the generic, formulaic, inane, mindless programming of the networks . . . Getting America to think beyond Fox News teasers and USA Today headlines is an ambitious undertaking" (F/GC, posting 274).

Great television shows generally require credible characters, well-scripted dialogue and compelling storylines—while *K Street* may have been able to substitute a sense of backstage realism for good scripts, it failed in its narrative structure (and perhaps was impeded by being only half an hour long rather than an hour long each episode) to deliver plots and characterization sufficiently comprehensible and accessible to attract a substantial audience. And when particular episodes did portray the workings of the firm and the characters' interactions with each other, often it was at the expense of any attention being paid to policy issues and the real world of Washington politics. Perhaps too much was being attempted at the same time in this television experiment, and in consequence too little was done successfully. As James Carville said, "the other thing about this TV series is, it is to a TV series what an anchovy is to food. You either like it or you don't" (quoted in Darman, 2003: n.p.). In the end, relatively few viewers seemed to like this version of a television anchovy.

That, too, tells us something about the relationship between HBO and its subscribers: while the channel is justifiably proud of being "not TV," it does still have commercial limits. Writing after HBO had announced that it would commission two additional specials of *Deadwood* to tie up the series' loose ends coherently, a journalist noted that:

> Viewer lobbying groups sprang up almost overnight when it was revealed that the third season would be the last. Unlike ad-supported TV, HBO is dependent on the feel-good vibe that its subscribers are getting something special. It likely behooved the network to reach some "Deadwood" finale deal rather than lose that "not TV" charm. (Bird, 2006: n.p.)

Thousands of *Deadwood* fans had protested the abrupt ending of that series; only a few hundred fans participated in the postings on the *K Street* online forums, not all of whom by any means enjoyed or supported the program. Even for a channel as jealously protective of its brand perception and reputation as HBO, numbers do count in the end. It could afford to dent its "not TV" charm for a relatively small band of *K Street* enthusiasts much more easily precisely because it was only a small band. In that respect at least, HBO shows itself as not being entirely devoid of the commercial considerations that characterize the larger networks.

## Notes

1   For those wishing to see *K Street* now, HBO released a two-disc DVD of the complete series in 2004.
2   For the sake of brevity and readability within the text, I have abbreviated the names of those forums from which quotes are taken as follows:

F/CGC Forums/Crew: George Clooney
F/CJC Forums/Cast: James Carville
F/CMD Forums/Cast: Michael Deaver
F/FPP Forums/Feedback Pre-Premiere
F/FW2 Forums/Feedback Week 2
F/FW3 Forums/Feedback Week 3
F/FW4 Forums/Feedback Week 4
F/FW6 Forums/Feedback Week 6
F/FW7 Forums/Feedback Week 7
F/FW9 Forums/Feedback Week 9
F/FW10 Forums/Feedback Week 10
F/GC Forums/General Comments
F/PTF Forums/Production: Technique and Format
F/QKSP Forums/Questions for K Street Producers

It should be noted that in quotes from forums, I have retained the original spelling and grammar, even where they included errors.

3    Bergstrom was played by Elliot Gould, Maggie Morris by Mary McCormack, Tommy Flannegan by John Slattery, and Francisco Dupré by Roger G. Smith.
4    Curiously, at the same time as the show was being aired, Mary Matalin was actually reported to be under investigation by the Department of Justice in a probe to discover the source of a leak that unmasked the identity of a CIA agent.
5    While the comments posted to the online forums have been taken down, much of the rest of the *K Street* website content could still be accessed at www.hbo.com/kstreet at the time of writing.
6    For those interested in "politainment," other productions worth viewing as comparisons with *K Street* include: Haskell Wexler's *Medium Cool*, which has a fictional story set against the backdrop of the 1968 Democratic convention in Chicago; Robert Redford's *The Candidate*, which presaged Ronald Reagan's election campaign eight years later; and *The War Room*, by D.A. Pennebaker and Chris Hegedus, which looked backstage at the 1992 Bill Clinton campaign (and which introduced viewers to the real-life romance between James Carville and Mary Matalin).
7    While HBO initially commissioned 10 episodes, those involved in the program had hoped that the series would prove popular enough that it would continue beyond 2003 to at least the presidential election the following year, and had apparently signed an 18-month lease on an office suite in Washington (Abramson, 2003; McConnell, 2003; White, 2003).

## Works cited

Abramson, J. (2003, August 24) "Hyperreality TV: Political Fact Meets HBO Fiction", *New York Times*. 2: 1, 8.

Allen-Mills, T. (2003, September 21) "Candid-Camera Clooney Dishes Washington Dirt", *Sunday Times* 1: 29.

Associated Press (2007, June 11) "Fan Protests Prompt CBS to Save 'Jericho' ", www.msnbc.msn.com/id/19078238/. Retrieved July 1, 2007.

Baym, N.K. (2000) *Tune In, Log On: Soaps, Fandom, and Online Community*. Thousand Oaks: Sage.

Bird, C.M. (2002) "Phenomenological Realities or 'Quinntown': Life in a Cyber Community", *Journal of American Culture* 25 (1–2): 32–37.

Bird, R. (2006, June 6) "HBO Bows to 'Deadwood' Fans", *Cincinnati Post* www.redorbit.com/news/technology/530270/hbo_bows_to_deadwood_fans/index.html. Retrieved July 1, 2007.

Borger, J. (2003, October 2) "George's Washington", *Guardian* 6.

Brooker, W. (2003) "Conclusion: Overflow and Audience", in W. Brooker & D. Jermyn, (eds) *The Audience Studies Reader*. London: Routledge.

Brower, S. (1992) "Fans as Tastemakers: Viewers for Quality Television", in L.A. Lewis (ed.) *The Adoring Audience: Fan Culture and Popular Media*. London: Routledge.

Darman, J. (2003, October 3) "Washington's Hollywood Moment", *Newsweek* Web Exclusive. www.msnbc.msn.com/id/3129932. Retrieved May 11, 2006.

Fiske, J. (1992) "The Cultural Economy of Fandom", in L.A. Lewis (ed.) *The Adoring Audience: Fan Culture and Popular Media*. London: Routledge.

Frey, J. (2003, September 13) "Hollywood Cues the Capital: On 'K Street', Real Washington Meets Reality Television", *Washington Post* C01.

Genauer, A. (2003a, September 16) "K St. Meets Hollywood: Part-Documentary Debut Fails For Many D.C. Insiders", *The Hill* 21.

Genauer, A. (2003b, September 17) "Washington, D.C., is Ready for its Closeup: Politics-Hollywood Trend Popping Up More Frequently", *The Hill* 37.

Gwenllian Jones, S. (2003) "Web Wars: Resistance, Online Fandom and Studio Censorship", in M. Jancovich, & J. Lyons (eds) *Quality Popular Television: Cult TV, the Industry and Fans*. London: British Film Institute.

Hagan, J. (2003, September 29) "On HBO's K Street, News, Moviemaking Are All Mixed Up", *New York Observer* 1.

Harris, C. (1998) "Introduction. Theorizing Fandom: Fans, Subculture and Identity", in C. Harris & A. Alexander (eds) *Theorizing Fandom: Fans, Subculture and Identity*. Cresskill: Hampton Press.

Havrilesky, H. (2003, September 15) "Instant 'K Street' Cred", *Salon*. www.salon.comy/ent/tv/review/2003/09/15/k_street. Retrieved May 11, 2006.

Hills, M. (2002) *Fan Cultures*. London: Routledge.

Jenkins, H. (1992) *Textual Poachers: Television Fans and Participatory Culture*. New York: Routledge.

Jones, M.L.F. (2003, September 15) "OK Street: HBO's *K Street* Has a Promising Concept But Still Needs Work", *The American Prospect Online*. www.prospect.org/webfeatures/2003/09/jones-m-09–15.html. Retrieved May 14, 2006.

Kurtz, H. (2003, September 15) "Beltway Hall of Mirrors", *Washington Post* Web Exclusive. www.washingtonpost.com/wp-dyn/articles/A12360–2003Sep15.html. Retrieved May 11, 2006.

Lee, J. (2003, October 5) "Good Morning, Senator! You Rocked on 'K Street' ", *New York Times* 9: 1.

MacDonald, A. (1998) "Uncertain Utopia: Science Fiction Media Fandom & Computer Mediated Communication", in C. Harris & A. Alexander (eds) *Theorizing Fandom: Fans, Subculture and Identity*. Cresskill: Hampton Press.

McConnell, B. (2003, September 8) "Hollywood Goes to Washington: HBO is Mixing Real-Life Politicos and Actors in Series about a Lobbying Firm", *Broadcasting & Cable* 18.

McGrath, C. (2003) "More Spinned Against Than Spinning? Representations of Political Lobbyists in Fiction", paper presented at the annual conference of the UK Political Studies Association, Leicester. www.psa.ac.uk/journals/pdf/5/2003/Conor%20Macgrath.pdf. Retrieved May 12, 2006.

Rich, F. (2003, September 28) "Travels With George and Carville", *New York Times* 2:1.

Rosenthal, P. (2003, September 16) "Political Reality, Fiction Intersect on 'K Street' ", *Chicago Sun-Times* 39.

Seitz, M.Z. (2003, November 16) "The Most Innovative Show You've Never Seen", *New Jersey Star-Ledger* 16 November. www.nj.com/printer/printer.ssf/base/entertainment-0/106899666388100.xml. Retrieved November 22, 2003.

Shister, G. (2003, October 1) "Matalin: 'K Street' Like a Campaign Minus the Paranoia", *Philadelphia Inquirer* E08.

Stanley, A. (2003, September 14) "Inside Washington Politics, Turned Inside Out", *New York Times*. Late Edition—Final 1: 40.

Taubin, A. (2003, November 3) "Quoted on HBO's *K Street* site", www.hbo.com/kstreet. Retrieved May 16, 2006.

Taubin, A. (2004) "K Street: Washington Inside-Out", *Film Comment* Online Exclusive. www.filmlinc.com/fcm/online/kstreet.htm. Retrieved May 15, 2006.

Tulloch, J. (2000) *Watching Television Audiences: Cultural Theories and Methods*. London: Arnold Publishers.

Van Zoonen, L. (2004) "Imagining the Fan Democracy", *European Journal of Communication* 19 (1): 39–52.

White, S. (2003, September 8) "It's Not a 'Real' K Street Office Building Lease; It's HBO", *Washington Business Journal*. www.washington.bizjournals.com/washington/stories/2003/09/08/newscolumn7.html. Retrieved May 16, 2006.

# Chapter 10

# Praise you like I should

## Cyberfans and *Six Feet Under*

*Rhiannon Bury*

From the airing of the pilot in 2001 to the series finale in 2005, *Six Feet Under* (SFU) received almost universal critical acclaim. When the first season was finally shown on regular cable in Canada in 2003, the summer television critic for the Canadian national newspaper, *The Globe and Mail*, provided a brief plot synopsis of that first episode for the viewers who had "somehow missed the oodles of press surrounding this show" and urged them to follow the lead of other critics and viewers and watch it for its originality (Dawson-March, 2003: R2). Two years later, the regular *Globe* critic began his review of the series finale as follows: "In the annals of American television, SFU will always stand apart. Certainly it will stand beside *The Sopranos* as an example of HBO's enormous impact on American TV drama at the turn of the twenty-first century" (Doyle, 2005: R29). He went on to describe "Everyone's Waiting" as "immensely smart and elegiac. It is a fitting conclusion to what has been a magnificent fifth season for the drama. The final three episodes stand with anything produced in Hollywood in the past few years as a statement about the contemporary American quest for happiness, stability and optimism." Similarly, fans such as the three quoted below who posted to HBO's fan forum for SFU echo the critics in their praise of the series:[1]

> This is truly one of the most thought provoking shows on TV. I began watching this a few years ago and have loved every episode! . . . I could go on for days about how each character has a depth to them and how spectacular the writing and so forth is but if you are here you already know that!. . . . I love anything that challenges me to think beyond and look deeper into the meaning of life. (HBO01)

> The writing and acting on this show is so taut and sharp that there is not one word, action or even silence that is unnecessary or gratuitous. It really is extraordinary. I don't know how people survive without HBO. (HBO02)

This show, like The Sopranos, is still so heads & tails above the usual crap on TV that I'd watch repeats of the shows I just saw two days earlier than most of what is on network TV. (HBO03)

At its broadest, this chapter sets out to destabilize the category of the "quality" television text and the interpretative practices that surround it. Given that a sizeable portion of television's *oral culture* (Fiske, 1987) has migrated online in the past 10 years (Bury, 2005) and that the network-administrated discussion boards have replaced the Usenet newsgroups as the point of entry into online media fandom in the past five, the HBO board was the logical site to yield a rich set of data on such practices. The SFU discussion forum is a multi-topic board accessed through a link from the SFU home page. It includes general discussion about the show, the characters and the actors as well as individual episodes. Topic areas for the latter were typically set up right after the airing of a new episode and fans could continue to post messages until the next season aired. I examined the messages posted to the episode topic areas for Seasons Four and Five, both of which were locked and archived by HBO in February 2006. I typically studied the first week of postings after the original broadcast date from June 2004 to August 2005, comprising several thousand messages. Based on my analysis, I argue that fans, commonly perceived as mindless consumers of mass culture, make a clear distinction between quality popular texts such as *Six Feet Under* and the usual network "crap," as one participant bluntly put it. In doing so, they mobilize a powerful discourse of modernist literary criticism learned in school. At the same time, they mobilize a populist discourse of personal response, emotional attachment and admiration associated with fandom. The ways in which they do so are indicative of the complexity of the meaning-making process as well as the pleasures and displeasures afforded by quality texts. More importantly, because the process of signification is intrinsically linked to the process of subject formation, such fans not only construct themselves as "quality readers" but also police the boundary of such a readership. Despite the commonsensical belief among elites and the middle classes about a societal decline in cultural literacy due to the ubiquity of media technologies and non-print-based mass culture, this research demonstrates that the panic button has been pushed needlessly.

## Leave it to Leavis: Ethical technologies and the quality television text

"The assumption that there [is] an unchanging object known as 'art', or an isolatable experience called 'beauty' or the 'aesthetic' " dates back to nineteenth century Romanticism (Eagleton, 1983: 21). Indeed, a Romantic education was distinguished from a classical education by its focus on the "aesthetico-ethical" organization of the individual (Hunter, 1988: 5). Until almost the end of the nineteenth century, such a project was one of "self cultivation" (5). Even one of its most prominent disseminators, Matthew Arnold, never advocated for the teaching of literature or literary criticism in schools, despite dire warnings that society would be "in danger of falling into anarchy" (quoted in Eagleton, 1983: 24) if the project of enculturation were to fail.

It was F.R. Leavis, an inheritor of Arnold, but influenced more directly by I.A. Richards and his notions of practical criticism, who would concern himself with popular education and teacher training. A "proper" literary education was for Leavis a moral imperative. Like T.S. Eliot, Leavis believed that postwar (I) England and America were in a serious state of decline. As he noted in his essay "How to Teach Reading" (Leavis, 1948: 106), the tradition of the Common Reader, who represented "the cultural tradition and the standards of taste," was dead. Similarly, the opening paragraph of *Culture and Environment*, written 15 years earlier with Denys Thompson, a former student of Leavis' and a Senior English Master, intones:

> Many teachers of English who have become interested in the possibilities of training taste and sensibility must have been troubled by accompanying doubts. What effect can such training have against the multitudinous coun- ter-influences—films, newspapers, advertising—indeed, the whole world outside the classroom? Yet the very conditions that make literary educa- tion look so desperate are those which make it more important than ever before; for in a world of this kind—and a world that changes so rapidly— it is on literary tradition that the office of maintaining continuity must rest. (Leavis & Thompson, 1933: 1)

Literature is positioned as all that remains of the organic community that formed the backbone of authentic English life and sensibility. The book is divided into a number of short chapters of topics such as "Advertising: Types of Appeal," "Tradition," and "Substitute Living." In each, Leavis takes aim at one aspect of modern life and provides passages to be read closely and critically by students. Follow-up questions are often included. The final chapter with a series of ideologically laden examples encapsulates Leavis' disdain for modern "low brow" culture. No. 17 states that "advertising created the cigarette habit," and then asks students not to prove or disprove the claim, but to come up with more examples. Two others are noteworthy:

29. "The best novel I've read this week is *Iron Man*." What kind of

standards are implied here? What would you judge to be the quality of the "literature" he reads, and the reading he devotes to it? (119)

34. "Clean cut executive type," "good mixer," "representative man," "short-haired executive," "regular guy" (Americanism). Why do we wince at the mentality that uses this idiom? (121)

While it would be easy to simply laugh off these examples as hopelessly outdated and quaint, Leavis' approach to literary education is still with us almost 75 years since the publication of *Culture and the Environment*. Beyond the book's direct influence and popularity among teachers in the UK (Hayman, 1976), literary education as advocated by Leavis and others needs to be understood as part of a larger set of pedagogical and institutional practices. "School instruction," warns Bourdieu (1990: 208), "always fulfills a function of legitimization, if only by giving its blessing to works which it sets up as worthy of being admired, and thus helps to define the hierarchy of cultural wealth valid in a particular society at a particular time." Aesthetics and "good" taste are but the ideological constructions of cultural elites, passed off as natural or universal as are their preferred methods of acquiring mastery of these cultural codes. To denaturalize this practice, Bourdieu uses the term *bourgeois aesthetics* (referenced in Jenkins, 1992), a term that I will appropriate in the pages that follow. However, more is at work than naturalization and universalization. In *Culture and Government* (1988), Hunter draws on Foucault's notion of *governmentality*[2] to examine the imbrication of literary education and the management of populations along with the formation and regulation of social subjects. He describes the emergence of English as an *ethical technology* drawing on existing "techniques for the moral management of experience and a new kind of teacher-student relationship" (68). He quotes one administrator as saying that the classroom "is the place where all that have been lived through can be put in order" (124). The English classroom became the privileged site of such "ordering," in part, through a "correction through self-expression" approach. While students were to be encouraged to respond to literature by drawing on their own experiences, preferably in writing, these responses were then to be refined and corrected by the teacher-critic. This meant that the literary text had to be constructed as possessing both a "surface" immediacy and accessibility simultaneously with "a 'depth', one which every reading would only serve to intensify" (128). The "good" student of "good" literature eventually becomes a "good" subject, or to use Miller's term, a "well-tempered self" (1993). As Leavis' writings made clear, such an ethical technology operationalizes a clear distinction between the high culture text and the popular text—to the "untrained" eye, popular texts have surface appeal even if only illusory.

As a result of the ever-existing disruptive potential of the popular, this mode of literary education relies on a logic of crisis. In the 1980s, for example, conservative academics such as Allan Bloom and Roger Kimball bemoaned the dumbing down of education, blaming not only television, video, and portable music players, but also supposedly radical leftist educators who had thrown out the canon in favor of popular culture and multicultural texts for the purpose of ideological inculcation. Their position is aptly summarized by Giroux and Simon (1989: 7): "the category of true culture is treated as a warehouse filled with the goods of antiquity, waiting patiently to be distributed anew to each generation. Knowledge in this perspective becomes . . . removed from the demands of social critique and ideological interests." Their own ideological interests are of course not mentioned, papered over with the language of objective inquiry. Such to their chagrin no doubt, as well as that of Leavis, who lived until 1978, middle school and high school English classrooms across North America have for the most part embraced albeit limited forms of "quality" popular cultural texts since the 1970s. Every new form of cultural expression whether visual art, music, cinema and television has set off a moral panic and yet over time, select texts from each genre are incorporated into an expanding version of a Cultural Tradition. American television programming can be considered to have first crossed the divide that relegated it to mindless entertainment for "the masses" in 1971 with the comedy/drama *All in the Family* and its portrayal of bigotry in America. The legacy of HBO as a producer of "quality" drama is preceded and indeed mapped out by the networks in the 1980s with *Hill Street Blues*, *Moonlighting*, *Northern Exposure*, *thirtysomething* and then in the 1990s with *ER*, *The West Wing*, *Homicide: Life on the Street*, and *NYPD Blue*. While HBO had success with series such as *Sex and the City*, it was *The Sopranos* that solidified its reputation as being "too good for television." In short, what has shifted is the positioning of texts on the high/low culture binary; the binary itself remains intact but redeployed to distinguish "quality" popular texts deserving of literary treatment from those that are not.

In reference to higher education, Rabinowitz (2000: 219) argues that what is needed is not only a diversity of texts to be studied, but a diversity of reading practices beyond close reading. By relying on this practice, "we not only reject many works that don't fit; more damaging, we also twist many others until they *do* fit." He then self-reflexively adds, "I'm exaggerating the power of teachers of course. When reading for class, many students read closely, but few continue the practice once they've left college" (220). While he is correct not to assume students are malleable subjects shaped exclusively by the teacher-critic, he has underestimated the workings of power of the ethical technology that is literary education. There is no reason to assume that the "well-tempered" students will not continue to self-cultivate and self-regulate outside the classroom. As with any form of practice of the self, there are always emotional, social and/or economic benefits. Leavis (1948: 133) points out one such benefit: "[h]aving trained one's sensibility and grasped firmly the significance of 'tradition' and a 'literature' in the literature of one's own language, one is equipped to profit by incursions into other literatures." In the contemporary context, these "incursions" can involve other cultural forms that are not necessarily print-based. While watching too much television leads to charges of being a "tv junkie," small doses of "quality" television are perfectly acceptable. When discussing HBO series like *The Sopranos* or *Six Feet Under*, the qualifications and/or self-depreciation required and, indeed, expected of the educated middle-class viewer when admitting to watching soap operas or reality programs, are unnecessary. Quality texts thus *produce* quality readers/viewers. By demonstrating their ability to recognize and appreciate the aesthetic standards of the quality text in a like-minded community, from the local book club to an internet forum, such readers/viewers mark themselves out as legitimate members of the cultured middle class.

The fan is in a precarious position vis-à-vis the "quality" text. A figure of ridicule since the term was first used back in the 1920s, she or he is deemed to be incapable of distinguishing "good" texts from "bad" because of his or her emotional attachment. In *Textual Poachers*, Jenkins (1992) vigorously challenged this assessment of fans' interpretative practices. Fan criticism may be "playful, speculative [and] subjective," but is also concerned with "the particularity of textual detail and . . . internal consistency across the program episodes" (278). Based on my previous research with female media fans, I would add that fans have differing levels of investment in the discourse and practice of bourgeois aesthetics and those like my participants, all of whom had completed at least one university degree, will regularly deliver detailed and rigorous criticism of the text in terms of writing, acting, production, direction, etc (Bury, 2005). Fans of a "quality" text are thus particularly susceptible to the pressures exerted by the dominant discourse of "objective" criticism to shore up their stock of cultural capital and prove themselves to be legitimate "quality" readers. At the same time, criticism, as Jenkins suggests, is not an end in itself and is usually handled with care: even among educated middle-class fans, too much criticism can spoil the pleasures of the text. At other moments, though, criticism of an episode deemed to be of "poor quality" can be particularly harsh.

## In praise of *Six Feet Under*

Although comments on the greatness of the series and its superiority to any other television programming were regularly made during discussion of specific episodes, they were the most numerous for discussions of premieres and finales. The sample I presented in the introduction refer to the Season Four premiere, "Falling into Place." Taken together, the comments addressing the specific qualities are in line with the literary standards informed by bourgeois aesthetics: depth of characterization, "taut and sharp" writing, and no "unnecessary or gratuitous" plotlines. Like HBO02, other posters also drew on cinematic/televisual aesthetics of acting, editing, direction and sound:

> . . . And that opening scene, if you have ever eaten acid was as close to a real trip I have ever seen captured on film. Unbelievable editing/ direction. Bravo HBO, Alan Ball, entire cast and crew. I love you! (HBO04)

> Last night's premiere reminded me why I have become such a devoted Six Feet fan. The writing is impeccable and the characters are very deep and complex (more than six feet deep, that's for sure!) Peter Krause was superb. The anguish he showed as he buried Lisa, alone in the desert was heart-wrenching. How he showed repulsion, grief and guilt at the same time was incredible . . . (HBO05)

> This show just keeps getting better and better. The final scene was one of such magnitude that frankly, it was almost too hard to take. My wife and I sat in stunned silence as Nate honored Lisa's wishes by burying her directly into the earth. When the credits began to roll, the impact of what we had just witnessed, along with the haunting music track, left us both in tears . . . (HBO06)

In a post that would made even Leavis proud, HBO07 offered his/her understanding of the impact of a "great" work like SFU:[3]

> The grace of this series is that it allows the viewer—as good literature does the reader—subtleties from which to find meaningful, depth-enhancing connections; also, that it often allows the open-endedness which provokes us to thought rather than smothering us in didacticism.

The above messages prompted HBO08 to exclaim, "I love this posting group. Treating this show like art."

This episode generated no negative criticism, most likely because it was a premiere in which the storylines were laid out and had yet to be developed in a direction that could raise objections. That fans had waited over a year between seasons and were relieved just to have the series back on the air is a factor that must be taken under consideration as well. A couple of posters had read the text closely enough to point out the "in-joke" on the lengthy gap:

Did anybody notice that Keith said "I feel like I've been eating this cake for 12 months?" (HBO09)

Yeah, wasn't that brilliant? HBO honors its viewers by assuming that we are intelligent. Thanks HBO. Thanks Alan Ball. Many of us are. (HBO10)

These replies reaffirmed the link between the "quality" text and the "quality" reader and enabled the posters to stake out their membership in the broader community of educated SFU fans. The few criticisms that were made are best categorized as minor quibbles. HBO06, for example, noted that a couple of scenes seemed too long but immediately qualified this remark: "But the fact is, all of these characters are so tightly drawn and subtly nuanced, I could watch them for hours on end." S/he then turned this aesthetic weakness into a strength:

> And, truth be told, life acts out in much the same way—there are long, awkward stretches of silence, where one person is trying desperately to find just the right words to help the other in their time of need. . . .

Hence the overly long scenes were justified on the grounds that they were "realistic." To paraphrase the old adage, art imitates life and the better the imitation, the better the art according to the logic of bourgeois aesthetics.

As the season progressed, more dissenting messages were posted although they made up a small percentage of the total. While some addressed the perceived failings of the particular episode, others commented on the season as a whole. Take HBO11's message posted on the topic about "Parallel Play:"

> I have the feeling that I'm not the only one who feels this season is swinging on the ropes. It is a cardinal rule in fiction to have conflict and tension fuel the course of a show, but because this is a season-to-season exercise, the writers are compelled to come up with more and more problems for their characters. Perhaps that's why Nate is becoming more and more of a 2-D character. (HBO11)

The characterization of Nate Fisher was to be a reoccurring complaint for the rest of the series run. In reference to "Can I Come Up Now," HBO12 posted:

> . . . I hate what they are doing with the character Nate. I don't think he should be so screwed up. He has issues but for him to be this crazed over his dead wife that he supposedly wasn't sure if he loved doesn't seem real. (HBO12)

Although a discourse of criticism was mobilized, the message also reveals an emotional investment in the character and a sense of frustration with the writers and producers. HBO13 explicitly advocates for fan input and in doing so, implicitly challenges the established authority of the writers to be the sole producers of authoritative meaning: "I miss SFU of old. Do they read these boards? Maybe if we complain enough, they'll listen."

## Hell hath no fury . . .

No episode generated more controversy among the HBO participants than "That's My Dog" and only the series finale generated more messages. It begins with David Fisher picking up a hitchhiker whose car has apparently run out of gas. Scenes of David chatting with Jake as they drive from one bank machine to another so the supposedly grateful passenger can pay for gas are intercut with narratives involving other central characters, as is typical of serial television drama. Once Jake pulls a gun on David, the focus of the remaining 40 or so minutes is David being terrorized over the course of the night until he is finally abandoned in an alleyway, doused with gasoline but not, in the end, torched alive by the carjacker. The posters were all in agreement that this episode was a deviation from the usual SFU fare in terms of content, tone and structure. However, opinion was sharply divided as to whether this deviation was brilliant or proof that the series had "jumped the shark" in the *Happy Days* tradition. The first set of posters were in the first "camp":

> My God! Was this not the most tense episode ever? So glad to see this season take some shape. Fantastic! (HBO14)

> I agree. This episode was very powerful and nerve wracking. It really gave you the feeling that David was going to be murdered. Another fantastic episode on a fantastic show. (HBO15)

> I posted this over in "About the Show" last night, and since I've basically grown stronger in my opinion on the episode. Anyhow here it is: "I didn't love the episode, but I didn't hate it. It was difficult to watch, but now upon reflection I get why they didn't cut away from David during the last 35 minutes, it wouldn't have been real. If they can show us a 'real' look at death, a 'real' look at a marriage, and a 'real' look at sex. Why shouldn't they show us a 'real' look at something traumatic a main character is going through? To cut away from his experience would have been totally dishonest and not what the show is about. I remember their original tag line waaaaaayyy back when, 'only real life is better'. Well, I think we got

a major dose of that real life last night, imho." Any other thoughts? (HBO16)

The importance of an uninterrupted storyline, as articulated by HBO16, echoes Postman's (1985) criticism of American network news programming. By cutting abruptly from one story to another with words like "now . . . this," the impact of the story is diminished, rendering it forgettable. Yet HBO16's response is also based on an emotional attachment to and respect for the character: cutting away would have trivialized David's "experience," not unlike getting up in the middle of a real friend's tale of assault to get a coke from the fridge.

Others joined the thread who felt just as strongly that the episode was unrealistic and manipulative:

What the hell was that? David smokes crack? What's next heroine? If David does become a crack-addict then this will indeed be the episode when SFU jumped the shark. I pray last night was just a halibut last night. (HBO17)

This episode was SILLY. Total soap opera . . . [It] wasn't fit for a "that's my dog" to sh-t on. The characters were completely off, the dialouge stilted . . ., and the freaking van thing-it was so silly and transparent that I was yelling at the show for getting so f-cking STUPID. So he doesn't leave when the guy gets out the van-smart move. It was all so bad and staged that I couldn't get into it or feel bad for David b/c David wasn't even acting LIKE David in the first place-all I could picture was the writing group saying-okay, how bout David gets picked up, acts completely stupid, etc. David is a smart, buff guy. What is going on with this show? The crack scene was so silly that we just started treating the whole scene like a bad B-movie comedy. Horrible decision on HBOs part-this episode should have NEVER happened and everybody affiliated with it should be fired. (HBO18)

. . . Last nights episode was the worst yet. Did they really need to spend half of the show on David's hijack? Really boring. What is going on with Six Ft. this year? It been on a steady decline, IMO. I used to plan my Sunday night around the HBO lineup and now it is very hit or miss. Mostly on the miss side I am sorry to say. Please get back to a more balanced story line. (HBO19)

The most common complaint was that the episode was badly written in terms of plot and characterization—the scene in which David is forced to smoke crack at gunpoint and his subsequent hallucinations was identified as one of the worst. Although HBO18 found the scene reminiscent of "a bad B-movie comedy," his message, like the previous poster's, was permeated by disappointment, anger and betrayal. He accused the writers of purposely dumbing down the character he respected for being both intelligent and handsome. On the other hand, the last message in the sample was bereft of emotion or affinity with David, the central narrative curtly dismissed as "boring."

The intense fan response also needs to be cast in relief against the *queerness* of the carjacking narrative. Doty (1993: xviii) defines queer texts or queer textual elements as "a range or a network of nonstraight ideas" in which the lesbian, gay and bisexual or other nonnormative sexualities are combined. Given the centrality of David as a male gay character to the series narrative, fan discomfort with such elements may seem surprising. Doty cautions us to recognize, however, that "queer reception . . . stand[s] outside the relatively clear-cut and essentializing categories of sexual identity under which most people function" (15). In Season Four, David and his lover/friend, Keith Charles, have entered into a committed relationship but it does not adhere strictly to heterosexual norms and expectations. "That's My Dog" has several scenes involving man on man sex and gay desire that disrupt these norms, the first being David casting a series of desiring glances at Jake when he first gets in the van. Jake, in a typical SFU fantasy scene, asks David if he is gay and then confirms that he is as well. After a confession of unconditional love from Jake to the surprised but delighted David, the scene cuts away to Jake staring at David blankly and repeating his offer of water. A later scene shows David hallucinating about receiving a blowjob from Jake after being forced to inhale from a crack pipe at gunpoint. HBO18 alluded to David's desire being problematic when he wrote "David gets picked up" rather than "David picks up a hitchhiker." The next posters was more explicit:

> . . . I understand David's a bit out of it due to Keith's leaving [on tour]— but c'mon? He's usually professional, except for the BJ [blowjob] he got from the plumber a couple episodes ago, which was WAY out of character. Maybe there's a point to his bad choices and lack of professionalism lately. But he wouldn't pick up a hitchhiker or stranger in need of help (when it was obvious he wanted it to be a trick) with a corpse in the back, not to mention drive around aimlessly for an hour or two and let the body cook and decompose.(HBO20)

Why is everyone saying that picking up the hitchhiker was out of character for David? Has everyone forgot about him having unprotected sex with a hustler in an alley during the Funeral Directors convention (first season)? . . . He may be outwardly uptight, but inside he is a total sex pig that fantasizes about (and sometimes acts out) very risky sexual encounters. This type of behavior is quite common amongst a significant segment of the gay population. Ever heard of "glory holes" or "cruising the park"? (HBO21)

Both posters interpreted David's motivation for picking up Jake to be based solely on sexual desire. The first characterized such behavior as "unprofessional" and therefore "out of character" even though s/he provides an example from Episode 41 (the blow job from the plumber) that would seem to suggest that it was in character, at least at this juncture in the series narrative. If this message can be understood as heterosexist, the one from HBO21 is overtly homophobic because of the way in which the character in particular and gay practices and gay sexuality in general were dismissed and pathologized.

Other posters rejected this interpretation of David's behavior:

Come on folks! 6FU has been and still is the best show on tv since day 1. I have no problem with David's moment of poor judgement—is a compassionate act really outside of his character? Yes, I was yelling at my tv, calling him a "wuss" among other things, but who really knows how they will act when staring down the barrel of a gun? Not me. In the end I was shaken and disturbed as if it had happened to a family member . . . (HBO22)

. . . I'm not sure why it's so difficult to distinguish his simply being gay from his acting out of behavior that ANY person could exhibit— loneliness, need, and insecurity.(HBO23)

David's actions were thus reframed as based on a shared set of human emotions. This interpretation draws on a liberal-humanist discourse that emphasizes commonality and plays down social differences. Such a move is well-intentioned and enables fans to identify and sympathize with characters from different social locations than their own. Yet, the erasure of social difference functions to shore up normative identities. In this case, David's gayness and gay desire has been erased. Only two posters interpreted David's actions as motivated by a complexity of emotion and sexual desire:

It's fascinating to read the intense and angry reactions to this episode. The writers have obviously struck a collective nerve . . . What made this episode so painful to watch is that David's a wonderful, sympathetic character—one we've come to know intimately—a genuinely kind guy who grapples with everday issues—responsibility, family, self worth—and—his own dark side (especially when he's feeling vulnerable aka "abandoned" by Keith). David is human; and way back when in the first season flirted with dangerous sex (in the Las Vegas parking garage). His choice to pick up the "stranded" motorist was fueled by fantasy and the hint of the forbidden . . . (HBO24)

Alright, come on people. You're talking about this episode as if someone came out of your T.V. and vomited on you . . . David has a kind heart. He let the guy in 'cause he feels sorry for him, and probably 'cause he thought he was cute. I loved this episode, it kept me on the edge of my seat the entire time. I don't see what was so wrong! (HBO25)

Only one poster directly confronts what s/he refers to as "a faint whiff of homophobia." Targeting posters such as HBO19, s/he notes that:

. . . I'm afraid that some of you hated the episode simply because you feel it wasted valuable air-time on one of its gay characters, time which you also feel could have been spent more wisely exploring the storyline of one of its many straight characters. So I think for many of you, your reactions have more to do with the "gay thing" than the fact that Alan Ball & his writer Scott Buck stooped to cheap melodramatics and shock value. And if that is the case, you need to get the f*** over it. David is and has been a major character on this show and he will continue to be. I need to point out that I don't feel this is the case for everyone who disliked the episode . . . (HBO26)

This response is all the more interesting given that HBO26 agreed that the episode was melodramatic.

As the debate intensified, the friction between the two "camps" intensified. In the previous data sample, HBO 25 seemed perplexed and frustrated by the reactions of the "betrayed" fans. HBO27 was more direct and dismissive, implying that fans with such emotional investments were not really capable of appreciating a "quality" show like SFU and whose viewing tastes would be better suited for the lower-rung network offerings:

Please stop the whining. If you guys really feel that SFU has jumped the shark, watch shows like "Hope and Faith" or "For Love or Money". That Kelly Ripa sure is funny. (HBO27)

The message below was addressed to those who liked the episode:

> I think the "6FU can do no wrong" crowd needs to stop idolizing this show.
> Like everything else, this show has flaws. Be objective. 6FU is usually 80%
> good & 20% bad, IMO. "That's My Dog" was the exact opposite. Let's
> examine why people thought it was such a step in the wrong direction . . .
> (HBO28)

After accusing the "supporters" of being subjective, this poster included two
lengthy numbered lists of previously stated arguments in addition to his/her
own in order to "objectively" prove that the kidnapping narrative was
unrealistic. HBO29 responded in a similar vein when feeling under attack by a
few of the episode's supporters:

> I really do like the show, and I was hoping that someone would have some
> thoughts about the issues I brought up. It does upset me a bit when people
> dismiss dissent out of hand, and that kind of got my dander up. Ad
> hominem and straw man attacks are another pet peeve of mine, and they
> seem to be a favored tactic used by regulars here to squash dissent.
>
> How about this: address specific issues that others raise along the lines of
> "When you say X, I disagree for reason Y. Here are some thoughts to back
> up my position: A, B, C." That way we can all learn something, and no
> one's feelings are unnecessarily hurt. Lines like "Grow up!" and "Don't let
> the door hit you on the way out." are not conducive to rational discussion.
> (HBO29)

HBO29 thus represents the fan critic most heavily invested in the type of
discussion sanctioned by a discourse of bourgeois aesthetics. This next poster,
however, rejected out of hand such detached engagement in the context of a
fan board:

> . . . You want us to address specific issues that others raise alone the lines
> of "when you say X . . ." ?: | I thought this was a friendly msg board and
> not one that required "conducive rational discussion". Also, I dont think an
> HBO msg board should be a place people would come to "learn" some-
> thing. Are you an english teacher on summer break by any chance?
> (HBO30)

This message implies that too much criticism takes away from the pleasures of
the text and the sharing of those pleasures (or displeasures) with other fans.

## Everyone's grateful

The outpouring of praise for "Everyone's Waiting" was even more intensive and extensive than for the Premiere of Season Four or, indeed, any other episode. In less than 48 hours, 1,486 messages had been posted (at which point my data collection ended). By the time the boards were locked, this topic area comprised 8,958 messages. A significant number posted on the day after the broadcast expressed gratitude to Alan Ball and the others associated with the show:

> Most definately the most spectacular and satisfying ending to a series that I have ever witnessed. I have been an avid SFU fan from day one and I am sure I will go through the grieving process now that its over. Thank you so much to Alan Ball and Carolyn Strauss at HBO for the creation as well as the writers, producers, cast and crew. Each of you have contributed to this phenomenon and I believe Freddy Rodriguez [SFU actor] hit it on the head when he said you changed the landscape of television . . . (HBO31)

> Kudos and praise to Alan Ball and his peers. The cast, crew, writers, directors, producers, caterers, grips, drivers, EVERYONE did a fabulous piece of work for five years and especially for the finale.

> The way the show was tied together from beginning to end, alpha to omega, if you will, just floored me. The pilot, Season One, was the beginning, but began with the ending of a life (Nathaniel), and the finale, Season Five, was the ending, but began with the beginning of a life (Willa). The oldest to the youngest, the yin and yang, it resonated perfectly for me. (HBO32)

As the above data sample illustrates, the strong emotional response is legitimated by reference to the "quality" of the text—a groundbreaking series whose narrative was appropriately "bookended." Others talked about the lessons offered by the series, lessons that all "quality" texts are expected to offer:

> I can go on and on about this show or finale. For those of us blessed by it, we will carry it forever. It is going to be so awesome purchasing the DVD set and watching it all over again and being touched by this great show. I think it is best to not "say much" but to take from the show what has touched you and be better for it. I just really feel sorry for those who thought the show was dumb, or are into reality shows or mindless dribble that is on TV now. This show was special. (HBO33)

It was a beautiful, spiritual, inspiring ending to one of the greatest TV shows ever made. A million thanks to Alan Ball and his team of writers for this fantastic series. The message of LIFE imparted by a show focused on death is extremely powerful. People, live your life the best way you can, make it count for something while you are on this Earth. We will all die eventually, but it's not necessarily a sad thing, if we use our valuable time to make meaning with our lives. (HBO34)

. . . [T]he last episode leaves me with a profound sense of grief tempered with hope and peace. It offers a challenge to seize the fullness of life while we are able. And it also issues a gentle reminder that no matter what choices any of us make for ourselves, the adventure of life continues on and on—long after we leave the room. (HBO35)

Like classic literature in the Leavisian tradition, SFU was understood to have enriched the lives of its viewers; hence the pity felt by HBO33 for those with "low culture tastes." Like a number of others not quoted, s/he also saw it as able to stand up to the scrutiny of multiple viewings over time on DVD. The posters generally agreed that the universal "message" was about living life fully and meaningfully but to recognize and accept the inevitability of death.

Unlike with other episodes, "That's My Dog" in particular, harsh criticism was almost nonexistent. The following message was the one exception:

Well, all I have to say is thank god this show is over. Nothing more depressing than watching a bunch of self-loathing narcissists bitch and moan about how horrible their lives are when they have it better than 90% of the world they live in. From manic depressive Ruth to self-righteous Claire, it was more than enough. You should all get over yourselves before it's too late and you die. Which was maybe the point all along. (HBO36)

The responses were immediate and made it clear that no real fan would post this type of message at this juncture. HBO37 did not mince words:

[HBO36]—you can voice your opinion all you want, but this probably isn't the best place to post a negative opinion. Everyone here clearly had a love for this tv show, and it seems with that comment that all you are looking for is attention . . . if you don't like the show, and how we feel—then GET THE FUCK OUTTA HERE and stop reading this board! (HBO37)

The only aspect of the finale that generated any qualified criticism was the final five-minute montage, which "fast forwards" through the lives of all the major characters to the moment of their deaths. Those critical of the montage on the grounds that the "happy" ending and aging make-up on the actors were silly and unrealistic, tended to flag their "minority status." HBO38 opened his/her message with "I think I am in the minority here" to which HBO39 replies, "Hello, there [HBO38]. You and I are 2 of a handful that were disappointed with this finale. I was beginning to feel very lonely :)." When one critic was mocked for being in the "1% group" that did not like the episode, s/he retorted:

> LOL . . . and your point is??? "you can kiss 1% of my ass!" don't get bent out of shape, that's a seinfeld reference. i still think the ending was cheese-tastic, and i really can't believe most people thought it was a great way to end the show but, there you go. pop-culture indeed. (HBO40)

This response points to the differing investments in bourgeois aesthetics when applied to a popular culture text outside the regulatory space of the classroom or other space to which admittance can be more carefully monitored by levels of cultural capital.

## Conclusion

As I hope my discussion makes clear, the SFU fans who posted to the HBO board positioned themselves as "quality" viewers of a "quality" text. To that end, they engaged with bourgeois aesthetics to both praise and criticize the show. Yet, they also had strong emotional investments in the show and unlike HBO28 and 29, most violated the rule of "objective" distance, their posts a synthesis of both critical and fannish discourses. Unlike professional critics, fans openly anticipate and seek out the pleasures of their text and to this end, their criticisms are tempered accordingly. If they are generally happy with the episode, as was the case with "Falling into Place," they tend to minimalize, qualify or rationalize perceived flaws. Messages that are dismissive or harshly critical are either ignored or challenged. On the other hand, an episode that offers few or no pleasures, as was the case for many with "That's My Dog," is not only harshly criticized, but taken as a betrayal by the writers for failing to meet the "standards" of the series. In the end, though, all is forgiven and the series' status as a great piece of art ready to take its place in the Great Cultural Tradition is confirmed.

Ultimately fannish investments and practices expose and disturb what Foucault (1972) would call the "will to truth" that pervades bourgeois aesthetics in contemporary culture. It is not that fans have failed the test of objectivity but rather that objectivity has failed the test to set itself outside of ideological-laden judgments and tastes based on cultural norms. The difference between fans and professional critics and other textual "authorities" is that the former are less willing and/or able to cover up the tracks they leave on texts. That said, fan practices should not be naively celebrated: as some of the responses to the carjacking narrative in "That's My Dog" demonstrate, the will of the truth that informs modernist criticism enables homophobic and hetero-sexist responses to be passed of as an objective discussion of plot and character development.

Finally, this research points to the effectiveness of the techniques of government—schooling in particular—to ensure cultural reproduction and subject formation in line with the dominant social order. Popular culture may disturb this order temporarily, as may pedagogies of transgression that seek to denaturalize normative discourses, particularly those of race, class, sexuality and gender (see Giroux and Simon, 1989; hooks, 1994). Yet over the long term, it is not the specific legacy of Leavis or the rantings of conservatives like Bloom and Kimball but the mundane practices of the classroom that will ensure that the more media technologies change, the more the ethical technol-ogy stays the same.

## Notes

1   Although these messages were posted to a public board and a membership is not required to access them, I have chosen not to use the "handles" of the posters and instead have numbering them according to the order of presentation in this paper. All ellipses are mine unless indicated otherwise. As I understand computer-mediation to be a hybrid form of communication (Jones, 1999), I have not corrected any spelling or typographical errors and so all errors should be assumed to be in the original message.
2   For more on governmentality see Burchell, Gordon, and Miller (1991) and Bratich, Packer, and McCarthy (2003).
3   Without any supplemental data from questionnaires or interviews, the only infor-mation I have regarding the gender identity of the participants is within the context of their posts included in the dataset. If they self-identified as male or female in any of their messages or had a "handle" that was gender-specific, I have chosen to use the pronoun in my discussion. Otherwise, I have used "s/he" and/or "his/her."

## Works cited

Bourdieu, P. (1990) "Artistic Taste and Cultural Capital", pp 205–216 in J.C. Alexan-der & S. Seidman (eds) *Culture and Society: Contemporary Debates*. Cambridge: Cam-bridge University Press.

Bratich, J., Packer, J., & McCarthy, C. (eds) (2003) *Foucault, Cultural Studies, and Governmentality*. Albany: State University of New York Press.

Burchell, G., Gordon, C., & Miller, P. (eds) (1991) *The Foucault Effect: Studies in Governmentality*. Chicago: University of Chicago Press.

Bury, R. (2005) *Cyberspaces of Their Own: Female Fandoms Online*. New York: Peter Lang.

Dawson-March, C. (2003, August 22) "Does Anyone take Decorating Shows Seriously?", *The Globe and Mail* R2.

Doty, A. (1993) *Making Things Perfectly Queer: Interpreting Mass Culture*. Minneapolis: University of Minnesota Press.

Doyle, J. (2005) "Six Feet Under Bows Out Gracefully", *The Globe and Mail* R29.

Eagleton, T. (1983) *Literary Theory: An Introduction*. Minneapolis: University of Minnesota Press.

Fiske, J. (1987) *Television Culture*. New York: Methuen.

Foucault, M. (1972) *The Archaeology of Knowledge and The Discourse on Language*. New York: Dorset Press.

Giroux, H. A. & Simon, R. I. (1989) *Popular Culture, Schooling, and Everyday Life*. New York: Bergin & Garvey.

Hayman, R. (1976) *Leavis*. Lanham: Rowman and Littlefield.

hooks, b. (1994) *Teaching to Transgress: Education as the Practice of Freedom*. New York: Routledge.

Hunter, I. (1988) *Culture and Government: The Emergence of Literary Education*. Basingstoke: Macmillan.

Jenkins, H. (1992) *Textual Poachers: Television Fans and Participatory Culture*. New York: Routledge.

Jones, S. (ed.) (1999) *Doing Internet Research: Critical Issues and Methods for Examining the Net*. Thousand Oaks: Sage.

Leavis, F. R. (1948) *Education and the University: A Sketch for an "English School"*. London: Chatto & Windus.

Leavis, F. R. & Thompson, D. (1933) *Culture and Environment: The Training of Critical Awareness*. London: Chatto and Windus.

Miller, T. (1993) *The Well-tempered Self: Citizenship, Culture, and the Postmodern Subject*. Baltimore: Johns Hopkins University Press.

Postman, N. (1985) *Amusing Ourselves to Death: Public Discourse in the Age of Show Business*. New York: Penguin Books.

Rabinowitz, P. (2000) "Actual Reader and Authorial Reader", pp 218–221 in D.H. Richter (ed.) *Falling into Theory: Conflicting Views on Reading Literature*. Boston: Bedford/St. Martin's.

# Chapter 11

# Fashion(able/ing) selves

## Consumption, identity, and *Sex and the City*

*Cara Louise Buckley and Brian L. Ott*

*More and more, what you wear and what you don't wear define who you are.*
—Juliet Schor (1999: 41)

*[S]hopping is not an inconsequential instrumental act but rather can be an expressive and even constitutive existential act.*
—Russell Belk (1999: 182)

We are a nation of consumers. So axiomatic is this view that it is tempting simply to end there. But to do so would be to ignore the way that our opening claim flattens history and erases the decidedly contextual character of consumption. Just as our economic system has undergone profound changes in the transition from industrial capitalism to informational capitalism, so, too, has the practice, purpose, and performance of consumption. To speak profitably of consumption, then, necessitates that one first situate it within a particular historical and cultural milieu. Our specific interest in consumption concerns the contemporary moment or postmodern condition—the media-saturated, information-driven, hyper-capitalist landscape in which Fordism has given way to flexible accumulation, manufacturing to processing, standardization to individualization, certainty to skepticism, foundationalism to contingency, progress to exhaustion, and authenticity to simulacrum. Recognition of this shift and its contours is also crucial to understanding the role consumption now plays in the endless (re)construction of identity.

In the transition from modernity to postmodernity, the notion of an essential self—of a rational Cartesian subject—has been displaced by a far more fragmented, fluid, and contingent understanding of subjectivity tied to image, style, looks, and hence consumption (Kellner, 1995: 231–247). Increasingly, the self is an outward performance of signs and codes borrowed and poached from culture, rather than an innate and unchanging core being. "Individuals" are, above all, consumers, who articulate a meaningful sense of self through consumer choice (in media, fashion, social commitments, etc.). The consum(er/ing) self is a paradox, at once hegemonic and resistive. In performing their personas, "individuals" simultaneously reproduce the codes of the dominant culture through adoption and assimilation, as well as undermine those codes through creative recombination and bricolage. Though acutely aware of this paradox, we are interested in the resistive side of the equation/contradiction, and more specifically, in how viewers can exploit it through their own media choices and consumptive practices.

Toward that end, we undertake a reading of Carrie Bradshaw—the lead character from the HBO hit series *Sex and the City* (1998–2004). We are not so much interested in what Carrie "means," as in demonstrating how Carrie, in fashioning her own identity, affords viewers the symbolic resources for (re)fashioning theirs. Our central contention is that Carrie's consumptive practices with regard to clothing and fashion both model a transgressive subjectivity (specifically a queer identity, we argue) and furnish actual cultural resources for enacting such a subjectivity. Before turning to our analysis of this process, however, we first discuss how television functions as equipment for living, and then illustrate how a queer subjectivity deconstructs prevailing and thus hegemonic subject positions. A concluding section of the chapter explores the wider social and political implications of consumption for identity in postmodernity.

## Television as equipment for living

Though it has become almost cliché to observe that television is society's principal mode of storytelling today—a sort of electronic bard, the claim is not without significance. Stories and their characters are a way of rehearsing prominent cultural themes and concerns. Simply put, society stories its hopes, dreams, fears, and anxieties as a way of coming to terms with them, of realizing and working through them. The famous twentieth century literary critic Kenneth Burke (1941: 304) was well aware of this process and regularly wrote about the way various literary and art forms operate as *"equipments for living."* For Burke, any discourse could provide the symbolic resources or stylistic medicines for confronting and resolving the challenges and difficulties of everyday living so long as it named (ie summed up) a situation with which an audience could identify. Since "public discourse in the United States is dominated [today] by the influence of television" (Brummett, 1991: 4), television serves not merely as frivolous entertainment, but also as an influential set of symbolic resources for making sense of ourselves and our world. As Barry Brummett (1991: xxi) elaborated, "People need to see their engagement with popular culture as participation in *rhetorical* struggles over who they are and how the world will be made."

Approaching discourse (televisual or otherwise) as symbolic equipment for living reflects a hybridized approach to media studies. While the approach employs textual analysis, it depends upon an understanding of what Burke (1953: 31) called "the psychology of the audience" to illuminate the text. The psychology of the audience, for Burke, describes the symbolic needs of society at a particular historical juncture. Operating from this perspective, "it becomes the task of the Burkean critic," explained Brummett (1984: 161), "to identify the modes of discourse enjoying currency in a society and to link discourse to the real situations for which it is symbolic equipment." As our chapter concerns the contemporary moment, we are interested in how *Sex and the City* and the character of Carrie specifically addresses itself to the real-life situations of postmodernity, namely concerns about consumption and identity. Thus we turn our attention now to an overview of the challenges posed by and for consumption in the postmodern condition.

United States society has long been described as a "consumer culture." But the contemporary culture of consumption is a far cry from the one that prevailed at the height of industrialism a mere 60 years ago. During modernity, consumption was tied to the mass production of highly standardized commodities. Within this economic model, consumption functioned to keep the social classes strictly separated and to perpetuate existing social imbalances (Marx, 1975: 326). In postmodernity, by contrast, consumption has shifted from an overindulgence in durable goods (whose differential costs located one in a particular class) to an insatiable appetite for symbolic or soft goods in the form of images and styles (re)produced by the culture and fashion industries. "The implication," according to Mike Featherstone (2000: 92–93), "is that we are moving towards a society without fixed status groups in which the adoption of styles of life (manifest in choice of clothes, leisure activities, consumer goods, bodily dispositions) which are fixed to specific groups have been surpassed. . . . [an] apparent movement towards a postmodern consumer culture based upon a profusion of information and proliferation of images which cannot be ultimately stabilized." Although postmodernity affords possibilities for resistive modes of consumption related to the play of images and styles (Fiske, 1989; Hebdige, 1979), it certainly does not guarantee them (Bourdieu, 1984).

Not only has consumption historically been associated with wastefulness, but fashion, glamour, and shopping have specifically been singled out as frivolous and shallow, particularly for women. In his writings on femininity, for instance, Sigmund Freud (1974: 132) identified vanity as the principal motivator for women's desire to consume clothing, adding that, "the vanity of women is a late compensation for . . . original sexual inferiority . . . and has as its purpose concealment of genital deficiency." Freud's assessment has been an influential one within our culture and the consumption of fashion remains highly stigmatized—the "trivial" pastime of women rather than the "serious" matters of men. The women who actively and openly admit their enthusiasm for fashion are commonly viewed as simple-minded Barbies who have regressed the project of feminism. But interest in fashion can also be damning for men, as it violates traditional notions of masculinity. As Kathryn Bond Stockton (2003: 268) elucidated, "Women wrapped in beautiful clothes may betray the vanity said to be their shame. Men who rush to their own cloth beauty likely suffer a woman's vain shame."

This shame is all the more stigmatizing for men because, as a woman's shame, it marks them as sexually inferior. Gay men, who are frequently associated with fashion through shows such as *Queer Eye for the Straight Guy*, are shamed along with women. This shared shame can become a shared bond, however, and thus offer opportunities for cultural restructuring. Stephen Maddison (2000: 97), commenting on the centrality of fashion in the relational bond between gay men and straight women, noted that it allows gay men to offer "the best advice to women on the right shade of lipstick." Though this may seem trivial, Maddison went on to say, it can be of vital cultural significance, as bonding over trivialities that have been used to stigmatize gay men and straight women suggests "possibilities for resisting the security of hierarchical gender authority and offer[s] profitable strategies for the acquisition of subjectivity" (97). It is through *Sex and the City's* use of fashion that these possibilities for resistance are illuminated, enacted, and validated. But before turning to the analysis, we pause briefly to examine the intersections of postmodern identity, queer subjectivity, and transgression.

## Queer transgressions

As society has transitioned from industrialism to informationalism, identity has become increasingly intertwined with the culture industries. Consequently, the relatively unified, stable, and essentialist identities of modernity have steadily given way to the more fragmented, fluid, and performative identities of postmodernity. But the character of postmodern identity is itself diverse and varied. As Ott (2003: 74) argued in his analysis of *The Simpsons*, "there is more than one mode for performing identity in a postmodern landscape." While, no doubt, many of these modes function hegemonically to maintain prevailing relations of power, others we contend offer more socially resistive and transgressive possibilities. One postmodern brand of identity that registers as more resistive is a "queer" subjectivity.[1]

The use of the term *queer* as a positive moniker arose out of the Gay,

Lesbian, Bisexual, and Transgendered (GLBT) community. Once a disparaging signifier in dominant culture, queer was (re)appropriated by the GLBT community and used as a marker of pride, rather than sexual deviance and cultural otherness. In the GLBT community today, the term is closely aligned with a critical sensibility and represents a break with the dominant desire to categorize and normalize. Queer recognizes the exclusionary potential of "normal" and seeks instead to find a space upon which the maximum amount of inclusion can be enacted by continually staying in the space of the abnormal. A queer subjectivity is one that breaks with traditional notions of identity, for as Moe Meyer (1994: 3) explained, "what 'queer' signals is an ontological challenge that displaces bourgeois notions of the Self as unique, abiding, and continuous while substituting instead a concept of the Self as performative, improvisational, discontinuous, and processually constituted by repetitive and stylized acts." The queer self is a postmodern self—constantly subject to change and contradiction, and therefore, unable to be definitively "nailed down." This mutability of self is paralleled by the definitional indeterminacy of the term queer itself, which continuously resists the imposition of a final signified.

Most queer theorists agree that the most destructive thing that could happen to queer would be for it to be decisively defined, forcing a loss of the shape shifting identity that currently marks it. In her discussion of queer, Annamarie Jagose (1996: 1) explained, "It is not simply that queer has yet to solidify and take on a more consistent profile, but rather that its definitional indeterminacy, its elasticity, is one of its constituent characteristics." Jagose further noted that this elasticity not only defines queer, but also creates it, allowing it to continually exist outside of the margins of normal. Its definitional indeterminacy is precisely what allows it to be such a highly inclusive subjectivity. As Michael Warner (1993: xxvi) asserted, " 'queer' gets a critical edge by defining itself against the normal rather than the heterosexual." And while it is largely agreed that queer must remain tied to the GLBT community out of which it grew, the same-sex desire at its core is an identification based upon fluid affinity and not absolute identity. According to Steven Seidman (1993: 133), "under the undifferentiated sign of queer are united all those heterogeneous desires and interests that are marginalized and excluded in the straight and gay mainstream." Therefore, just as there is no central queer identity, there is no central identity to which queer is opposed either, it is simply (and complexly) opposed to exclusion.

The act of "queering" then, is an act that denormalizes and destabilizes, moving identities placed within the margins of normal to spaces outside its margins. Queering can be understood as an instance of what Judith Butler (1993: 4) termed "collective disidentifications," or a demonstration of the inability of traditional categories to adequately name or contain the infinite subject positions that exist. As Butler (1993: 4) noted:

The mobilization of the categories of sex within political discourse will be haunted in some ways by the very instabilities that the categories effectively produce and foreclose. Although the political discourses that mobilize identity categories tend to cultivate identifications in the service of a political goal, it may be that the persistence of disidentification is equally crucial to the rearticulation of democratic contestation . . . Collective disidentification can facilitate a reconceptualization of which bodies matter, and which bodies are yet to emerge as critical matters of concern.

The collective disidentification brought on by queering draws attention to the poor "fit" of some selves to the subjectivities available to them. It is in this way that consumption/fashion can be seen as operating within *Sex and the City*. The character of Carrie utilizes fashion to perform her disidentifications with the dominant identities of heterosexual and woman, and in doing so, she queers these identities.[2]

## Queering consumption (in heels)

Carrie Bradshaw is obsessed with fashion. One need only look in her closet to see it. From floor to ceiling in the room that connects her bedroom to her bathroom are the racks and shelves of evidence, replete with sequins, sashes, and silk. While the names that adorn the tags on the dresses, shirts, skirts, scarves, belts, hats and pants—names such as Gucci, Prada, and Dolce & Gabbana—are evidence enough, it is the boxes that fill the majority of this space that are the most telling. Under lid after perfectly placed lid rest stilettos, pointed toes, rounded toes, and strappy sandals, while the ubiquitous moniker "Manolo Blahnik" exposes the indulgent impracticality of it all. Upon taking in this spectacle, there is little doubt that Carrie Bradshaw is a shoe glutton, a clothing coveteuse, a fashion whore. Although her soul may seem irredeemable to the devout ideologue (Christian, Marxist, Feminist critic—take your pick), it is her very practices of consumption that provide audiences a glimmer of resistance. To understand how, however, requires that we first take a step back and look at Carrie in context.

*Sex and the City* follows the lives of Carrie Bradshaw and her three best friends, Miranda Hobbes, Samantha Jones, and Charlotte York, all single at the show's inception and all living Helen Gurley Brown's dream life of *Sex and the Single Girl* (1962), with independence, money, and sexual freedom. The four women at the show's narrative center represent diverse lifestyles and personalities within, of course, the confines of the White, upper middle-class identity. Carrie (played by Sarah Jessica Parker), a sex columnist for a New York City newspaper, is the agent that holds these personalities together, both within the show's diegesis and through voiceover narration of the weekly adventures that are the basis of her columns. Carrie dates continuously throughout the show's run, at times carrying on serious, long-term relationships and at times dating men casually, though never expressing a desire to get married. In fact, in an episode that follows her acceptance of a marriage proposal from a boyfriend, she speculates that she may be "missing the bride gene," as she breaks out in a rash the moment she tries on a wedding gown. Carrie's most successful relationships within the show are clearly with her girlfriends, whom she is seen with far more often than men. Another, equally intense relationship exists between Carrie and fashion.

Pivotal to the life of *Sex and the City*, Sarah Jessica Parker has even been quoted as referring to fashion as the show's "fifth character" (quoted in Bruzzi & Gibson, 2004: 117). The unique manner of dress, supplied by Patricia Fields, the show's stylist, has made Parker a fashion icon, and the show itself a must-see for fashion devotees. Items featured on the show often become best sellers, and Carrie's obsession with Manolo Blahnik's shoes has made the brand a household name. Interestingly, fashion has even been used within the show to recreate the body of Parker, who, during season five, was far along in her first pregnancy during the filming. Through creative dressing, which was already a large part of the character of Carrie Bradshaw, the show was able to avoid the awkwardness of shots used to disguise a protruding belly that often accompany the pregnancy of a star whose character is not pregnant.

In many episodes, the consumption of fashion can also be read as serving a resistive purpose within the show, allowing for traditional gender and sexual roles to be questioned and even queered. Events such as Charlotte's indecision, in season four, over what to do with her prized Tiffany engagement ring from her failed marriage, stand as an example of consumption's unique nature within the show. Carrie is about to be kicked out of her rented apartment if she cannot make the sizable downpayment to buy it, as the building it is in is owned by her ex who recently moved out after the breakoff of their engagement. Charlotte decides, in the end, to give the ring to Carrie to make her downpayment with, causing the traditional use of diamond ring consumption—binding women to men in marriage—to be queered, allowing it to stand as a symbol of freedom, and a symbol of friendship. However, the two episodes that highlight fashion's significant nature occur in season four and season six, respectively, with "The Real Me" and "A Woman's Right to Shoes."

## The Real Me

Fashion comes to represent, in "The Real Me," Carrie's identity/character, in much the same way that Butler (1990, 137) discusses outward acts as markers of personhood, stating:

acts, gestures, and desire produce the effect of an internal core or sub-stance, but produce this *on the surface* of the body, through the play of signifying absences that suggest, but never reveal, the organizing principle of identity as a cause. Such acts, gestures, enactments, generally con-strued, are *performative* in the sense that the essence or identity that they otherwise purport to express are *fabrications* manufactured and sustained through corporeal signs and other discursive means.

It is in such moments that a postmodern and queer identity, specifically, is enacted allowing for a fluidity of self.

"The Real Me" begins with Carrie and her gay best friend, Stanford, together in a trendy Manhattan bar on a Saturday night, Carrie's voiceover instantly marking the spot as fashionable, as she dubs it "the place to see and be seen," and, hence, she and Stanford's consumption of fashion in this episode begins here. Against the backdrop of beautiful people, the two of them stand out, Stanford wearing a salmon colored suit with a blue shirt and tie combo under it, Carrie in a black lace dress that has a cream colored bra on the outside, as opposed to beneath it. Their bold fashion marks them as different from the others and simultaneously brings them together, as something of a unit, and the conversation they have solidifies this unity. They both peruse the people that wander by, and as Stanford spots a beautiful man at the top of the stairs who he guesses to be a model, which Carrie speculates on jokingly, he comments on how unattractive he feels in comparison, which Carrie refutes. He looks knowingly at Carrie and states, "I know what I look like," to which she replies, just as knowingly, "Then you can't see what I see." Stanford appears touched, offering Carrie his cheek, which she kisses. Carrie and Stanford are closely aligned both with fashion and the fashion industry at this moment, given their style of dress, and their topic of conversation, in particu-lar, models. However, their words and actions of affection change the valence of these topics, from one of vanity to one of kinship. Carrie, by commenting on Stanford's appearance, what she can *see*, is also commenting on his character, demonstrating the link between the two and the productive nature of fashion in her mind.

Furthermore, the issue of models versus "real people" that runs throughout the episode begins here, for when Stanford suggests that the hot guy in the bar is a model, Carrie's response is to ask, "A model what? A model citizen? A model home? A model airplane?" This line of questioning instantly connects the normative understanding of fashion models both with the idea of perfec-tion, but also with Carrie's sense that these are not real people, just as model airplanes are not "real" airplanes. This distinction becomes important after the two interact with Lynn Cameron (played by Margaret Cho), who asks Carrie to be a model in her upcoming fashion show. When Carrie hesitates at the offer, Cameron bluntly states, "You're fucking doing my show if I have to hunt you down, skin you alive and have one of the other models fucking wear you." Cameron's statement gets at the heart of how the fashion industry is represented throughout the rest of the episode, as only concerned with outward appearances, even to the extreme of believing it is only a model's skin, their outward appearance that is necessary to make the clothes "work."

Carrie's use of fashion, we soon learn, is different. After Cameron huffs away, Stanford smiles excitedly and states, "I am so coming!" expressing his desire to support Carrie in her move to the next level of fashion. Carrie, however, is not as excited and states, "To what? I'm not a model," asserting her view of herself as not model material and as more than a hanger for her clothes; she is created through her clothes; they form her identity; and are much more than simply appearance. Stanford returns Carrie's knowing smile from earlier and quips, "Then you can't see what I see," reasserting their kinship based partly in the bond of their belief in the outward expression of identity.

What changes Carrie's mind and makes her decide to do the show, in the end, is the prospect that she will get to keep the clothes that she wears. This begins to demonstrate more clearly how Carrie's consumption of fashion involves postmodern, paradoxical "use." Carrie consistently demonstrates an art in utilizing the fashion produced by the dominant fashion industry, making it her own, and making it an expression of her own queer identity. This would of course be stifled if she became a model in the fashion show, where her style would be dictated by the will of the designers, and she would, as she explains to her girlfriends as she tries to decide, be judged, because we as a culture, "judge models all the time." Carrie's understanding and use of fashion becomes clearer in this moment, as she does not see herself, though a fashionable body, as one who is to be judged based upon her appearance. She challenges this traditional understanding of feminine vanity and sexuality as desiring attention and positive judgment, and instead makes it something done for personal satisfaction and expression, echoing Simone de Beauvoir's (1988: 545) assessment of the "woman of elegance," stated as, "what she treasures is herself adorned, not the objects that adorn her." Though Carrie may adore her clothing, she is truly enraptured with the identity that she creates from them, one independent of the heteronormative notions of femininity and its need for the gaze of admiration.

Carrie's sense of fashion goes head to head in this episode with those of the fashion industry, seen most clearly in her fitting for the show. The industry is symbolized in this episode through the head designer for Dolce & Gabbana, Oscar, who announces, "we're just calling me 'O' now, love," played brilliantly by British actor Alan Cumming. As she tries on a dress for the show, O immediately begins the process of judgment Carrie feared, deeming within seconds what looks good—her bust and waist—and what looks not so good—her height. Furthermore, he treats her body as if he owns it in this moment, touching and prodding her in his assessment, fluffing her hair, patting her on the butt when he changes his mind, and even forcing her to walk away from him and then trot back in a ridiculous fashion that seems purely designed for his amusement. This comments upon the control that the fashion industry has over women's bodies, determining what looks good and what does not through the types of clothes they produce and the models that they use to display them. These strategies of the fashion industry, spurned on by the beauty myths of the dominant culture, keep women in a position of being looked at, and their love of fashion in a place of frivolity, adding to their subservient position. Carrie's attempts to interject her subversive use of fashion, as well as her identity as a writer and not a model—an attempt to allow the fashionable body to signify more than just looks—go unheeded throughout the scene and in many ways she seems bested by the dominant ideologies encapsulated by the fashion industry.

As the episode continues, Carrie gets caught up in the fantasy of being a model, even admitting her own fascination with models to a fashion photographer she becomes friendly with, stating, "they're just beautiful." The use of the word "just" in this statement becomes important, as it signifies the simplicity of appearance in the fashion industry. There, being beautiful is enough, and there is no need for other attributes, which would only complicate and perhaps get in the way of beauty. This continues as she and Stanford—her single chosen guest backstage at the fashion show, demonstrating his fashionable nature with a bright orange suit—joke about her status as a model, both clearly excited by this idea, and Carrie begins to appropriate O's terminology, stating proudly afterward, "that's a fashion term." Her bubble is soon burst, however, when the dress she was supposed to wear becomes a pair of jeweled panties and an overcoat. This shocks her back to her identity as a writer, which she tries in vain to assert to the variety of fashion industry stylists who make her "fabulous" for the show. Carrie's continual assertions of "I'm a writer" to the various designers, hair stylists, and make-up artists, who accost her with beauty, reinforces her belief in the ability of fashion to signify much more than appearance. And though they ignore her, she inadvertently brings her own use of fashion into the show.

During an emergency visit from Samantha backstage, who assures her that she is a model, Carrie brags about the addition of super high heels to the outfit, a gesture to the trademark Manolo Blahnik stilettos she frequently wears on the show. It is these heels, Carrie's insertion of her use of fashion, that queers this moment of perfected beauty. Carrie makes her grand entrance onto the runway as Cheryl Lynn's disco hit, "Got to Be Real," begins playing. Carrie's strut down the runway lasts only a few feet, however, as one of her shoes comes undone and sends her flying to the floor, prompting a frustrated exclamation of "fuck me hard!" from Lynn Cameron in the control booth, who orders supermodel Heidi Klum, awaiting her turn backstage, to "go." As Heidi steps over Carrie, still sprawled out on the floor, a horrified Stanford exclaims, "Oh my God! She's fashion road kill!" In this moment Carrie does, in Cameron's words, fuck the fashion industry hard, interrupting its moment of perfect, to-be-looked-at beauty with imperfection, the insertion of "fashion road kill." Carrie's fashionable body, sprawled out on the floor at this moment a subversion to the role of woman as perfect object to be looked at, asserting instead, as the song playing overhead states, Carrie's desire "to be real." And even though the fall was an accident, it was brought on by her conscious addition to the outfit—the super high heels that are a part of her trademark style. As she lies on the runway, her voiceover asserts, "I had a choice. I could slink off the runway and let my inner model die of shame, or I could pick myself up—flaws and all—and finish. And that's just what I did, because when real people fall down in life, they get right back up and keep on walking." Carrie manages, in the end, to make fashion her own, as she completes her strut with only one shoe, disrupting the perfection of the fashion world for this moment, and resistively appropriating its space to demonstrate that there is more to clothing than outward appearance. In a way, it was fashion itself that helps her to do this, her strappy heels reminding her who she is and what fashion means to her. And, it is in this way that Carrie asserts her postmodern identity over the more modern—perfect, static—identity that the fashion industry attempts to make for her.

The episode closes with Carrie in her closet in her regular underwear (men's briefs) and a tank top, placing her clothes gained from the fashion show—the pair of jeweled panties—in her drawer, the voiceover stating, "I tucked my jeweled underwear and my inner model away, where they belonged, and went back to my life as a real person." As she says this, Carrie turns to the camera and struts toward it, model-style to the beat of "Got To Be Real," then turning and heading back toward her bathroom as if she were on a runway, swaying her hips, arms gracelessly side to side over her head as she gets to the door, closing it behind her. Carrie demonstrates that she has taken her role in the fashion industry and made it her own, demonstrating the importance of, in de Certeau's (1984: 31) words, "what the consumer *makes* of these images [of the dominant culture]." Carrie is still able to appreciate fashion, and even modeling, as long as she does it her way, queering the runway strut through her awkward dance with her hips and arms at the runway's end, not unlike her fall on the real runway. The song continues to play as the credits roll over her closed bathroom door, a break from the usual fade to black and theme song that accompanies the credits, symbolizing the significance of this song and the importance of this experience to Carrie's identity. This episode pulls Carrie's sense of self in a variety of directions, not unlike the postmodern culture of which she is a part. But it also demonstrates, as Anthony King (2006: 120) explains, that the postmodern "self is realized in the act of consumption. The self is established temporarily in effervescent fusions with commodities. Commodities become the vehicle of externalization." Carrie enacts various visions of her self throughout the episode and as the credits end, and the song sounds its horn finale, Carrie peeks her head out of the door, offers a big smile and slams it shut once more, letting us know that the runway ends *her* way.

### A woman's right to shoes

Another example of the productive nature of Carrie's fashion consumption occurs in season six with the episode, "A Woman's Right To Shoes." The title immediately draws attention to the female body, as it is a parody of the pro-choice statement, "A Woman's Right To Choose." Though the episode does focus specifically on the issues of the right to have and not have children, it is Carrie's feet that bear the most bodily significance and possess the most resistive force in this episode. But, before we even get to her feet; consumption is foregrounded as a central theme of power and hierarchy.

The episode begins with Carrie, shopping bags in hand, moving from store to store while the voiceover explains, "The single New Yorker's weekend is all about buying. The latest *Vogue*, fresh flowers, and gifts for previously single New Yorkers." In what follows, we witness Carrie purchase gift after gift from various bridal and baby registries, in support of her friends. In the next scene, Carrie and Stanford ride the elevator to a friend's apartment for a baby shower, each bearing gifts and discussing what they bought for the baby. The two are paired together as outsiders, both in their own ways breaking the rules of heteronormativity—Stanford by being gay, Carrie by being single, and both of them for choosing each other instead of a romantic partner for this outing. However, they are able to "pass" in this instance through consumption—in buying gifts, they have, in a sense bought their way into the realm of the dominant, if only for one night. In this moment they illustrate Fiske's (2000: 323) understanding of the potential of commodities, "Commodities are the resources of the woman (or man) who is exercising some control over her look, her social relations, and her relation to the social order." Shopping has allowed Carrie and Stanford to control their relation to the dominant social order of heterosexual family in this moment.

As they enter the party, they are greeted by Margo, the aunt of the new baby, and are told where to put their gifts and where to put their shoes, the latter causing both Carrie and Stanford to freeze, and look down at the rows of shoes in horror, the camera following their line of vision. Carrie voices their shared concern as she lifts her present over her head to show off her clothes, stating plainly, "But this is an outfit." Both Carrie and Stanford are dressed in their usual eye-catching manner—Carrie in a fuchsia and green strapless dress with black bra straps protruding and a pair of silver Manolo Blahnik sandals, Stanford in a blue and green wide-plaid suit with green shirt and tie combo and a pair of black wingtips. Neither is excited about the prospect of removing the shoes that complete these outfits. Margo then explains, "Keira and Chuck [the parents] don't like outside dirt coming in. The twins are always picking stuff up off the floor." In this moment it becomes clear that Carrie and Stanford's consumption revolving around what might be considered "appropriate" reasons, such as gifts that support people conforming to heteronormative standards, *will* be accepted at this party. Their consumption around more trivial "inappropriate" reasons, such as being fashionable, *will not* be accepted. In fact, it is identified as posing a threat to the heteronormative family.

At the evening's conclusion, Carrie and Stanford appear bored and out of place as the couples remaining discuss buying summer homes and Carrie states, "Well, it's getting late. It's midnight. He's gay and has to start his night," identifying she and Stanford's queer lifestyle in opposition to the lifestyle of the married couples. As they reach the door to be reunited with their shoes, Carrie discovers that her shoes have gone missing, and is forced to borrow a pair from her hostess with the promise that her shoes will surely "turn up." The next shot is of her feet, awkwardly making the walk home in a pair of old tennis shoes, as the frivolity of her Manolos is contrasted with the practical nature of these shoes, a *mother's* shoes. Her voiceover narrates the experience, stating, "They say you shouldn't judge until you've walked a mile in someone else's shoes. I made it six blocks," reinforcing the differences she sees between herself and her family-based friend.

The next day, Carrie returns to the site of her loss to ask if her shoes have "turned up" only to discover that they have not. Keira offers to pay for the shoes, and invites Carrie in while she writes the check, eyeing Carrie's shoed feet meaningfully as Carrie steps into the house, and Carrie awkwardly removes her shoes so as not to dirty the children's environment. When Keira asks Carrie how much the shoes cost, and Carrie replies, "$485," Keira looks shocked and declares the number ridiculous, claiming that she only spent that much money on shoes before she had a "real life," and states, "I really don't think we should have to pay for your extravagant lifestyle." In this moment, Carrie's shoes, a central focus of her life, become Othered. They are opposed to the central focus of Keira's life, children, and the shoes come out on bottom, being deemed extravagant. Extravagant, of course, denotes something unnecessary, in fact, ridiculously unnecessary, marking Carrie's lifestyle as silly and frivolous in comparison to Keira's lifestyle replete with children and conformity. Furthermore, Carrie's body gets marked as useless in this exchange, as hers can only be used as a tool of consumption, with no creative ability of its own. Keira's body, on the other hand, has produced children, and therefore no longer requires the extravagance of fashion. Whereas Keira has made the appropriate move by the dominant culture by getting married and having children, Carrie is in a long-term relationship with her clothes, and because of this she is not worth compensating when this relationship is disrupted by someone else's actions. Carrie later identifies this as a moment of "shoe shaming," her feet betraying her inadequacy in the eyes of the larger culture.

The choice of Carrie's feet as the site of bodily power struggle in this episode is significant on several levels. It is the primary site of Carrie's fashion fetish, as she is seen most often admiring, adoring, and buying shoes, and therefore, it represents a highly important site of identity for her as well as perhaps the most painful site of loss. On a different level though, the feet represent one of the more shame-inducing parts of the body, after the genitalia of course, and the forced baring of her feet at a party, especially for someone as shoe savvy as Carrie, comes close to the type of shame experienced in nightmares of high-school nakedness. As Mary Douglas (1996: 37) explains, "our pollution behavior is the reaction which condemns any object or idea likely to confuse or contradict cherished classifications," and in this episode, Carrie's feet—already a polluted body part—come to represent the threat the queer body poses to the cherished classifications of heterosexual family. Carrie's feet become a synecdoche for her whole body, which is dirtied and shamed by its inappropriate use, and the consumption used to cover this shame is stripped away in this moment, leaving her bare feet behind. It is significant that we never see Keira wearing shoes in this episode until the end, as she is always in her house, where no shoes are allowed. Keira's body, through her feet, is marked as natural in this way, as she doesn't need shoes to cover up any shame or unnaturalness. It is Carrie, however, who is used to remind the viewer that the "natural" body is a myth, that "the body is always-already encoded by culture" (Negrin, 1999: 104). Though Carrie is shamed by Keira for her shoes and chastised by the heteronormative structure of family to which she does not conform, her use of consumption allows her to resist these shamings and enact proudly a postmodern/queer identity.

When Carrie realizes that she has spent $2,300 celebrating Keira's life choices, such as her engagement, her marriage, and the birth of her three children, her shame turns to righteous indignation. As she comes to the realization that there are no landmarks to celebrate for single people after graduation, she becomes angered that she is put in the space of the other merely because she chose not to get married, and more angry that a woman she considered her friend was the one to put her there. In a moment of clarity, Carrie calls Keira, and leaves a message, stating, "I just wanted to let you know that I'm getting married," pausing to add, "to myself. Oh, and I'm registered at Manolo Blahnik." The next scene shows Keira buying the shoes that Carrie registered for—the silver sandals lost at the party—and being shamed herself, as the woman in the store asks her to watch her children because the owners don't want them "touching the shoes." Not only does consumption allow Carrie to retain her queer lifestyle in this instance, but it also places the heteronorm, in Keira, in the space of the other momentarily. The card that accompanies Carrie's wedding gift reads, "Congratulations! We couldn't be happier for you and you," demonstrating that Carrie's queerness is not just intact, but it has brought about a moment of acceptance within dominant modes of understanding. As Carrie prances down the street in her shoes at the episode's close, the voiceover explains, "The fact is, sometimes it's hard to walk in a single woman's shoes. That's why we need really special ones now and then, to make the walk a little more fun." Carrie's self-identification as single, given her adamancy about it throughout the show, queers her, placing her on the outside of normativity. By identifying the difficulty in this identity, she opens up a space for acceptance to break through. Moreover, by using consumption to assuage this difficulty, Carrie engages in what de Certeau (1984: 26) terms "trickery," or the opening of a space in which the "order can be *tricked* by an art"—in this case, the art of consumption as a means of fashioning a fulfilling lifestyle outside of the boundaries of normal.

## Reflections

In her examination of the fashion industry, Dorinne Kondo (1997: 106) has noted the importance of moving beyond the conception of fashion as "frivolity," citing not only its constructive power in culture and identity, but also "the aesthetic pleasures, desires and political possibilities that can open up within particular regimes of power" as a result of fashion's role within our culture. It is specifically these particular "aesthetic pleasures, desires and political possibilities" that the character of Carrie engages in through her consumption of fashion. Clothes become for Carrie a site of identity and the reclamation of power in a culture that denies a space to queer bodies, to bodies that refuse to conform to heteronormative standards. The bond that Carrie shares with fashion on the show and her own assertion of identity through the consumption of fashion gives *Sex and the City* moments of uniquely resistive character that rupture the show's place, nestled firmly in the grip of the dominant culture and dominant ideologies of gender, class, race, and sexuality. In watching Carrie literally fashion her identity, viewers are taught how to (re)fashion theirs. They are shown how to use fashion to create their own sense of personal style.

But the character of Carrie on *Sex and the City* does more than simply model a queer subjectivity and thus transgressive consumption. She provides actual symbolic resources in the form of styles and fashions that viewers can (re)appropriate and put their own personal stamp or spin on. As Sasha Roseneil (1999: 165) has pointed out, "Postmodernity is the era of enhanced reflexivity, in which processes of detraditionalization and individualization mean that people are increasingly aware of creating their own life narratives." As viewers creatively (re)combine the images, styles, and looks offered up by their favorite TV shows and characters with their own wardrobes and tastes, they can exercise some degree of self-awareness in the construction of their identities. None of these practices occurs, of course, within a cultural vacuum, and viewers cannot simply eschew the heavy cultural baggage carried by many signs. As such, future studies ought to more carefully investigate the complex mediation of semiotic openness with prevailing cultural codes in the lives of everyday viewers. Nevertheless, as our analysis has shown, "it is in this [queer] marginalized area of the contingent, the decorative, the futile that not simply a new aesthetic but a new cultural order may seed itself" (Wilson, 1987: 107). Such, then, are the stakes in fashion(able/ing) selves.

## Notes

1   While clearly not every mode of postmodern identity qualifies as "queer," we argue that a queer subjectivity is necessarily postmodern.
2   It is interesting to note that the GLBT community has responded in largely positive ways to the show, noting its "gayness." In an article in *The Advocate* extolling the show's gay virtues, one fan stated, "I really feel like it comes from a gay man's perspective. They all go to the gym, have sex, drink cosmos, and shop. They are gay men" (Hensley, 1999: 88). Beyond what might be considered more superficial elements of gay/straight alliance, the show also has been noticed for its queer politics, winning the Gay and Lesbian Alliance Against Defamation's (GLAAD) 2004 Media Award for "Outstanding Comedy Series," and in discussions of cable drama/comedy involving gay characters, *Sex and the City* is often dubbed the "queerest," beating out shows like *Queer as Folk* and *The L Word* (Adams & Rawi, 2004).

## Works cited

Adams, N. & Rawi, A. (2004, April 13) "Julianne Moore, Cherry Jones, *Sex & the City, People en Espanol*, Honored at 15th Annual GLAAD Media Awards Presented by Absolut Vodka in New York", http://www.glaad.org/media/release_detail.php?id=3652. Retrieved September 15, 2007.

Belk, R. (1999) "I Shop, Therefore I Am", *American Anthropologist* 101 (1): 182–185.

Bourdieu, P. (1984) *Distinction: A Social Critique of the Judgment of Taste*, trans. R. Nice. Cambridge: Harvard University Press.

Brown, H.G. (1962) *Sex and the Single Girl*. New York: B. Geis Associates.

Brummett, B. (1984) "Burke's Representative Anecdote as a Method in Media Criticism", *Critical Studies in Mass Communication* 1: 161–176.

Brummett, B. (1991) *Rhetorical Dimensions of Popular Culture*. Tuscaloosa: The University of Alabama Press.

Bruzzi, S. & Gibson, P.C. (2004) " 'Fashion Is the Fifth Character': Fashion, Costume, and Design in *Sex & the City*." In K. Akass & J. McCabe (eds) *Reading Sex & the City*. London: I.B. Tauris.

Burke, K. (1941) *The Philosophy of Literary Form: Studies in Symbolic Action*. Baton Rouge: Louisiana State University Press.

Burke, K. (1953) *Counter-Statement, 2nd edition*. Los Altos, CA: Hermes Publications.

Butler, J. (1990) *Gender Trouble: Feminism and the Subversion of Identity*. New York: Routledge.

Butler, J. (1993) *Bodies That Matter: On the Discursive Limits of "Sex"*. New York: Routledge.

de Beauvoir, S. (1988) *The Second Sex*. London: Picador.

de Certeau, M. (1984) *The Practice of Everyday Life*, trans. S. Rendell. Berkeley: University of California Press.

Douglas, M. (1996) *Purity and Danger: An Analysis of the Concepts of Pollution and Taboo*. New York: Routledge.

Featherstone, M. (2000) "Object Domains, Ideology and Interests", in M.J. Lee (ed.) *The Consumer Society Reader*. Malden: Blackwell Publishers.

Fiske, J. (1989) *Reading the Popular*. Boston: Unwin Hyman.

Fiske, J. (2000) "Shopping for Pleasure: Malls, Power, and Resistance", pp 306–328 in J.B. Schor & D.B. Holt (eds) *The Consumer Society Reader*. New York: The New Press.

Freud, S. (1974) "Femininity", in *New Introductory Lectures on Psychoanalysis*, (ed.) and trans. J. Strachey. London: Hogarth.

Hebdige, D. (1979) *Subculture: The Meaning of Style*. London: Routledge.

Hensley, D. (1999, November 23) "Hooked on Sex: HBO's Sex & the City Revolves around Straight Women, but the Saucy Sitcom Has a Gay Sensibility All Its Own", *The Advocate*.

Jagose, A. (1996) *Queer Theory: An Introduction*. New York: New York University Press.

Kellner, D. (1995) *Media Culture: Cultural Studies, Identity and Politics Between the Modern and the Postmodern*. New York: Routledge.

King, A. (2006) "Serial Killing and the Postmodern Self", *History of the Human Sciences* 19 (3): 109–125.

Kondo, D. (1997) *About Face: Performing Race in Fashion and Theatre*. New York: Routledge.

Maddison, S. (2000) *Fags, Hags, and Queer Sisters: Gender Dissent and Heterosocial Bonds in Gay Culture*. New York: St. Martin's Press.

Marx, K. (1975) *Early Writings*. Harmondsworth: Penguin.

Meyer, M. (1994) "Introduction: Reclaiming the Discourse of Camp", pp 1–22 in M. Meyer (ed.) *The Politics and Poetics of Camp*. New York: Routledge.

Negrin, L. (1999) "The Self as Image: A Critical Appraisal of Postmodern Theories of Fashion", *Theory, Culture & Society* 16 (3): 99–118.

Ott, B.L. (2003) " 'I'm Bart Simpson, Who the Hell Are You?' A Study in Postmodern Identity (Re)Construction", *Journal of Popular Culture* 37 (1): 56–82.

Roseneil, S. (1999) "Postmodern Feminist Politics: The Art of the (Im)Possible?", *European Journal of Women's Studies* 6: 161–182.

Schor, J.B. (1999) "What's Wrong with Consumer Society? Competitive Spending and the 'New Consumerism' ", pp 37–50 in R. Rosenblatt (ed.) *Consuming Desires: Consumption, Culture, and the Pursuit of Happiness*. Washington, D.C.: Island Press.

Seidman, S. (1993) "Identity and Politics in a 'Postmodern' Gay Culture: Some Historical and Conceptual Notes", pp 105–142 in M. Warner (ed.) *Fear of a Queer Planet: Queer Politics and Social Theory*. Minneapolis: University of Minnesota Press.

Stockton, K.B. (2003) "Cloth Wounds: Queer Aesthetics of Debasement", in P.R. Matthews & D. McWhirter (eds) *Aesthetic Subjects*. Minneapolis: University of Minnesota Press.

Warner, M. (1993) "Introduction", pp vii–xxxi in M. Warner (ed.) *Fear of a Queer Planet: Queer Politics and Social Theory*. Minneapolis: University of Minnesota Press.

Wilson, E. (1987) *Adorned in Dreams: Fashion and Modernity*. London: Virago.

# Chapter 12

# "No country for the infirm"

## Angels in an unchanged America

*Joanna L. Di Mattia*

> *This is how one pictures the angel of history. His face is turned toward the past. Where we perceive a chain of events, he sees one single catastrophe which keeps piling wreckage upon wreckage and hurls it in front of his feet . . . This storm irresistibly propels him into the future to which his back is turned, while the pile of debris before him grows skyward. This storm is what we call progress.*
>
> Walter Benjamin (1992: 249)

> *For gay people to be truly public, they would have to be able to display their sexual orientation—and discuss their sexuality within the same parameters laid out for heterosexuals . . . Until gay sexuality is removed from the realm of "privacy," gay people will never be full citizens.*
>
> Michael Bronski (1998: 184)

> *For AIDS is not only a medical crisis on an unparalleled scale, it involves a crisis of representation itself, a crisis over the entire framing of knowledge about the human body and its capacities for sexual pleasure.*
>
> Simon Watney (1996: 9)

### The world only spins forward

At the close of "Bad News," Chapter One of HBO's *Angels in America*, Roy Cohn (Al Pacino) is diagnosed with AIDS. It is October 1985 and Roy employs the same AIDS lexicon as the mainstream media. Despite the visibility of the virus on his body after the removal of several Kaposi sarcoma lesions, Roy rejects the diagnosis, because as he and the wider community understand it, AIDS afflicts mostly homosexuals and intravenous drug users. Like the real Roy Cohn on whom this dramatized version is based, *Angels in America*'s Roy Cohn remains closeted until his death, perpetuating the fiction that he has liver cancer (a more heterosexual and manly illness). Roy insists that he cannot possibly have AIDS because, as he defines it, he cannot possibly be a homosexual. He tells his doctor, Henry (James Cromwell), that unlike a homosexual,

Roy Cohn is a *citizen* with social and political power. He explains that being gay doesn't define who you sleep with but rather:

> Like all labels they tell you one thing and one thing only: where does an individual, so identified, fit in the food chain, in the pecking order. Not ideology, or sexual taste, but something much simpler: clout. Not who I fuck or who fucks me, but who will pick up the phone when I call, who owes me favors.

Unlike most homosexuals, Roy has clout and as a result is *not* invisible within the public domain. For Roy Cohn, what his body desires and does plays no part in his self- or social identification. As Roy explains, sexuality defines more than participation in certain sex acts, but importantly, one's social and political status: "Homosexuals are not men who sleep with other men. Homosexuals are men who in fifteen years of trying cannot pass a pissant antidiscrimination bill through City Council. Homosexuals are men who know nobody and who nobody knows." Disowning the role his own body and its desires plays in defining who he is, Roy's rant nevertheless raises key questions about the status of the gay male body and gay sexual practice in demands for citizenship. In addition, Roy sets up a vital dichotomy that resonates throughout *Angels in America* between visible/invisible, known/unknown bodies. Crucially, this scene reinforces the centrality of the gay male corpus in *Angels in America* and in the public domain at this time in history. The gay male corpus, both sick and healthy, is critical to true progress in debates about gay men's social, cultural, and political power and privilege.

When it first screened on HBO in December 2003, *Angels in America* was heavily promoted as an "HBO Event." A $60 million dollar, two part, five-and-a-half hour, star-studded television film of Tony Kushner's Pulitzer Prize- and Tony Award-winning play, HBO President Colin Callender explained that the network "has never had an event like this" (Gener, 2003: 31). Further, Callender categorizes *Angels in America* as "groundbreaking" and "rule breaking" for both HBO programming and television history (31). Callender locates the film in the context of "risk-taking" that is often associated with HBO programming: "We offer a safe haven, a protected environment, in which creative talent can take risks and make movies that would otherwise not be made and released in theatres" (32). *Angels in America* is not only an "HBO Event" but represents a major cultural event that has *reappeared* at a crucial juncture in American social history. First screened in the lead-up to Bush's re-election in November 2004, it is viewed within the tone of conservative Christian rhetoric that saturated American public life at this time. A context of panic and anxiety about all things sexual and aligned with the body defines "the year of living indecently," as Frank Rich (2005: AR1) referred to it in the wake of "Nipplegate." It is my position here that *Angels in America* takes risks and breaks television rules in a number of ways, not only related to its length and star-power, but that are specifically courageous in this particular cultural and political climate. But why, in the year 2003, when nearly anything goes on both network and cable television, would a film like *Angels in America* still be considered provocative?

This chapter argues that the desire for "normalcy" evident in President Bush's America is in conflict with the increasing visibility of gay issues in the political realm and the presence of gay men (in particular) and lesbians in popular cultural narratives. This chapter explores the role played by gay men's bodies in visibility debates. I use *Angels in America* to look critically at how knowledge about bodies is formed by media technologies and why some bodies remain invisible in media culture. Refusing to acquiesce to the rules of hetero-normativity, Kushner's world is populated by characters fighting to be visible, seen, and known. It is my position that AIDS prompts a theoretical and dis-cursive crisis, but is also a representational crisis that challenges how we *look at, see*, and come to *know*, the gay male body as a sexualized corpus. In short, AIDS problematizes images of gay men's bodies and sexual practice. In this context, I argue that accepting the fundamental role the body plays in the articulation of gay identity is essential. *Angels in America* illuminates the limitations of demands for media visibility of gays and lesbians that remain confined to those images that are palatable and comfortable for mainstream, heterosexual audiences.

The body is the primary medium by which Kushner's characters come to know each other, and by which the audience in turn comes to know them. As the crisis that triggers its action, *Angels in America* is primarily an AIDS narra-tive. As AIDS remains largely a sexually transmitted virus, it is an illness inextricably tied to a sexualized body. This chapter understands AIDS as a disease that makes an invisible sexual difference *visible* on the body's surface. It is my position here that only when heterosexual audiences deal with the real-ities of gay male sexual practice—its pleasures *and* its risks—can they engage with gay men as human beings and not monstrous, marginalized others. *Angels in America* reveals that the visibility of the body that is defined as deviant, abnormal, and infirm, is essential to this process. *Angels in America* reinvests the infirm, marginal body with subjective experience.

The AIDS body, when gay and male, is for better or worse, perceived as a sexualized body. The sexual corpus to which this chapter refers is not simply a body that has sex. Nor do I refer to images of a body engaged in explicit sex acts; although we see gay men kissing, touching, dancing, and lying together in bed, graphic sexual images are absent from this text. This does not, I would argue, diminish the important and radical nature of the images of the gay male body on display here. What matters is the way in which *Angels in America* simultaneously intellectualizes and materializes the role that the gay male body plays in visibility and citizenship debates. It does this via a sexual corpus that is a sensual, sensory body—a body that senses and experiences, that makes things intelligible, a body that exists in the world. Unrestricted by the fears and anxieties of advertisers, HBO can play a key role in defining a new representational terrain for gay men's bodies.

*Angels in America* is concerned with the antithetical concepts of stasis and movement, or progress. Change is the key throughout this narrative. Change is also implied by our viewing. As Michael Bronski (2004: 58) explains, with this humanistic narrative, "we see the possibility of change through empathy." Stasis, on the other hand, is aligned with death and stagnation, opposed to both individual and large-scale social progress. Parts One and Two of HBO's *Angels in America* are divided along these lines: part one, *Millennium Approaches*, shaped by a growing sense of anxiety, fear, and dread at personal and social change, and *Perestroika*, as its name suggests, driven by acceptance of and desire for movement, change, and progression. Importantly, as the narrative reveals, physical pain and suffering are fundamental to this process. When he discovers that he has AIDS, Prior Walter (Justin Kirk) is convinced that he will die. When he is abandoned by his lover, Louis Ironson (Ben Shenkman), he *wants to* die, and conjures an Angel (Emma Thompson) who decrees that humankind has driven God away and as a result, "You must stop moving!" For Prior to progress towards acceptance that he is sick and commit himself to "more life," he must let go of the past and step into an unknown future, in a world that only spins forward. As he later tells the assembly of angels in heaven, suffering equals visibility in the world. Despite our fear of the future, "We can't just stop. We're not rocks. Progress, migration, motion, is modernity. It's animate. It's what living things do. We desire. Even if all we desire is stillness, it's still desire *for*." And finally, and most importantly, Prior affirms that, "Even sick, I want to be alive."

As a cultural text, HBO's *Angels in America* reminds us that social and political progress for gays and lesbians demands a concurrent shift in the realm of representation. Richard Dyer (1993: 1) persuasively argues for the continued importance of image analysis: "How we are seen determines in part how we are treated; how we treat others is based on how we see them; such seeing comes from representation." For Simon Watney (1996: 8), "we can only ultimately conceive of ourselves and one another in relation to the circulation of available images in any given society." Toby Miller and Justin Lewis (2003: 2) explain that cultural institutions produce cultural citizenship "and nurture a sense of belonging." As much as they format this "public collective subjectivity" cultural institutions can foster a sense of isolation and disenfranchisement that leads to certain groups never being represented. For Miller (1998: 5), media technologies create truths (or accepted facts) through which the cultural citizen is "formed and reformed on a routine basis through technologies of truth—popular logics for establishing fact." If the "truth" is created by the media functions to "build citizens" (1998: 7), then it is essential to question the type of citizen it builds: Who is included in these power relations? Who is rendered docile and invisible? As an instrument of the state, television shapes the ways in which we come to *know* by privileging some bodies and excluding others from the field of knowledge. It decides which bodies matter.

As noted, the history of images of homosexuality on American television is a history of policing the "comfort levels" of heterosexual viewers, often via humour. Network television productions such as *Ellen, Will and Grace*, and *Queer Eye for the Straight Guy* reveal that what we see of gay bodies and gay lives continues to operate within limits of what is deemed palatable to the tastes and values of "middle America." As Debbie Novotny (Sharon Gless) on *Queer as Folk* explains, "Let's face it honey, most viewers don't want to think about gays having sex. It just makes them uncomfortable." This policing of the sensual and sexual gay corpus is most apparent on network television, where throughout the 1990s network stations had a "broadcasting tradition that said that shows could imply as much just-off camera kissing as they liked, as long as none of it spilled into the *visible frame*." (Capsuto, 2000: 361, emphasis mine).

Although it seems that there are greater numbers of gay and lesbian characters on US television screens, across dramas, comedies, and "reality" offerings, than ever before, visibility for its own sake is ineffective. Visibility is about more than being seen. As Suzanna Danuta Walters (2001: 10) has argued, while gays and lesbians are *seen* in a variety of "non-threatening" poses throughout the vastness of popular culture, they are not really *known*. Writing about the invisibility of lesbians on U.S. television, Stacey D'erasmo (2004: 2.1) notes that gays and lesbians live in a "representational desert" that leads to a "ferocious desire not only to be seen in some literal sense" but also "to be seen with all the blood and angst and magic you possess." D'erasmo's argument interrogates the limits of a cultural visibility that does not address the ways in which we come to *know* the bodies of gay men and women. Referring specifically to HBO's *Angels in America*, she suggests that *knowledge creation* requires visibility of a particular mode: bold and uncompromising. D'erasmo (2004: 2.1) asks: "Visibility is a tricky thing; is someone visible when you can point her out in a crowd, or when you understand what her life feels like to her?"

On cable television stations, a number of recent shows have reconfigured the representational terrain of homosexuality on American television, and as a result have enlarged the parameters of what we *know* about being gay. Programs such as Showtime's groundbreaking *Queer as Folk* and *The L Word*, HBO's *Six Feet*

*Under* and, more recently, the hyper-masculine *The Sopranos* offer something other than images of gays and lesbians that are easy for straight audiences to stomach. Importantly, they have achieved this through direct engagement with the sexualized body. *Queer as Folk*, in particular, has expanded the iconography by presenting gay men and lesbians as multidimensional, flawed, and sexual human beings for the first time in an American television drama. Representations of gay men on premium cable stations HBO and Showtime can be contrasted with the sexless, inoffensive eunuchs and clowns most often found on network stations. On *Six Feet Under* and *Queer as Folk*, for example, gay men are visible doing what defines them as gay in the first place: loving and fucking other men.

## Bodies that matter

Throughout American history, the sexual body has been a key site of conflict. Kathleen Kennedy and Sharon Ullman (2003: xiii) suggest that "sexuality helps define the boundaries and hierarchies of gender, class, and race difference by encoding beliefs about normalcy and degeneracy" that are "integral to the process by which Americans produce new identities, social practices, and structural changes." Similarly, Elizabeth Bernstein and Laurie Schaffner (2005: xiii) suggest that social panics about sexuality "often serve as a barometer of more generalized social tensions—in times of economic and cultural flux, sex may become an easy and frequent target of campaigns for state regulation." Further, they remind us that, "the state serves to shape our erotic possibilities and to impact a particular normative vision. The state, in short, has a sexual agenda" (xiii).

It is clear that social panics about sex are, more often than not, panics about the transgression of "normal" gender and sexual roles. A concern with what is "normal" requires a distinction with an entity that is not normal, or deviant. Those bodies categorized as "abnormal" are also implicitly seen as un-American. Because homosexual bodies cannot be contained within or regulated by heteronormativity and its attendant institutions of marriage and, ideally, monogamy, they are conceptualized as deviant and un-American.

Bodies are monitored, disciplined, and normalized by culture. As culture regulates women and their bodies, so too does it regulate men into appropriately masculine forms, in particular, those men whose bodies cannot be contained by heteronormativity. Throughout history the bodies of homosexual men have been subjected to stringent social controls that render them invisible and powerless in the public domain—the history of the gay and lesbian liberation movement is about this struggle for public visibility and viability. Feminist theories of the body revaluate the denigrated role that the body, or corporeality, has played in knowledge formation throughout the Western tradition, a tradition that has prized the mind, or reason, above corporeal knowledge. As Susan Bordo (1989: 13) notes, the body is both a "medium of culture" and "metaphor for culture." Drawing on Michel Foucault's concept of disciplinary regimes of the body, Bordo (13) notes that, "The body is not only a *text* of culture. It is . . . a *practical*, direct locus of social control."

In *Discipline and Punish: The Birth of the Prison*, Foucault (1979: 11) writes a history of the creation of docile bodies through state regulated practices of punishment, discipline, and surveillance. Foucault notes that in these disciplinary systems, the body is monitored and "caught up in a system of constraints and privations, obligations and prohibitions." As instruments of the state, media technologies, such as television, can be seen as regulating bodies and inscribing these with a series of power relations. Bodies are coerced to remain within the boundaries of appropriate or normal behavior attached to culturally proscribed practices or face expulsion from the social order. These punishments are often silent, or subtle, existing within, what Foucault (1979: 25) calls, a " 'political economy' of the body" that serves a distinct social function. As Foucault (1979: 25–26) explains:

> the body is also directly involved in a political field; power relations have an immediate hold upon it; they invest it, mark it, train it, torture it, force it to carry out tasks, to perform ceremonies, to emit signs . . . the body becomes a useful force only if it is a productive body and a subjected body.

Social discourse and practices institute a series of regulatory laws in which men and women who do not articulate a gender identity that conforms to their biological sexual identity risk exclusion from the cultural and political domain. In *Gender Trouble*, Judith Butler (1990: 33) extends this vision to explain that the body, culturally inscribed with gender through "a set of repeated acts within a highly regulatory frame," is subjected to narrow practices that exclude certain bodies from a social matrix that accrues privileges (17). This "matrix of intelligibility" is heterosexual in nature and requires a coherent relationship between sex, gender, and sexuality in order that an identity can exist. It is a matrix that:

> assumes that for bodies to cohere and make sense there must be a stable sex expressed through a stable gender (masculine expresses male, feminine expresses female) that is oppositionally and hierarchically defined through the compulsory practice of heterosexuality. (151)

As she famously notes (1990: 139–140), while "genders are part of what 'humanizes' individuals within contemporary culture . . . we regularly punish those who fail to do their gender right." Gay men, whose bodies often produce a gender and sexual identity discontinuous with "proper" masculinity, are among the bodies most frequently, and publicly, punished for this failure. Butler (1990: 17) accounts for the existence of those bodies that cannot be contained within this logic of gender norms, suggesting that these bodies "provide critical opportunities to expose the limits and regulatory aims of that domain of intelligibility and, hence, to open up within the very terms of that matrix of intelligibility rival and subversive matrices of gender disorder."

Timothy Landers (1988) argues that images of AIDS on television are also designed to reinforce a self-other binary, or the existence of bodies that do and don't matter in the audience. He defines this as a visual variation on the normal/abnormal paradigm, the distinction between Bodies and Anti-Bodies (1988: 211). Landers (1988: 281) explains that the Body is manifestly normal, healthy, and whole, part of a homogenous group, "white, middle-class, heterosexual, and healthy, grouped in cozy, stable families." AIDS attacks those outside these values and unable to be disciplined by this regime:

> The Anti-Body becomes, specifically, gay, black, Latino, the IV drug user, the prostitute—in other words, *sick*. Tinged with the stigma of illness, that dramatically destroys the body, what was usually absent from representation becomes spectacularly and consistently *visible*. (282)

These Anti-Bodies are the bodies that threaten straight, white, middle-class values, and it is these bodies that are most often *absent* or *invisible* in representation (282).

Landers' paradigm is also concerned with the persistent identification of AIDS and gay men, noting that the fact that the first reported cases of AIDS were in gay men has shaped people's understanding of the disease. He (1988: 282, emphasis mine) explains that:

> the extant discourse on homosexuality provides the shape, *the invisible framework*, the explanation-by association for AIDS. It is the reigning idea of "homosexuality" that is never represented but upon which representations of AIDS rely.

Landers' concept of an "invisible framework" is an important one, suggesting that AIDS defines gay sexual practice in the popular imagination, and adds "color" to an otherwise sketchy form. Paradoxically, this sexual body, despite its negative marker, remains unknown and invisible, living secret lives and dying secret deaths.

## We won't die secret deaths anymore

Citizenship often comes with conditions, and for gays and lesbians in America, this condition is assimilation, or the denial of difference. Urvashi Vaid (1995: 202) notes that the desire to be citizens of the mainstream can be an appealing one for many gays and lesbians, where, "To be mainstream is to be a part of the majority, to be safe, respectable, maybe even respected." As Roy Cohn suggests, society enfranchises those willing to pretend or play at being straight; that is, those who succeed in keeping their difference invisible. Bodies are visible or invisible within social networks and in terms of homosexuality this manifests as the space inside and outside the figurative "closet." The "closet" remains a highly contested space in queer life and politics and looms large throughout *Angels in America*, in both personal struggles and on a national level. The closet regulates boundaries between normal and deviant bodies, maintaining the insider/outsider status that many homosexuals experience in relation to their citizenship. Vaid (1995: 31) notes that gays and lesbians are often asked to "pass" as something they are not in order to be citizens and access the privileges this accrues: "The more open and comfortable we are about our homosexuality, the farther outside the cultural, political, and religious norm we are kept." If inclusion in mainstream society requires a careful negotiation of this divide, it remains dependent on one's willingness to remain hidden and unknown. Homosexuals are *tolerated* if they stress what is the *same* between gays and straights. Bronski (1998: 183) argues that it is openness about gay lives and bodies that is the threat, where "the overt presence of homosexuality and more public displays of gay culture engendered a backlash intended to reinforce the closet."

Structured around value-laden binaries such as gay/straight, sick/healthy, dirty/clean, and weak/powerful, *Angels in America* interrogates the process of *othering* that shapes most images of gay men. It succeeds at making what was once invisible *visible*, and in challenging conventional terms of reference for both gay bodies and bodies afflicted by AIDS. *Angels in America* is structured around a tension between the visibility and invisibility of the gay male body: to itself, to others, and to the nation as a whole. Corporeality is essential to this process of making visible what remains hidden and therefore *unknown*. The body is a *corpus* as in a collection of texts, the text of identity, a record of experiences. This is not an essentialist truth to which I allude here, rather, a conceptualization of the body as a map or corpus of an individual's experience. The body reveals an individual's status in the social network that embraces or rejects it.

Throughout both stage and screen versions of *Angels in America*, Kushner imagines that homosexuals are at the center of American history, relocating gay men's bodies from margin to center. The bodies of gay men occupy the center of the screen and each of the major characters has a distinctive relationship to their own body and to the bodies of those around them. Because he has AIDS, Prior initially struggles with his body, before resolving to live in it. His lover, Louis, has a contrasting engagement with corporeality. Louis is verbal, cerebral, and runs from how he feels, rationalizing pain and guilt with politics and philosophy. Roy, unable to accept the chasm between his political clout, the disease he is dying from, and what this might say about his position on the food chain, becomes increasingly conflicted with the limitations of his body. Joe Pitt (Patrick Wilson)—a married, closeted, Mormon, Republican lawyer—also battles to reconcile the things he believes with who his body and its desires tell him he really is.

In *Angels in America's* opening scene, Prior and Louis attend the funeral of Louis's grandmother, Sarah. They sit at the rear of the chapel, next to each other, but separated from the rest of the Ironson family. They are positioned as outsiders, their bodies physically located on the margins. For those unversed in the *Angels* story, in this opening scene Prior and Louis's *difference* is hidden from the audience. They could simply be two men seated together, not lovers, but friends, or brothers. After the service, their difference is visible, as Louis says goodbye to his family and Prior stands, excluded and isolated on the street corner. It seems that Prior is unknown to Louis's family and is not introduced on this occasion. The family is leaving together for the burial, but as an outsider, Louis is going alone, by bus. He and Prior walk together, and it is only when they turn the street corner, and are invisible to Louis's family, that we really understand the nature of their relationship. Prior puts his arm around Louis and makes visible both their individual homosexuality and their specific relationship as gay men to each other.

Both Prior and Louis find themselves negotiating the space between visibility and invisibility. As they walk to the bus stop Louis notes that he gets "closety" at these family things. Prior, on the other hand, suggests that Louis gets "butch," introducing himself as "Lou, not Louis, cause if you say Louis they'll hear the sibilant 's'." Prior concurs that Louis was "hiding" from his family, but doesn't blame him for doing so, knowing he would do the same. In Part Two, "Perestroika," a sick Prior is taken to the hospital by Hannah Pitt (Meryl Streep), Joe's mother. Hannah asks him if he is a homosexual, and Prior jokes, "Oh, is it that obvious?" Prior says yes. While this is clearly Hannah's first close encounter with an openly gay man, Prior is not presented here as "obviously" or visibly gay, and despite his illness, it is not named, in their initial exchange, as AIDS. Hannah wants to know if Prior is a "typical homosexual," which Prior interprets as this is generally defined, like a hairdresser. Prior says that he is "stereotypical," but as we see throughout *Angels in America*, he is not stereotypical, but rather fractures stereotypes. These exchanges reveal the often self-imposed closet in which gay men are forced to live, and their aware-ness of the dual space in which their bodies exist.

In a state of far greater self-denial is Joe Pitt, Hannah's son. Louis first encounters Joe the day after the funeral. Louis is in the bathroom of the Federal courthouse at which they both work—Joe as the chief clerk of the chief justice, Louis as a word processor. He is crying, distressed by the discovery that Prior has AIDS. Hidden away in the bathroom, unable to deal with Prior's illness, Joe is the first lawyer to enter and actually ask Louis if he is okay. Their exchange reveals a compelling tension between what is visible and invisible to each man about the other. Although Joe remains invisible to himself, Louis correctly reads him as gay. Beyond "gaydar," there is something about who Joe *really is* that is visible here. When Joe admits that he voted for Reagan, *twice*, Louis is surprised: "Well, oh boy, a gay Republican." While the incongruity of these terms surprises Louis, Joe seems confused and says, "I'm not gay." Louis plays along, claiming that he could tell, from the sound of Joe's voice, that he sounded like a Republican. Despite the denial, Joe is intrigued by his visibility to Louis, and a series of incomplete inquiries ensues: "Do I, sound like *a . . .?*" That this exchange takes place within a sort of closet (a rather small, stuffy men's bathroom) is important to note. It is an odd space—at once public, yet hidden, and filled with mirrors that both fracture and reveal the self. Joe's image throughout this exchange is split between his actual body and its blurred reflection in the dirty mirror behind Louis. Fascinated by Louis's recognition of his true self, it is this image that Joe is left to contemplate when Louis kisses him on the cheek and leaves.

In contrast, Roy Cohn has seized public power because he is not truly public. Roy remains closeted until his death. As a result he is able to reinforce and maintain his social and political clout. Ironically, he does this throughout *Angels in America* via homophobia, toward himself and toward others. Michael Warner (2000) argues that the politics of assimilation depends on the politics of shame, which includes disgust with the queer body, its desires, its fluids, its pleasures, and its risks. Warner (2000: 32) writes that, "On top of having ordinary sexual shame . . . the dignified homosexual also feels ashamed of every queer who flaunts his sex and his faggotry" and as a result, blames "the fuckers who deserve it: sex addicts, bodybuilders in Chelsea or West Hollywood, circuit boys, flaming queens . . ." This notion of a sexual hierarchy plays itself out in the antagonistic relationship that develops between Roy and his night nurse, "flaming queen" Belize (Jeffrey Wright). Belize is an African-American ex-drag queen, and Prior's best friend. He is also *Angels in America's* most visibly queer character: he is flamboyantly dressed, camp, and boldly honest. When Roy is admitted as a liver cancer patient to the AIDS ward in which Belize works,

Henry notes the "inappropriateness" of Belize's colourful attire: "Why are you dressed like that? Nurses are supposed to wear white." Henry's comment on Belize's difference illuminates not only his homosexuality, but also his blackness, which he cannot hide. Belize celebrates both differences, challenging those who wish him to disappear to deal with him. As a visibly gay male, Belize is the antithesis of the invisible homosexual embodied by Roy.

It is important to note the representational challenge the film presents by offering the character most at ease in his own body as the most flamboyant and "stereotypical" homosexual male. Belize is the gay male whose visibility marks him as the most potentially ostracized and powerless. In many ways, Belize has nowhere to hide. While Prior, Louis, and Joe are on a journey toward acceptance, Belize arrives in the narrative already having achieved his full humanity. It is this humanity that allows him to emphasize his solidarity with Roy and dispense justice to him in the film's second half, even though he would "rather suck the pus out of an abscess" than sit and talk. Belize puts Roy in his place, reminding him that he too is living on the margins. When Roy wants a white nurse, "my constitutional right," Belize reminds him, "you're in a hospital, you don't have any constitutional rights." Belize also advises Roy to use whatever clout he has left to make sure his AZT trial contains no placebos. When Roy asks why he should believe Belize over his "very expensive WASP doctor," Belize reminds him, "he's not queer, I am."

## Americans have no use for sick

In the age of AIDS, homosexuality is reimagined as contagion. As noted, the spectacle of illness renders both the gay male body, and the gay male body with AIDS, *visible* in a political and cultural climate in which the representation of both bodies remains problematic. Early AIDS narratives and news coverage quantified this concern by contrasting those bodies that were healthy, and therefore "normal," with those that were "infirm" and therefore deviant. Emile Netzhammer and Scott Shamp (1994: 98) note that prime-time programs like *21 Jump Street* and *Designing Women* drew a "distinction between guilty and innocent victims" where "sympathy is garnered for those who have been infected through no fault of their own." Importantly, if a television show introduced a character with AIDS, as *Beverley Hills 90210* did in its fourth season, a causal link was suggested between the disease and gay men's "unnatural" sexual practices (while those practices continued to remain hidden and taboo) (93–94).

AIDS narratives are conventionally constructed around the corporeal punishment of the homosexual male who resists heteronormativity. Within such narratives, the gay male body that reveals *visible* signs of the virus is forced out

of the invisible closet, made public through shame and the danger of contamin-
ation. AIDS is a health crisis, but, as *Angels in America* suggests, it is also a
political crisis, thrusting the gay male body into the public domain, compelling
us to question its status. Chapter Four, "Stop Moving!" sees once powerful
Roy Cohn in hospital, dying, delusional, and hallucinating the ghost of Ethel
Rosenberg (Meryl Streep), whom he put in the electric chair in the 1950s. He
tells Ethel that "Americans have no use for sick," realizing that his grasp on
power is slipping. He elaborates on the relationship between illness, otherness,
and powerlessness:

> The worst thing about being sick in America, Ethel, is you are booted out
> of the parade . . . Look at Reagan: he's so healthy he's hardly human . . .
> he takes a slug in the chest and two days later he's out west riding ponies
> in his PJs. I mean, who does that? That's America. It's just no country for
> the infirm.

AIDS renders Roy irrelevant and invisible and has required him, because of his
closeted nature, to amplify this invisibility at the very moment when some
"truth" about himself is legible on his body. Despite his role as villain, Roy's
demise forces us to question the complex ways in which AIDS reconfigures his
body's social and political status. Roy is simultaneously visibly gay because of
his illness and invisible because he is gay.

Since the first cases of "gay cancer" were reported in North America in
1981, the AIDS epidemic has made gay bodies more visible than ever. As Vaid
(1995: 81) explains, "AIDS outed our entire community. Perversely put, we
won visibility for gay and lesbian lives because we died in record numbers."
Watney (1996: 3) argues that AIDS is a disease that cannot be divorced from
the media technologies that have defined it: "Fighting AIDS is not just a medical
struggle; it involves our understanding of the words and images which load the
virus down with such a dismal cargo of appalling connotations." If AIDS, as
Watney (1996: 9) suggests, initiates a "crisis of representation" "over the entire
framing of knowledge about the human body and its capacities for sexual
pleasure," then this crisis exists, in part, because AIDS manifests as a legible
mark of difference on the body itself. AIDS makes it effectively "easier" for
those society classes as healthy and normal to pick out those that are sick,
dangerous, and queer.

In her work on purity, cleanliness, and taboo, Mary Douglas (2002: 149)
suggests that bodily waste, such as urine, vomit, faeces and blood, is both a
source of danger and power in some societies. Maintaining the margins of
bodies that threaten to leak out and contaminate the rest of "clean" society is
paramount in this scenario. As Douglas (2002: 152) writes, "the symbolism of

the body's boundaries is used . . . to express danger to community boundar-ies." If the AIDS body is viewed as dirty, impure and polluted, it is in part because it is seen as a result of impure, unclean and taboo sexual practices. Douglas contends that "Sex is likely to be pollution-free in a society where sexual roles are enforced directly" (174). Coherence between sex roles and sexual practices (which homosexuality disrupts) becomes vital in the mainten-ance of both bodily and social purity. Richard Meyer (1991: 275) conceptual-izes AIDS as a disease that compels homosexuality to virtually "leak out" of the body. Writing specifically about Rock Hudson, Meyer notes, "Closeted though all the years of his celebrity, Rock Hudson's secret finally registers, Dorian Gray-like, on the surface of his body" (275). As Meyer (1991: 283) suggests, Hudson's infirm body became a signifier of homosexuality, where the real "terror" of AIDS is visible: "the collapse of a particular fantasy of male con-tainment and sexual safety—a fantasy once attached to Rock Hudson's body, a fantasy once embodied by Rock Hudson's closet."

In *Angels in America* conventional representations of illness and taboo are challenged. Here, AIDS is a virus that provides the opportunity for progress within the gay community and United States as a whole—it is "the virus of prophecy" and Prior Walter its prophet. It is his suffering that enables us to see the body of a gay man with AIDS as more than an invisible framework for our own misconceptions. *Angels in America*'s most compelling scene occurs in Chapter Three, "The Messenger," and involves the juxtaposition of images that illuminate the importance of the gay male body in visibility debates. It is a scene that literally questions gay men's status as Anti-Body in America. It counters Roy's declaration that "Americans have no use for sick" by revealing what can be learned from the marginalized corpus. In an outpatient clinic, Prior is examined by Emily (Emma Thompson), a nurse. In a coffee shop, at the same time, his now ex-lover Louis sits with Belize, and discusses the nature of American democracy and citizenship. The juxtaposition of Prior's examin-ation with Louis and Belize's dialogue makes clear what is really at stake for the democratic ideal in not granting gays and lesbians full enfranchisement and protection under the law. Here, there is a frank discussion of the gay male body, while that body is made visible on the television screen. Importantly, Kushner has altered the order of action here from the play, so that the relation-ship of the body to these political questions is unambiguous.

Emily removes Prior's IV. Louis tells Belize that he cannot bear to hear George Bush (Sr) talking about human rights since this is something he knows nothing about. Louis elaborates that conservatives in America "don't begin to know what, ontologically, freedom is, or human rights, like they see these bourgeois property-based Rights-of-Man type rights, but that's not enfran-chisement, not democracy, not what's implicit, what's potential in the idea, not the idea with blood in it." At this point, the camera returns to the clinic, and we see Emily examine Prior's lesion-covered torso. It is this body with blood in it—conceptualized by mainstream society as infirm, other, and deviant—which offers the basis for reconfiguring our ideas about democracy and freedom. It is this body that must be confronted directly for progress to occur, acting as a catalyst for important questions about gay citizenship. This is how freedom and human rights are articulated—not in abstractions and ideals, but via the body's actual experience of the world.

Prior removes his pants and appears completely naked, lying on the examination table. Emily gently touches his body, examining his lesions, checking his lymphatic glands. Back in the coffee shop, Louis develops one of Kushner's major themes. Over the image of Prior's naked corpus, Louis explains that, "what I think is, that what AIDS shows us is the *limits of tolerance*, that it's not enough to be tolerated, because when the shit hits the fan you find out how much tolerance is worth. Nothing. And underneath all the tolerance is intense, passionate hatred." Louis concludes: "*Power* is the object, not being tolerated. Fuck assimilation!" Louis is not only angry that gay men lack social or political power, but that they are required to hide their difference as a condition of enfranchisement.

As Prior dresses, he provides Emily with a catalogue of his corporeal complaints: "Ankles sore and swollen, but the leg's better, the nausea's mostly gone with the little orange pills. BM's pure liquid but not bloody anymore, for now . . ." Prior sees himself as society sees him—as polluted and monstrous— despite the fact that we are now seeing him as something else. When he later meets Hannah and she sees his lesion-covered body, Prior describes it as an inhuman "horror" from which he runs. But rather than run from his body, Hannah sees his corpus as one involved in the most human struggle, his lesions "a cancer—nothing more human than that." Conventionally, Anti-Body status is aggravated by the image of the AIDS body as a body further marginalized through the denial of human touch. But Emily's examination of Prior's body is imagined as much more than a cold, medical inspection; as both nurse *and* angel she cares for and touches his body in a way that reinvests Prior with, what Landers (1988: 294) calls, "subjectivity—individuality, emotions, a biography."

Prior's naked physical examination effectively removes the taboo associated with the "untouchable" AIDS body. Emily is not polluted by this contact. In addition, his corpus is humanized by not hiding its difference but defiantly displaying it in the television frame. This process expands our understanding of these categories, and promotes something other than tolerance of that body, but a new way of looking at, seeing, and knowing it. In this scene, Prior who feels "dirty" and believes his "heart is pumping polluted blood," becomes a

Body and in doing so reverses the accepted meaning attached to the gay male body as sick and unclean. We are reminded of what Joe's wife, Harper (Mary-Louise Parker) tells Prior in their shared hallucination, that there is a part of him, "the most inner part, entirely free of disease."

## The body is the garden of the soul

Humanizing the gay male body, healthy or sick, normalizes and politicizes it. By returning subjectivity to this body it becomes something other than deviant or infirm. Throughout *Angels in America* the body is a source of self-expression and knowledge, a record of an individual's life. Corporeal knowledge is repeatedly connected to what is real and most human in people's experience of the world. As the Angel tells Prior, "the body is the garden of the soul," elevating it from its reviled position as a base, unholy entity. *Angels in America* places subjective, corporeal experience at the core of its narrative. Bodies here carry irrefutable truths. When Joe tries, one last time, to be a good heterosexual and husband, Harper stands before him, naked. She asks "what do you see?" and Joe replies that he sees "nothing." Harper's body is a body that Joe feels no sexual desire for, and this, finally, is the truth they have both been seeking.

*Angels in America* attempts to restore order to a world disordered by AIDS and does this by confronting, not fleeing, from the source of that disorder—the gay male body—for resolution. As they wait for the bus that will take Louis to bury his grandma, Prior reveals a lesion on his torso and that he has AIDS. While Louis thinks it is just a burst blood vessel, Prior says that the body doesn't lie, "no wall like the wall of hard, scientific fact." Preceding this revelation, Prior and Louis argue about the disappearance of their cat. Louis says that he prefers dogs because they have brains; Prior prefers cats because they have intuition and "know when something's wrong." An opposition is immediately set up that is played out throughout the entire narrative, between the head and heart. Louis, the cerebral, idealistic voice of the playwright/screenwriter, flees from the heart, the emotions, and the body through the head. Louis tries to rationalize the guilt he feels at abandoning Prior with intellectualism and philosophical values. His verbosity offers a significant point of contrast to the corporeality and materiality of human experience that Prior embodies at the center of the story. Theirs is an opposition that reveals different ways of knowing via differing engagements with the body. While Prior's illness forces him to inhabit and experience his body, Louis, at various stages in the narrative flees from bodies. In Part Two, Prior first encounters Hannah Pitt when he is trying to advise Joe to be careful about Louis. As he explains: "I wanted to warn your son about *later*, when his hair goes and there are hips and jowls and all that human stuff. That poor slob there's just going to wind up miserable, fat, frightened, and *alone*, because Louis, he can't handle bodies."

Louis's guilt leads him to the realization that there is something more genuine and accurate in a pain that is felt by the body and not rationalized by the head. When he abandons Prior in the hospital, knowing he "can't incorporate sickness into his sense of how things are supposed to go," Louis wants to be punished for his "sins." He goes to the park and picks up a hustler who he wants to hurt him, infect him, and make him bleed. Later, as he and Belize leave the coffee shop in Chapter Three, Louis shows Belize a cut on his forehead: "I don't know what to do anymore. Last week at work I screwed up the Xerox machine . . . and then I tripped on the subway steps and I fell, and my glasses broke and I cut my forehead, here, see . . ." Louis's "Mark of Cain" is emblematic of his increasing inability to rationalize his behaviour and, more importantly, his feelings. There is a conflict, here, between the body and the mind, which will not resolve itself for Louis until he reads Kaddish for the dead Roy in Part Two. When Louis seeks forgiveness from Prior in Washington Square Park, Prior is critical of Louis's abstracted existence in his own skin. Although Louis's guilty misery makes him cry, Prior is not convinced that the tears are anything more than an "idea" of crying: "You cry, you endanger nothing to yourself when you do it." Prior needs to see physical evidence of Louis's suffering; for Prior to believe that Louis is in pain, he needs to see corporeal proof. Although Louis claims that he is bruised on the "inside," Prior insists: "Come back to me when they're visible. I want to see black and blue, Louis, I want to see blood. Because I can't believe you even *have* blood in your veins till you show it to me."

Like Louis, Joe resists living in his body. Although Harper suspected the true nature of Joe's sexual identity even before marrying him, Joe struggles, stoically, to maintain control of his desire, his beliefs, and ultimately, his body. After crossing paths with Prior in "Bad News," and receiving the prophecy that "your husband's a homo," Harper insists that Joe tell her the truth. Rootless and restless, Joe is afraid of stasis, of stillness, so goes walking through Central Park at night, and up and down 53rd St., running towards a more complete occupation of his own skin. Harper explains that Joe's body is "unfamiliar" to her when he comes home from his night walks: "When you come through the door at night, your face is never exactly the way I remembered it . . . even the weight of you in the bed at night, the way you breathe in your sleep is unfamiliar." When she asks Joe if he is indeed a "homo," Joe answers, "No, I'm not. I don't see what difference it makes."

But it does make a difference, and the inability to be truthful about who he is, is presented as a struggle of biblical proportions for Joe. Harper knows that the body cannot be denied. Even his "mentor," Roy Cohn, provides Joe with valuable advice, encouraging him to transgress and progress, goading, "you want to make the law or subject to it?" When Harper asks the question again Joe becomes increasingly upset: "What do you want from me? There's nothing left. I'm a shell. There's nothing left to kill." Joe experiences his body as hollow and completely disconnected from what he really is and wants. Joe believes that he can escape the confines of his own skin by walking and moving and behaving in a moral, normal way. He struggles with what his church and political party tell him is sick, deviant, and un-American: his own body and its desires. But as Joe walks to escape he is also walking towards acceptance and understanding of that body: to the men who cruise for tricks in the park, to the hustlers who display their bodies for rent on 53$^{rd}$ St, to the realization that homosexuality is not a "lifestyle" choice but as intrinsic as his own skin. For Joe, walking magnifies the tension between completely annihilating his body, praying "for God to crush me, to break me up in little pieces and start again," and his need to be seen and known.

As Joe gets to know a gay man he is able to "normalize" his perception of himself and what it means to be gay. Three weeks into a sexual relationship, Joe and Louis walk on the beach and talk about the one-piece undergarment that Joe wears. Joe explains that it is a "temple garment," or a protective "second skin." Joe offers to stop wearing it, but Louis doesn't understand, "How can you stop wearing it if it's a skin? Your past, your beliefs . . ." When Louis confesses that he misses Prior and needs to see him, Joe begs him to stay. He removes his clothes and his protective underwear, revealing what really lies beneath. Joe says he will give up anything for Louis, "My skin . . . I'm flayed. No past now. I can give up anything . . . I want to live now. I can be anything I need to be, and I want to be with you." Finally living in his own body, Joe has "blossomed," as Louis says, and can stop running from himself. For Joe, unlike Prior, stasis is not death, but the stillness of self-acceptance that he has never previously had.

This progress into self-acceptance must also include acceptance of the body's sexual desires. After Joe leaves Harper he meets up with Louis in the park. Admitting to following him from work, Joe recognizes the sameness he shares with Louis. Joe takes a trepidatious leap into an unknown future—for the first time in his life, he believes the truth located in his body. He follows his desire, and this desire leads him to Louis, who takes him home. Part Two of *Angels in America* begins with Chapter Four, "Stop Moving!" in which Joe and Louis do just that: they arrive at Louis's new apartment in the East Village, stop running from themselves, and begin to explore each other's bodies. The sensuality of the scene that follows cannot be undervalued in a time in which scenes of such genuine intimacy remain absent between male bodies on American television.

In Louis's messy new home, the men stand before each other and while Joe is initially uncomfortable, Louis reassures him that gay sex can be safe, clean, and pleasurable: "We can cap everything that leaks in latex. We can smear our bodies with nonoxynol-9, safe, chemical sex. Messy, but not dirty." As Joe slowly acquiesces to his decision to be here, Louis tells him that he smells good and that smell is "inextricably bound up with sex." For Louis, the nose is a sexual organ: "The nose tells the body—the heart, the mind, the fingers, the cock—what it wants, and then the tongue explores." And Louis begins to explore: licking Joe's face, he tastes salt, kissing his mouth he tastes iron and clay; placing his hand in Joe's pants, he tastes chlorine, copper, earth. The body is earthy and elemental. While they remain fully clothed their bodies are instruments for knowing self and other. As Louis explains, smell is made up of the molecules of a person, "little molecules of Joe." In this way, the sensual, sensory event of two bodies coming together to touch, taste, and smell one another promises to reveal some elemental truth about each person. With the possibility of finally living in his own skin, Joe agrees to stay. Louis has connected the body of the gay man in America to the exploration of and articulation of an "unmapped terrain" and new way of corporeal being. Here, the body is more than a collection of bones, muscle, organs, and skin; the body is a vehicle for self-expression that tells the world the place that body occupies within it. Exploration and discovery give things a name, making what was unknown and invisible, visible and known.

## We will be citizens

Vaid (1995: 32) argues that "in order to change homosexual status, we must be forthright and open about what it means to be and live as homosexuals. Nothing will change as long as we pretend to be people we are not." Television plays a vital role in this potential for wider social change. I disagree with Andrew Billen (2004: 47) who suggests that "the great questions posed by *Angels* have mostly been answered by the passage of time." It is my position here that rather than reveal how much progress has been made for gays and lesbians in America since the 1980s, when the plays are set, and the early 1990s, when they were first performed, HBO's *Angels in America* reveals stasis around the issue of full enfranchisement and the development of a more inclusive and authentic media visibility. *Angels in America* is a vital bridge between two repressive Republican regimes intent on pushing the bodies of its gay "citizens" back into the closet. Prior's final prophecy at the film's conclusion, that gays and lesbians "won't die secret deaths anymore, the world only spins forward, we will be citizens, the time has come," remains unfulfilled.

As a queer text, HBO's *Angels in America* challenges Hollywood's commitment to heteronormativity, assimilation, and self-censorship. It is a "risky" slice of cable programming because it confronts and contests the representational limitations for the gay male body on American television. It takes "risks" by compelling audiences to question the status of that body today, and throughout American history; to wonder just how much or how little has changed in the post-Stonewall era. As a deeply political, intellectual, empathetic, and humorous exploration of national themes from a queer perspective, *Angels in America* must be viewed not only as a product of its original production, or the period in which it is set, but also the era of its most expansive dissemination (2003–). It is a conduit for dialogue between these times.

*Angels in America* visualizes the paradox between visible and invisible bodies and their social status, and as a television film text, it makes what is often invisible brightly, fantastically, and emotively real. In doing this, it also highlights the inconsistency between network and cable approaches to these bodies. It encourages important questions about gay images and the relationship between how these images are regulated for mainstream audiences and the limited knowledge they produce about gay lives. And it reveals that demands for the increased visibility of gays and lesbians in the media reman static, anxious, and un-revolutionary when restricted to images that render their bodies asexual and non-threatening. HBO, as the self-anointed home of innovative original programming, offers a unique intervention into this complex terrain. Both inside and outside the television screen, *Angels in America* magnifies a health crisis that has prompted a representational crisis only now being addressed, with the hope that these can lead to real, revolutionary progress. This upheaval, so specific to the early years of the AIDS epidemic is mirrored in the continuing panic over same-sex marriage and the questions about enfranchisement that this raises. It is evident, also, in the resistance to assimilating and "normalizing" gays and lesbians, both inside and outside the gay community, and the denial of difference that these processes entail. At the center of this movement for change is the need to shift the status of the gay male body in the public domain, by unveiling and revealing its difference across a variety of media technologies. Taking flight in the Bush era, *Angels in America* participates in this movement for change.

## Works cited

Benjamin, W. (1992) "Theses on the Philosophy of History", pp 245–258 in *Illuminations*. London: Fontana Press.

Bernstein, E. & Schaffner, L. (eds) (2005) *Regulating Sex: The Politics of Intimacy and Identity*. New York and London: Routledge.

Billen, A. (2004, February 16) "Wings of Desire", *New Statesman* 47.

Bordo, S.R. (1989) "The Body and the Reproduction of Femininity: A Feminist Appropriation of Foucault", pp 13–33 in A.M. Jaggar & S.R. Bordo (eds) *Gender/*

*Body / Knowledge: Feminist Reconstruction of Being and Knowing*. New Brunswick: Rutgers University Press.

Bronski, M. (1998) *The Pleasure Principle: Sex, Backlash, and the Struggle for Gay Freedom*. New York: St. Martin's Press.

Bronski, M. (2004, Fall) "Angels in America Review", *Cineaste* 57–59.

Buhle, P. (2005) "Redemption When We Need it Most", *Tikkun* 20 (1): 75.

Butler, J. (1986) "Sex and Gender in Simone de Beauvoir's *Second Sex*", *Yale French Studies* 72: 35–49.

Butler, J. (1990) *Gender Trouble: Feminism and the Subversion of Identity*. New York: Routledge.

Butler, J. (1993) *Bodies that Matter: On the Discursive Limits of "Sex"*. New York: Routledge.

Capsuto, S. (2000) *Alternate Channels: The Uncensored Story of Gay and Lesbian Images on Radio and Television*. New York: Ballantine Books.

D'erasmo, S. (2004, January 11) "Lesbians on Television: It's Not Easy Being Seen", *New York Times* 2.1.

Douglas, M. (2002) *Purity and Danger: An Analysis of Concept of Pollution and Taboo*. London and New York: Routledge.

Dyer, R. (1993) *The Matter of Images: Essays on Representations*. London: Routledge.

Foucault, M. (1979) *Discipline and Punish: The Birth of the Prison*, trans. A. Sheridan. New York: Penguin.

Franklin, N. (2003, December 8) "America, Lost and Found", *The New Yorker*. 125.

Gener, R. (2003, December) "Angels Takes Flight as a Film", *American Theatre* 30–33.

Kennedy, K. & Ullman, S. (2003) *Sexual Borderlands: Constructing an American Sexual Past*. Columbus: Ohio State University Press.

Kushner, T. (2003) *Angels in America. A Gay Fantasia on National Themes. Part One: Millennium Approaches. Part Two: Perestroika*. New York: Theatre Communications Group.

Landers, T. (1988) "Bodies and Anti-Bodies: A Crisis in Representation", pp 281–299 in C. Schneider & B. Wallis (eds) *Global Television*. New York: Wedge Press.

Lewis, J. & Miller, T. (2003) "Introduction", pp 1–10 in J. Lewis & T. Miller (eds) *Critical Cultural Policy Studies: A Reader*, Malden: Blackwell.

Meyer, R. (1991) "Rock Hudson's Body", pp 259–288 in D. Fuss (ed.) *Inside / Out: Lesbian Theories, Gay Theories*. New York and London: Routledge.

Miller, T. (1998) *Technologies of Truth: Cultural Citizenship and the Popular Media*, Minneapolis: University of Minnesota Press.

Netzhammer, E.C, & Shamp, S.A. (1994) "Guilt by Association: Homosexuality and AIDS on Prime-Time Television", pp 91–106 in R.J. Ringer (ed.) *Queer Words, Queer Images: Communication and the Construction of Homosexuality*. New York: New York University Press.

Rich, F. (2005, February 6) "The Year of Living Indecently", *New York Times* AR1.

Vaid, U. (1995) *Virtual Equality: The Mainstreaming of Gay and Lesbian Liberation*. New York: Anchor Books.

Walters, S.D. (2001) *All the Rage: The Story of Gay Visibility in America*. Chicago: University of Chicago Press.

Warner, M. (2000) *The Trouble with Normal: Sex, Politics, and the Ethics of Queer Life*. Cambridge: Harvard University Press.

Watney, S. (1996) *Policing Desire: Pornography, AIDS and the Media, 3rd edition*. Minneapolis: University of Minnesota Press.

# Contributors

**Kim Akass** is Research Fellow (TV Drama) at Manchester Metropolitan University. She has co-edited and contributed to *Reading Sex and the City* (IB Tauris, 2004), *Reading Six Feet Under: TV To Die For* (IB Tauris, 2005), *Reading The L Word: Outing Contemporary Television* (IB Tauris, 2006), *Reading Desperate Housewives: Beyond the White Picket Fence* (IB Tauris, 2006) and *Quality TV: Contemporary American TV and Beyond* (IB Tauris, 2007). She is currently researching the representation of motherhood on American TV and is one of the founding editors of the television journal *Critical Studies in Television* (MUP) as well as (with Janet McCabe) series editor of "Reading Contemporary Television" for IB Tauris.

**Cara Louise Buckley** is a doctoral candidate in the department of Communication and Culture at Indiana University and a lecturer at Emerson College. Her research is focused on rhetorics of transgression and queer theory. She is currently in the process of completing her dissertation, which examines the possibilities offered for reimagining traditional notions of "family" within mediated representations of the straight woman/gay man, or "fag hag," dynamic.

**Rhiannon Bury** has taught Communication Studies and Women's Studies at several universities in Ontario, Canada since receiving her PhD from the University of Toronto. She is currently Assistant Professor of Women's Studies at Athabasca University in Alberta. Her research interests include online identity, community and media fan culture. Her book, *Cyberspaces of Their Own: Female Fandoms Online* (Peter Lang, 2005), is part of the Digital Formations series edited by Steve Jones.

**Joanna Di Mattia** has a PhD in Women's Studies and is currently an independent scholar. She has published widely in the field of gender studies and popular culture, including work on *Sex and the City, Six Feet Under,*

*Seinfeld, Queer Eye for the Straight Guy* and *Queer as Folk*. Her current research addresses the importance of images of sexual practice and pleasure in debates about queer visibility.

**Blake D. Ethridge** is a doctoral candidate at The Johns Hopkins University. He studies political theory and urban politics. His dissertation addresses the role of image and identity in the development of American cities in the latter half of the twentieth century.

**Tony Kelso** is an Assistant Professor in the Department of Mass Communication at Iona College. He is co-editor of the book, *Mosh the Polls: Youth Voters and Popular Culture* (forthcoming), as well as co-author of *Show Business: The Encyclopedia of Politics, Media, and Popular Culture* (forthcoming). His research on advertising has appeared in the journal *Implicit Religion*, and in the ARFT *Encyclopedia of Religion, Communication, and Media*.

**Marc Leverette** is an Assistant Professor of Media Studies in the Department of Speech Communication at Colorado State University. He is author of *Professional Wrestling, the Myth, the Mat, and American Popular Culture* and co-editor of *Zombie Culture: Autopsies of the Living Dead* and *Oh My God, They Deconstructed South Park! Those Bastards!* His writing has appeared in journals such as *Communication and Critical/Cultural Studies*, the *Journal of Communication Inquiry*, the *Western Journal of Communication, Explorations in Media Ecology, Cultural Studies ↔ Critical Methodologies, Image & Narrative*, and *Studies in Popular Culture*.

**David Marc** is a freelance writer, editor, and teacher. A four-time winner of the Syracuse Press Club Award for Informational Feature Writing and member of the national editorial board of *Television Quarterly*, he recently completed work on his sixth book, which concerns the little-known role of Upstate New York in the invention of cinema and its development as an American industry.

**Janet McCabe** is Research Fellow (TV Drama) at Manchester Metropolitan University. She is author of *Feminist Film Studies: Writing the Woman into Cinema* (Wallflower, 2004), and is co-editor of *Reading Sex and the City* (IB Tauris, 2004), *Reading Six Feet Under: TV To Die For* (IB Tauris, 2005), *Reading The L Word: Outing Contemporary Television* (IB Tauris, 2006), *Reading Desperate Housewives: Beyond the White Picket Fence* (IB Tauris, 2006) and *Quality TV: Contemporary American TV and Beyond* (IB Tauris, 2007). She is a co-founding editor as well as the managing editor of the television journal *Critical Studies in Television* (MUP). Along with Kim Akass, she is series editor of "Reading Contemporary Television" for IB Tauris. Her research interests include policing femininities and cultural memory on television.

**Conor McGrath** is now an Independent Scholar, having previously been a lecturer (assistant professor) in political lobbying and public affairs at the University of Ulster, Northern Ireland. He is the author of *Lobbying in Washington, London and Brussels: The Persuasive Communication of Political Issues.* He has published in such journals as *Journal of Public Affairs, Irish Political Studies,* and *Journal of Communication Management*; and in edited books including *The Handbook of Public Affairs, When Elections are on the Horizon: Marketing Politics to the Electorate in the USA and UK,* and *Encyclopedia of Activism and Social Justice.*

**Shawn McIntosh** is a lecturer in the Strategic Communications Program at Columbia University's School of Continuing Education. He is co-author (with John Pavlik) of *Converging Media: Introduction to Mass Communication,* and (with Marc Leverette) of *Zombie Culture: Autopsies of the Living Dead.* He has been an editor and freelance writer for 10 years for various newspapers and magazines in the U.K., U.S., and Japan.

**Toby Miller** is Professor of Media & Cultural Studies at the University of California, Riverside. Previously editor of the *Journal of Sport and Social Issues* and co-editor of *Social Text,* he is currently editor of *Television and New Media* and co-editor of *Social Identities.* Among his more than 20 authored or edited books are *The Well-Tempered Self: Citizenship, Culture, and the Postmodern Subject, Technologies of Truth: Cultural Citizenship and the Popular Media, Spyscreen: Espionage on Film and TV from the 1930s to the 1960s, Global Hollywood 2, Cultural Citizenship: Cosmopolitanism, Consumerism, and Television in the Neoliberal Age,* and the five-volume *Television Studies: Critical Concepts in Media and Cultural Studies.*

**Brian L. Ott** is an Associate Professor of Media Studies at Colorado State University. He is an award winning scholar and teacher, who has published widely in national and regional journals, including *Critical Studies in Media Communication, Communication and Critical/Cultural Studies, Cultural Studies ↔ Critical Methodologies, Rhetoric and Public Affairs, Western Journal of Communication, Women's Studies in Communication,* and *The Journal of Popular Culture.* His previous book, *The Small Screen: How Television Equips Us to Live in the Information Age,* is published by Blackwell.

**Avi Santo** is an Assistant Professor in the Department of Communications at Old Dominion University. Along with Christopher Lucas, he is the co-creator of *Flow: Television and Media Culture.* He is also co-Coordinating

Editor and founder of *MediaCommons: A Digital Scholarly Network*, home of *In Media Res*. He is currently working on a book manuscript about licensing and corporate authorship in the U.S., 1930–1970.

**Lisa Williamson** is a postgraduate research student in the Department of Theatre, Film and Television Studies at the University of Glasgow. She is currently completing her thesis, entitled *Contentious Comedy: American Sitcoms in the Post-Network Era*.

# Index